Praise for
Married People: Staying Together in the Age of Divorce

"Takes a close look into the living rooms and bedrooms of couples who have managed to make their vows last."
—*Associated Press*

"Francine Klagsbrun takes us on a profound journey into a series of intimate relationships to discover how they work. . . . Her observations and emotions are keen."
—*Working Woman*

"A beautiful, touching book that is long overdue. Rarely do writers communicate complex psychological notions with such clarity and sensitivity. The couples she has interviewed reverberate in one's thoughts for days. Her book rings continually with the sound of truth."
—Dr. Samuel L. Pauker,
Department of Psychiatry,
Cornell University Medical Center
New York Hospital

"Not a book of statistics. . . . What it does tell us is how couples have navigated their lives, how they have coped in good times and bad, why they have chosen to stay together, and what they all have in common. It provides a rare look inside some ordinary marriages."
—*New York Daily News*

"*Married People* . . . a shining contemporary . . . . mane ideal. The epilogue— . . . . nole—is as beautiful and . . . . in Chekhovian humanity."
Cynthia Ozick,
hor of *The Cannibal Galaxy*

Married People

STAYING TOGETHER IN THE AGE OF DIVORCE

Francine Klagsbrun

BANTAM BOOKS

TORONTO · NEW YORK · LONDON · SYDNEY · AUCKLAND

MARRIED PEOPLE:
STAYING TOGETHER IN THE AGE OF DIVORCE

A Bantam Book

Bantam hardcover edition / July 1985
2nd printing . . . July 1985
3rd printing . . . September 1985
*A selection of Book-of-the-Month Club, October 1985 and Psychotherapy
& Social Science Book Club, March 1986.*
Serialized in Ms. *magazine, July 1985;* Family Circle, *July 1985;*
Glamour *magazine, August 1985;* New Woman, *August 1985;*
Reader's Digest, *October 1985;* Modern Bride, *August/September
1985; and* Woman, *December 1985.*

Bantam paperback edition / September 1986

*Grateful acknowledgment is made for permission to reprint
"The Common Wisdom" by Howard Nemerov from* The Collected
Works of Howard Nemerov, *University of Chicago Press, 1977.
Reprinted by permission of the author.*

Library of Congress Cataloging in Publication Data

Klagsbrun, Francine.
Married People.

Bibliography; p. 351
Includes index.
1. Marriage. 2. Communication in marriage.
I. Title.
HQ734.K57 1985   646.7'8   84-91731
ISBN 0-553-25684-X

Published simultaneously in the United States and Canada

For Sam,
and for Sarah

CONTENTS

~

ACKNOWLEDGMENTS

~

The dozens of individuals and couples who opened their lives to me are discussed and presented under fictionalized names. This is my chance to thank them publicly for their trust, their candor and their belief in a project that could not have happened without them.

A real name I can use is that of my research associate Cynthia Epstein Smith. She possesses a special blend of intelligence, wit and empathy that makes working with her a joy. I'm grateful for the professionalism of her research and for the warmth of her friendship.

My thanks also to the many social scientists and therapists who graciously met with me to discuss their work and ideas, and to a few especially: Drs. Salvador Minuchin, Henry Spitz, Alexander Levay and the late Aaron Stein.

Nessa Rapoport, my editor, whose curiosity sparked so much, has tended this project with patience, wisdom and love. I thank her for all those qualities and for not believing me on those days when I told her this book could not be done.

My husband, as always, read and reread every section and every version of the manuscript, offering his unique insights and perceptions. From him I have learned much about psychiatry and much more about how people think and feel. Without him nothing would be possible.

INTRODUCTION

~

Married People

This book grew out of a question and a statement.

"How have you managed to stay married for so long?" an unmarried woman in her late twenties asked me, referring to my marriage of almost thirty years. She went on, "I look at people like you and I wonder, 'How is it possible?' Maybe if I knew I wouldn't be so leery of marriage myself."

The statement was made by a divorced man in his midthirties. "Single people," he said, "think all long-married people are cowards."

Coming just a few weeks apart, both the question and the statement puzzled me. I had thought we were past the days when marriage and family life were under heavy and steady attack, those days of the 1970s when the future of marriage seemed shaky at best, more often desolate. I had thought marriage was fashionable again, that "commitment" was the favored word of the 1980s, and that—judging from the numbers of traditional weddings I had been attending—even bridesmaids in look-alike dresses were back to stay. Why then the wonder at my long marriage? Why the label of coward for couples in lasting matrimony? I realized as I pursued the matter further that while *getting* married seems to have made a comeback, *staying* married is still suspect. By now I have heard long-married couples accused not only of cowardice (meaning a fear of striking out on one's own), but of lack of imagination, of complacency, of inertia and of possessing a desperate need for security over excitement.

I suppose it is the steep rise in divorces that has made marriage seem an impossible dream for all but a few. Even those who have stayed married have inadvertently contributed to the prevailing attitude. Yet, if almost one of every two marriages ends in divorce, more than one of every two remains intact. Statistics actually show that 58% of first marriages last more than fifteen years. While a certain number of these marriages may be troubled or unhappy ones, most would not have lasted unless they were working—and working well. Isn't it time to hear that side of the story? Isn't it possible now, after almost two decades of emphasizing the negatives, that we might find we have more to learn from focusing on the positives—on why marriages succeed rather than why they fail?

That, then, is the rationale for this book. Its goal is to investigate how married people go about making their unions last over time and why they do. This is not, however, a "happily ever after" saga about fairy-tale marriages. It is a real-life study of couples who have experienced bad times along with good, who have suffered problems and conflicts, sadness and setbacks as well as great joys. In other words, it is a book about ordinary people who choose to be married, not because they feel they have to, but because their marriage is more important to them than any of the stresses or struggles that interfere with it. And it is a book not about cowardice but about the courage and convictions of married people, and about their optimism in staying married in an age in which divorce sometimes appears the easier solution.

For me, the book was a journey into the lives of many couples and at the same time an exploration of my own marriage and attitudes toward married life. I did not set out with a fixed thesis about what makes some marriages work and others not. My thoughts evolved with the work, as I gathered information and sorted out impressions.

It would be nice to say I uncovered *the* secret of lasting marriages (and am now bottling and distributing it as a wedding gift), but I always knew that marriage is far too complex a matter to be reduced to one secret. Instead I have tried to determine those qualities that many successful marriages share. My findings and viewpoints are woven throughout the text along with discussions of couples' lives, and are more concisely organized in the conclusions.

The couples whose stories served as sources for the book live many kinds of lives. Initially I investigated more than a hundred marriages, mostly long-lasting ones, but also some of newlyweds, some that were several years old and some that had broken up. In the last category were marriages that had dissolved after a few years and others that had ended after many years—seemingly lasting marriages that didn't last. After screening, I narrowed my investigation of the long marriages to eighty-seven that had lasted fifteen years or more. Later I returned to look again at couples from the initial group whose marriages had seemed problematic, in order to use them as contrasts to the stronger marriages.

Fifteen years seemed a logical baseline to use as a measure for long marriage, not because divorces don't occur after fifteen years—they do, of course, even after fifty years—but because the majority of marital splits take place earlier. A marriage that has lasted fifteen years is more likely to continue than to break up. Fifteen-year marriages are of particular interest because those marriages, begun during the late 1960s and early 1970s, were subject in their earliest and most vulnerable years to sweeping social changes, among them a dizzying rise in the divorce rate. That these marriages survived when so many others faltered is an indication of their strength.

Because my purpose was to tap into the stories of couples' lives, to the heart of their marriages, I was not interested in gathering vast amounts of statistical data or constructing a scientific survey; such things had been done. As it turned out, however, the couples interviewed came from a broad spectrum of American society and from a variety of geographic regions. A few years' stint on lecture circuits led me through many parts of the country, where

I recruited couples for interviews (sometimes by asking a lecture audience for volunteers and for the names of others to contact, sometimes by gathering names and references from community leaders, and sometimes simply by approaching people in different occupations). Other volunteers were sought out by Cynthia Epstein Smith, a gifted social worker who served as a superb researcher.

All the couples fall into that vague category we call middle class, but it is a middle class that ranges from a truck driver, a gardener, a police officer, several nurses and a farmer to an archaeologist, a plastic surgeon and a real–estate tycoon. Most couples had children; a few did not. Most marriages were the first for both partners, but a substantial number—about twenty—were second marriages for one or both partners.

Interviews with couples usually lasted four or five hours, and as often as possible additional discussions were held with each partner (to get their separate views, and a better understanding of them as individuals). Everyone was offered anonymity. Some people didn't care, but I changed their names in the book anyway, as well as geographic locations, occupations or other identifying details.

To learn as much as I could, I posed open-ended questions: about feelings and closeness; about who makes decisions; about sex and extramarital sex; about children, parents and in-laws; about family backgrounds; about fighting and making up and about staying married. The questions were designed to develop the themes explored in the book, but sometimes couples would go off in another direction, telling the story of their lives and becoming caught up in ideas of their own. And that was fine; the richness of those life stories often turned out to be more important than the specifics of the questions posed.

What else about these couples? Just this: I came away from interviews with many of them profoundly moved, often awed and humbled. Some of them spoke about struggles and problems I wondered how I could have handled. They told me about the devastations of alcoholism. They described illnesses and the death of children and financial pressures that had nearly choked them. They were not feeling sorry for themselves, and they were not complaining. They were simply explaining who they were, including their defeats and their victories. "We're kind of proud of ourselves," said a woman whose marriage had been fraught with difficulties. "We're proud of where we are now and we don't mind talking about where we've come from."

None of them minded talking; they were delighted to be asked. In fact, no one whom I invited to participate in this study turned me down. For years these people had heard the divorce stories and the naysayers. Now *their* turn had come, and they wanted to be heard. Did they tell the truth when they spoke into my tape recorder? I believe they did. Maybe not at first, when they might have tried to present themselves as they would have liked to be seen. But soon they would relax and get caught up in the moment, often surprised at what they discovered about themselves and their marriage in the course of talking.

As for me, I discovered how many ways there are to be married. There were marriages that would seem impossible to an outsider that worked beautifully for the people involved. There were men I might have found too patronizing or too weak for my taste, women too bossy or too clinging, yet they fit comfortably into the context of their own marriages, and that is what mattered. I drew the line on this nonjudgmental attitude, however, when partners were hurtful and destructive toward one another, reasoning that while such a relationship might satisfy in some twisted way, I could not equate it with other satisfactory marriages.

None of the couples was involved in marital therapy at the time of the interviews, although a few had had individual or marital therapy in the past and a few had attended marital encounter or enrichment groups. I knew from the beginning that I did not want this book to be about clinical cases or based on histories taken from a psychiatrist's or social worker's files. Plenty of such books exist—and I read them all. I wanted to learn how couples deal with difficulties themselves, how they shape their lives—the good and the bad—together. But I did meet with therapists and social scientists to know the thinking of experts in the areas of marriage and family living.

*   *   *

When I began this project I anticipated a certain amount of skepticism from friends and colleagues. And I did get some, the most common statement in that category being: "A book about long marriages? It's going to be awfully thin, isn't it?"

But what surprised and delighted me was that far more often the reaction was one of encouragement and pleasure. "Wow," said a photographer, married twenty-five years, "it's about time we came out of the closet. Maybe the rest of them will find out now what they've been missing."

With the work completed, I have two hopes for this book.

First, I hope couples of all ages will be able to recognize themselves in it. In spite of the unprecedented openness of our society, married couples still guard the intimacies of their lives from the gaze of others, as well they should. Yet knowing how other people live can help us understand how we live. The people who spoke so candidly to me told their stories in the belief that what they had to say might be of use. So I hope the lives and thoughts presented here will touch many couples, and bridge, somewhat, the isolation that separates married people from one another.

And second, I hope the qualities described here, those qualities that help keep marriages going, will have positive meaning for couples contemplating marriage as well as those deep into their own married lives.

No marriage presented in this book claims perfection. These marriages work because they have been given the chance to work. And they work because, of the many choices available for living in society today, staying married is seen by these couples as the happiest choice of all. This book is a tribute to that choice.

CHAPTER ONE

~·

Forever

They were getting married in a week, and they had agreed to let me interview them. Both tall, they were extraordinarily beautiful. Maggie, the bride, carried herself with the long-limbed grace of a dancer. Robbie, her husband-to-be, strong-jawed, with just a touch of sullenness, might have stepped out of an F. Scott Fitzgerald novel. They were both twenty-seven. They had known each other for five years, living together for three. She had recently begun working at a small, general law firm. He earned a fairly good living as a television writer.

For months before, I had been meeting with couples married fifteen, twenty, twenty-five or more years. I had collected their stories and shared their lives in my effort to learn about their marriages, both the joys and the problems. Although many of those people were beautiful in their own right, they no longer boasted the fresh-faced glow of youth. Rather, they were people who had known heartache and anger, who had begat children and lost children, whose faces were marked by age or illness or overexposure to the sun. But these two before me now were dazzling in their unself-conscious happiness, almost

1

intimidating in their confidence and the clarity with which they stated their views.

They were not the first young couple I had interviewed who displayed a sense of certainty and control. Whatever happened to shy brides and nervous grooms? I wondered. I wanted to know where this couple's self-possession came from and how they could be so sure of themselves as they embarked on their marriage. I wanted to know what they expected of the future. Mostly, I wanted to know whether a book about lasting marriages could touch the lives of people about to begin marriage. Or were they too far apart, these assured young people and the dozens of couples I had met who had been married decades earlier, decades so different from our own that they might have been centuries?

"Why are you getting married?" I asked them.

Robbie answered immediately. "It's an affirmation of my love for her, a public affirmation within a legal framework. It's a statement of my commitment."

"For me it's a little different," Maggie said. She looked at him as she spoke. "I always felt I had that commitment, marriage or not. Getting married is Robbie's way of saying he's definitely going to be there all the way."

"That's true," Robbie went on. I felt as if I were listening in on a conversation between them, an observer rather than a participant. "Even though we've been together for so long, part of me always knew I could just as easily walk out the door as not. Now I've decided there are no other houses I want to walk into. If there's any place I want to be, it's home, and home is Maggie."

"There's something else," Maggie said, pausing to find the words. "It's something about the fact that now we're adults. I always thought of myself as a kid, and getting married is a grown-up thing to do. I'm affirming my feeling of being an adult now, ready to take large steps into the future."

She stated it so well. Of course marriage is an affirmation of adulthood. Nobody asked why you were getting married back in the 1950s when I was a bride. It was assumed you were adult enough to marry when the time came, and the time came early then. When I was twenty, my father had what he called a "heart-to-heart" with me.

"You're not getting any younger," he said seriously. "You know what I mean?" I knew. Within a year I was engaged. At about the same age, so were most of my friends, as were most of the people I had interviewed, people married in the 1950s, 1960s and early 1970s. Couples really are different today, I thought. They are so much more thoughtful, so much more knowledgeable than we were. But then, why is this generation divorcing at twice the rate their parents did?

"Are you planning to have children?"

"Oh, I can't go into it." Maggie held her head with both hands. "That's something that makes me crazy."

"Why?" I asked.

"Yeah, why?" Robbie echoed. "I have exactly the same decision to make as you."

"No, you don't," Maggie answered. "You don't have to carry the baby for nine months."

"But I come from a tradition in which the male has always been the breadwinner, so I have a bigger responsibility." They were off into their own conversation again.

"That's different. What am I going to do, take off three years from work to have the fucking baby?"

The word jolted me. Are they so tough, these new professional women? When I married, it was assumed that within a year or two of marriage the beaming young couple would announce the expected arrival of an addition to the family. I had to acknowledge that I had not done the usual. I had worked while my husband was in medical school, and by the time he was finished, I was deep into a career of writing and editing. Did I really want to interrupt that career to have a child? It was the same dilemma Maggie would face, and with a flush I remembered myself responding not dissimilarly: "Okay, I'll have a damned baby," I had shouted at my mother (using the strongest profanity of which I was capable), "but let me fulfill myself first." The idea of "fulfillment" was not the cliché it would later become, and the women's movement had not yet arrived to tell me I was not the only woman struggling with this issue. "I'll have a baby; you'll be a grandmother; don't worry," I had cried. "But leave me alone."

Robbie turned to me. "I love kids. My father was

always too busy for me. I intend to be involved with my child from the beginning, changing diapers and . . ."

"I'm not talking about changing diapers and making meals," Maggie interrupted quickly. "I'm talking about who's going to get up at 8 A.M. and go to the office and who's going to get up at 6 A.M. and stay with the baby? I'm talking about am I going to spend the next five years getting somewhere in my law firm and then have to stop?"

"It won't be like that." Robbie spoke with conviction. "If I have to take time off from work, I'll take time off from work. I don't mind taking a few years off from my career to take care of my kid."

Maggie was pleased and surprised. Apparently, this was the first she had heard of Robbie's convictions. "Oh, if that's how you really feel, that's great. I mean that's so good. I'll stop worrying."

It sounded good to me, too. When I struggled with that issue, it did not occur to me or to anyone else that my husband would take time off from work to care for a baby. But if it's so different now, why do so many professional women seem tortured by this decision? Why do newspaper surveys consistently ask women, not men, how they plan to juggle career and family? Was Robbie exceptional, or were his intentions better than his deeds would prove?

"In what ways would you like to see each other change?" I asked, moving on to another subject.

Robbie answered this time. "There's no point in going into that. We're as different as two people can be and we'll never change."

"Yeah," said Maggie, smiling mischievously. "He's serious and introspective, ambitious and compulsively hard-working."

"And she wants immediate gratification. She doesn't like to work hard. She likes to get work over with quickly so she can play for the rest of the day. But it's okay, we respect the differences between us."

"Of course," said Maggie, still smiling, "we also fight about them all the time. In my family, everybody always held things in. Robbie is used to yelling and screaming. I've learned to yell and scream too, and it feels good. But then . . ." She hesitated. "I haven't gotten to the point of twisting umbrellas into knots and throwing dishes on the floor."

Robbie sounded testy now. "And I haven't gotten to the point of storming out for hours without saying where I'm going!" He relaxed. "We drive each other crazy, but I wouldn't want her to change."

"Do you think you'll fight as much after you marry?" I persisted.

"I don't know," Robbie answered, looking serious. "Fighting is a big part of our relationship. We never stop fighting."

"It's not really fighting," Maggie explained. "We bicker a lot. It's more like teasing. It amuses us both and we make up quickly. It keeps us from getting bored."

I had met older couples who fought all the time, but their bickering lacked the charm Robbie and Maggie seemed to feel their fights had. Will the fighting still feel like "teasing" five years from now? Ten?

"Are you concerned about getting bored with each other?"

"Not at all," Robbie said. "We both have strong personalities, and we don't depend on one another for stimulation."

"In fact," joined Maggie, "we spend very little time together. Robbie works every night on his scripts, so I go to the theater with friends. Sometimes we have lunch together, and we go out on weekends, but if he's working, we don't go out. That's our life-style, and I'm sure it will continue."

Togetherness was the buzz word of the fifties. The family that prays together—plays together, shops together—stays together. We had togetherness up to our ears, and many a later marital split came from being smothered by togetherness. But I wondered about a "life-style" in which a couple sees each other once in a while on weekends, and about the kind of closeness that arrangement can bring to a marriage that is just beginning.

"Do you believe in marital fidelity?"

They had expected a question about that, and I expected the answer they gave.

"Oh yes." They spoke almost in unison. "What's the point of getting married otherwise?"

"I trust Robbie," Maggie said. "I think he's gorgeous, and I like it that other women find him attractive."

"It hasn't been that easy for me," Robbie admitted. "I used to be angry as hell at men who flirted with Maggie. I'm just beginning to get used to the idea that she has a lot of male friends. And I'm just beginning to have some female friends myself. But if we looked for outside stimulation and thrills, it would not be because we were bored with sex itself, but because we were unhappy with each other."

"Absolutely." Maggie nodded her agreement. "I think we will be able to be honest with each other and lay it on the table before it happens. That would be my goal. If I felt something was wrong, I hope I would be able to say, 'Robbie, something's the matter,' before anything happens."

"Even though Maggie and I have been going together for so long," Robbie summed up, "I don't feel I've missed out on anything. Sure, I can't say I've had five serious relationships with five different women over the past five years. But there aren't four other women I would like to have had a relationship with."

It was a nice note on which to end our interview for the day. I shut off the tape recorder. Maggie reached for her purse, and I noticed the delicate, shiny engagement ring she wore on her left hand. "It belonged to Robbie's grandmother," she said, following my glance. "I still can't believe I'm wearing it. I ordered a gold wedding band to go with it. I wonder what it's going to feel like, wearing rings on my finger for the rest of my life."

For the dozenth time my mind flicked backward. I saw myself, more than a quarter of a century earlier, my hands immersed in water as I helped my mother wash dishes after my engagement dinner. On my left hand my new diamond ring glistened under the faucet. I had not wanted to wear a ring ("conspicuous consumption," I had called it), but my husband-to-be had insisted, proud that he had been able to save enough money from odd jobs to pay for the ring himself. He had chosen it himself too, and in spite of my principles I felt a surge of excitement when he gave it to me. Something about getting that ring made me feel part of a secret clan—the clan of the married. Something about it made me feel grown-up and responsible.

What was it Maggie had said? As an adult she was ready to take large steps into the future. I watched them prepare to leave. They were so much more sophisticated than I had been, or than most of the people I interviewed had been when they married. They had lived together; they didn't hesitate to say things to each other that none of us ever had. They used profanities we knew but had never dared mouth. And yet they were marching into a future that was as unknown to them as ours had been to us.

Did Maggie know, any better than I, what it would be like when there was a child she loved even more passionately than her career? Was Robbie any more sure than my new husband had been about how to get along with his wife's friends, about when to hold her close and when to let go of her? Was she any more certain than I that the ring on her left hand, so treasured now, would not one day itch or pinch, or seem unbearably heavy?

The circumstances were quite different, but the expectations, hopes and blind spots were more alike than I had thought. As they opened the door to leave, Maggie turned around. "You want to know why we're getting married?" she said. "Because now we're making a public statement. This is forever."

Every couple who marry expect their marriage to last forever. In spite of the bad name marriage received in the last decade, in spite of startling divorce rates and "alternative" ways of coupling, in spite of dire predictions about the death of the family, women and men continue to marry and remarry, each couple convinced that they will live happily ever after.

Statistics show that more than two million couples take marriage vows every year, and that marriage rates have increased steadily over the decades. According to the National Center for Health Statistics, the rate of marriage during the 1980s was higher than it had been during the 1960s and most of the 1970s. Unfortunately, as almost everybody knows, the divorce rate more than doubled during those same decades. The steep rise in divorces seems to have leveled off some during the 1980s, with 4 percent fewer divorces registered in 1984 than in 1981. But nobody is wildly optimistic about that small drop. For one thing, marriages decreased during the mid-1970s, and the lower divorce rates of the 1980s might simply reflect that decrease. For another, the poor state of the American economy during the early 1980s made divorce seem a luxury fewer people could afford. Some sociologists and demographers have even predicted that the divorce rate might rise again, although not as sharply, in the 1990s, as the economy continues to improve and marriages increase.

Sociologist Andrew Cherlin, in his book *Marriage, Divorce, Remarriage*, points out that divorce has been on the upswing for decades, at least since the mid-1800s. Studying statistics over the years, Cherlin argues that the 1950s, with their low divorce rate, were exceptional times, brought on by people's desire for stability and security after the tumultuous years of World War II. The steep climb in divorces that began during the 1960s, Cherlin maintains, was really a continuation of patterns that had started earlier. In our time, however, the divorce spiral has been accelerated by new factors in society, among them the increasing number of women who have entered the work force and have gained the economic freedom to be able to leave unhappy marriages they might otherwise have been tied into.

Why? Why such unhappiness? Why do so many people who promise and sincerely believe, as do Maggie and Robbie, that they will love one another until death, leave one another, convinced with equal sincerity that they can no longer stay together? And why so early in the game, not only long before death parts them, but long before a trace of silver threads their hair, long before either face is marred by frown lines or sags of skin? Data, again from the National Center for Health Statistics, indicates that most marriages that end in divorce do so within the first six and a half to seven years, giving concrete evidence for the "seven-year itch."

The greatest number of divorces occur during the first three years. In fact, the divorce rate at three years of marriage is more than double the rate at eleven years, more than four times the rate at twenty years and eleven times the rate at thirty years. Yet one might have supposed that the glow of love would last through those very early years and that the greatest difficulties would come later, when familiarity replaces the excitement of discovery, or when children, financial problems or worries over ailing parents might wedge through the closeness a couple had established.

For years now, social scientists have been placing much of the blame for the steady increase in divorce on the great importance our society gives to romantic love. The excitement of love, they say, the sexual thrills and the haze of rosiness blind lovers to reality and prevent them from making intelligent decisions about themselves and their lives together. Encouraged by poems, books, songs and movies, the sweethearts float away into a make-believe world that has little connection with the everyday world they will inhabit. Some of my feminist friends also knock romantic love and its effects on marriage by portraying it as a creation of men used to distract women from the powerlessness that will later limit their married lives and cause them great unhappiness.

Neither argument is altogether false, but neither encompasses the entire truth. Men are the victims of romantic love as equally as women are, and men are equally unable or unwilling, during those idyllic days of courtship, to focus hard on what will come later. As for those days themselves, as for being in love, well, what is there to say except that it is a wonderful state to be in? When you're in love, you're filled with a sense of completeness, of being inside, outside and wrapped all around your beloved. You know that everything is possible, and you brim with ideals, hopes and visions. Who would want to banish romantic love from our lives? Who would want to deprive oneself of the excitement and thrill, even the bittersweet pain of wondering whether you are loved as much as you love? My father, married to my mother for sixty years, once told me that if he could choose two weeks in his life to relive, they would be the week before and the week after his wedding—the week before because of "the anticipation," the week after because of "the sheer happiness."

Blaming romantic love when marriage turns difficult is like blaming a child for being too bright when she doesn't live up to expectations: "If she hadn't done so well all along, we wouldn't have been angry when she didn't get into Yale." More to the point if we are looking for culprits in the early dissolution of a marriage, are the expectations themselves—not all of them, of course, but the more exaggerated illusions and simplistic attitudes that people acquire in their youth and bear with them into their marriages.

Maggie and Robbie are a good example. They have known one another for years. They are not carried away in transports of romantic blindness about one another, nor does either deny the other's faults. But they are so pleased about getting married, so wanting to be adults now, that they happily gloss over those faults. "We're as different as two people can be, and we'll never change," Robbie says, as though his acknowledgment makes the differences unimportant. "We fight all the time," Maggie laughs, shoving aside the anger that must lie behind the constant bickering. "Of course I'll take off from work when we have a baby," Robbie asserts, denying to himself the drive of ambition that makes him spend every evening working at his desk, leaving little time for the two to be together. And Maggie accepts his assertion, pretending to herself and to him that he will be able to put aside his ambitions when the time comes.

All marriages, not only those that fail, begin with unreal expectations that color much of what happens between partners. Although these expectations and illusions may come in part from the tingling romance of love, in larger part they come from each partner's needs, wishes and dreams, some of them conscious, some of them less so.

Clifford Sager, a psychiatrist and marital therapist, has written extensively about his theory of marital contracts, a theory that has nothing to do with contemporary agreements that spell out such niceties as who takes out the garbage and who washes the dishes. The contracts in which Sager is interested are the often unspoken ones between husband and wife that reflect what in their heart of hearts the partners expect or hope for from the marriage, and which, because they are hidden, may become a source of trouble. A man marrying a professional woman, for example, may be wonderfully supportive of her work and career before they marry. He may truly believe in the principle of an egalitarian marriage and in his wife's right to work outside the home just as he does. Yet another part of him harbors the expectation, carried over from his own family, that once married, she will make her career secondary to her domestic life. His secret contract with her might be, "No matter what else you do, I want you to make a comfortable home for me, as my mother did for my father." A woman with a domineering father marries a soft-spoken gentle man, and speaks about her relief in getting away from the repressive strictures of her childhood. But her secret contract, buried someplace in the recesses of her consciousness, is, "I'm going to push you into being more bossy and assertive toward me because that's the only way I can feel safe and secure."

There are many kinds of expectations with which people begin their marriages. "I'll change him/her after we marry" is one of the most common of these—trite, actually, because it is so widely known and often laughed at. But it is there, for many newlyweds: that hope that the other person will change after marriage, or at least change just a few "little" habits. One man I know who loves skiing is about to be married to a woman whose idea of a perfect ski vacation is sitting in the ski lodge in front of a fire, reading. The man has decided to surprise his love on her birthday with an array of ski clothes, convinced that if she dresses warmly enough, she will change her mind about skiing and like it as much as he does. An expectation of a small change, but one that could lead to big disappointment. Robbie and Maggie hold the opposite expectation—that neither of them will need to change at all, no matter how much they fight about their differences. It is an expectation that will surely have to be modified with time.

The "I'll be happy once I'm married" illusion is also widely held, an anticipation that marriage will take care of all one's emotional needs. In good marriages each partner does fill some of the other's emotional gaps. But many people in long marriages told me that one of the hardest things they had to learn was that their spouses could not turn them into happy people, or satisfy their every wish, no matter how supportive the spouse. "I thought marriage was a ticket to heaven," one woman said. "It took me a long time to realize that *he* can't make me feel different. Only *I* can make me feel different."

Then there is the illusion that "if she loved me, she'd know how I feel," which may begin before marriage and continue well into it. This is the expectation that in some fantasy land of love you never have to tell your partner how you feel or what you want. Reinforced by love and understanding, she or he will be able to read your mind and intuitively know whether something is wrong. If the reading is incorrect or the knowledge doesn't exist, there is a serious flaw in the partner, the marriage or both. Actually what is flawed is the thinking itself. It's a way of looking at marriage that places the responsibility for closeness and understanding on one spouse and leaves the other a passive receptor. It's a way of relating that constantly tests the partner's love, a test that partner is bound to fail at some point.

A corollary to this expectation is the belief that true love is unconditional, meaning that if you are loved, you can say anything or act any way because your partner will understand and forgive—the old saw that "love means never having to say you're sorry." It's a nice ideal. The only condition for such unconditional marital love, however, is that it needs to be reciprocal. Each partner has to be equally accepting of the other; one-way acceptances don't work. A recently divorced woman told me: "He assumed I would always be there, no matter what he did. The table was there, the chair was there, and I was there. He could kick the chair when he was mad, hit the table or yell at me, and none of us would fight back or demand anything of him. Whatever he did, we would always be there, always accepting. Well, the table and chair are still there, but I'm not."

Underlying all the other expectations is the expectation of perfection. All of us begin marriage with such high hopes, it is hard to believe that anything about our life could be less than perfect. When imperfections appear (as they must), most couples look around at other marriages and wonder what is wrong with them. They are sure that everybody else's sex life is wonderful, while they have had trouble adjusting to one another; everybody else knows how to communicate feelings, while they have had vicious battles; everybody else is adept at handling finances, while theirs are in constant chaos. Since their marriage isn't perfect, as everybody else's is, they conclude that it is probably no good at all.

Expectations of perfection are especially true of couples marrying today. Couples like Maggie and Robbie, who have lived together before marriage, as many couples have, or slept together, as many more have, feel they know one another as well as anyone could. Many of them are older when they marry than their parents were. They have thought through, and discussed in great depth, what marriage is, whether they should marry and why they should marry. They cannot imagine that issues could arise that they have not considered, and there seems to be no reason why their marriage should not be perfect. In fact, those who come from homes of long-lasting marriages often marvel at the ability their parents had to stay married, considering how ill-equipped they had been for marriage compared to their children.

Yet their very assumption that they can achieve perfection is probably one of the reasons their marriages are failing at higher rates than their parents' marriages had. Because these couples know each other so well, because they are older and presumably more mature, their expectations of emotional fulfillment are greater than were those of earlier generations. That is not to say that their parents and grandparents did not expect to find happiness in marriage. They did, as did generations of couples before them, even those in arranged marriages. But social and economic pressures led those earlier generations of young men and women to temper their drive for perfection. With divorce as acceptable as it is, with many women less dependent economically on marriage than ever before, couples today are not willing to accommodate each other as readily if their illusions turn out to be false.

And often the illusions do turn sour. The idea that

many people hold, for example, that marriages of older couples—people in their late twenties or early thirties—have better prospects of lasting than marriages of younger couples may be true in individual cases but is not borne out statistically. During the 1970s, when divorce rates rose to an all-time high, couples' ages at marriage were also higher than they had been in decades. Age was no guarantee against divorce.

The even more popular belief that living together before marriage helps assure compatibility after marriage has not panned out so well either. As far as anyone can tell (since there are no exact statistics), there seem to be as many marital breakups among couples who live together first as those who do not. Some sociologists suspect there may be more. That's because some couples carry their "before" attitudes right into their "after" life. That is, they attach the same kind of impermanence to marriage that they did to living together. They don't mind walking out when things get tough. Others, on the contrary, find the adjustment to marriage especially difficult just because they feel so boxed in and weighted down by their newfound commitment. Temper tantrums and bad jokes, bathroom manners or bedroom habits that did not seem significant before suddenly take on new importance because they have become permanent. And that sense of permanence can frighten or disillusion a partner. "It's like looking at your life through a telescope turned backwards," said one man, who had lived with his wife for four years before they recently married. "Now everything each of you does seems to stretch far into the future, and you think it'll never change."

But today's generation of marrying couples is not the first to discover that the realities of marriage do not always correspond to the illusions and secret contracts brought into it. Probably every couple that ever existed has looked at one another at some point during or after the honeymoon and wondered, "Who are you?" and "What am I doing here?" For every couple there are expectations and dreams that go unfulfilled. Those who remain married and satisfied with their marriages are willing to discard the fantasies and build a richer and deeper life beyond the illusions.

Marital therapist Carl Whitaker, who has written and lectured a great deal, believes that a real marriage doesn't begin until that time when the illusions wear off, or wear thin. It takes a couple about ten years, says Whitaker, to realize that the expectations with which they began marriage and the assumptions they held about each other are not quite the way they seemed. At this point they see themselves as having "fallen out of love." He no longer thinks he can change her, and she no longer thinks he can understand her. The characteristics that had once seemed endearing—his fear of flying, her fear of failure—now drive them crazy. They have come to see each other as real people, neither saviors nor therapists, saints nor charming rogues. Each knows the other's vulnerabilities, and knows well how to hurt the other. Now their marriage is at a crossroads. They can become locked into a pattern of fighting and making each other miserable; they can become involved in outside affairs; they can decide that this is not what they bargained for and split; or they can create a true marriage. That is, they can come to accept the frailties and vulnerabilities each has, accept them and respect them, and in doing so, discover a much more profound love for the real person whom they married.

It may not take ten years for Whitaker's "ten-year-syndrome" to occur. It may take three weeks or five months or two decades for the exaggerated expectations and fantasies to fall away and for a couple to find themselves face to face with one another, confronting the realities of their marriage. I also don't agree with Whitaker's contention that all the illusions fade with familiarity. The person we come to know during the course of a marriage is flawed and human, but that person still retains some of the stuff around which the illusions were built. I know my husband's pains, self-doubts and powerful emotional needs, for example, but I know him also as the confident and calmly secure young man I married years ago. He is an amalgam of both, and the two together make up a strongly textured whole that is far more complex than either part alone.

In any event, a day will come when Maggie will not be able to smile indulgently at the twisted umbrella Robbie has hurled to the ground in a fit of temper. A moment will arrive when Robbie will not be able to see the charm of Maggie's inability to stick to a job. A week will present itself when both will wonder what they ever saw in each other and how they could have made the terrible mistake of marrying. They will despair of wanting to be near each other, to look at one another, to hear the other's voice. When that time comes—and it does in every marriage—they will have to decide, each of them, how deeply they care about one another, and how far they are willing to stretch toward each other. They will have to decide whether they want to live with the selves that have emerged and with the marriage as it has evolved and as it will continue to evolve over time. It's not a decision they will necessarily sit down and make one day, although they may, but it's one that will grow out of what they learn about each other, and how they come to feel toward one another.

If they make the decision to stay together, they will begin the real process of marriage. Marriage is a process because it is always in flux; it never stays the same and it never completes itself. It is a process of changing and accepting change, of settling differences and living with differences that will never be settled, of drawing close and pulling apart and drawing close again. Because it is a process that demands discipline and responsibility, it can bring frustration and pain, but it also can plumb the depths of love and provide an arena for self-actualization as nothing else can.

The one unchanging and constant in a marriage is the attachment of the couple to one another—the commitment, to use today's terminology. Yet even that is not static, but is constantly in motion. At the heart of that commitment lies an irresolvable tension, a pull between oneself and one's partner. It's a pull between loving yourself and loving your partner, doing for yourself and doing for your partner, satisfying yourself and satisfying your partner. If you don't love yourself, you cannot love another person, because how can you value the other's needs when you don't place value on your own needs? But if you love yourself too much, how can you give love to another? So there is a pull back and forth. At times self-love takes over and one partner makes incessant demands on the other. And then the positions reverse. At times one partner becomes ill or weak and depends on the other for health and strength. And then the positions reverse. In every marriage, there are shaky periods and calm ones, balancing themselves out over time. But at any given moment, there is a pull between the needs of one partner and the needs of the other and the paradoxical needs of both to be whole people in themselves and part of the whole that is the marriage.

People who make the decision to stay married because they find their marriages satisfying are people for whom the attachment to one another is more important than any disillusionments they encounter. In the pull and tug between self-love and love of the other, they are willing to extend beyond themselves to meet the needs of their partner, not always, but often enough, aware that their turn will also come. And in moving outward they sometimes discover that what started out appearing to be self-sacrifice becomes in the end self-enhancement.

If Maggie and Robbie stay married, their marriage will have a special kind of romance. It will not only be the romance of loving one another, and it will not only be the romance of sexual excitement—although those will be part of their marriage. The romance of a marriage that lasts beyond the illusions comes in its incompleteness, and in the adventure of exploring the unfolding process together.

CHAPTER TWO

~:~

Intimacy
"She's There to Listen to My Good Times and My Bad Times"

In the weeks before she died, my mother-in-law resembled a tiny marble figure, lying straight and flat on her hospital bed like one of those reliefs of saints that adorn the sarcophagi so often found in medieval churches. Every night my husband and I stood at that bedside in St. Luke's Hospital in New York City and helplessly watched her life ebb away as the cancer she had fought for five years won complete mastery over her body.

We found her especially fragile one Friday night, her skin the color of melted wax now and stretched so tight across her face that the cheekbones seemed to be pushing through, too rude to wait until death eased them out. She struggled to keep her eyes open as she listened to the trivia we brought to her. We talked to maintain the semblance of normalcy, about ourselves, our daughter, the incidents of the day. Although she no longer had the energy to speak, occasionally she could pull her thin lips back from her teeth in the semblance of a smile. Before we left, my husband asked if she would like some applesauce. She nodded, and he propped her in his arms, feeding her from a cup she was too weak to hold herself. Like a baby bird opening its mouth wide for the life-giving

18

worm its mother is about to feed it, she dutifully opened her mouth to receive bits of nourishment from the son she had once nurtured. Finished, she slid down into the bed again. Her eyelids sank, leaving only a sliver of color, a hint of wakefulness. Then she turned her head toward my husband and whispered, "Good-bye, *Schatzie*." They were the last words we would hear from her. She died exactly a week later.

Schatzie is a playful term for darling or dear one in German, a language my mother-in-law knew along with her native French. Born in Belgium, she had escaped the Nazi invasion and come to America together with her husband and her young son, her only child. He, my husband, was the apple of his mother's eye, the source of her deepest joy, her pride, her gem. A warm and gracious woman, she had embraced me with love and accepted me from the moment of my marriage. She had cherished my daughter, her granddaughter, with a love that brooked no competition from the other grannies eager to parade their grandchildren's virtues. Yet only my husband was called *schatzie*, her dear one. Her love for him was total, unequivocal, untarnished by doubt. He could do no wrong. It became something of a joke in our family that if ever I tried to complain to my mother-in-law about her son, she simply nodded her head, smiled sweetly and said, "Uh huh." No word of criticism would cross her lips about the boy turned youth turned middle-aged man whom she loved equally at every point in his life.

My husband and I left the room together that night. Suddenly I became aware I was walking alone. I turned and saw him leaning against a wall, head in hands, sobbing uncontrollably. I walked back to him, slipped my arm into his and waited for the tears to subside. I had seen him cry before, tears of sadness or joy on various occasions, but never had I seen these body-wracking sobs. Even when his mother first became ill, even when he took her, himself, to the hospital for what he knew would be the last time, he did not cry this way. Nor would he cry later—at her funeral or afterward when he sorted through her belongings—the way he cried that night at the hospital.

I knew why. For so long he had been the calm, composed psychiatrist, the wise doctor, the cool professional who was also an expert in the field of death and dying. In our home the phone rings constantly with the calls of people sorrowing over sick friends or relatives. My husband gives them practical advice, discusses hospice care, proffers sympathy, yet remains distant enough to help them keep some distance themselves. He had dealt with his mother's illness, as he does with all family problems, using the same professionalism, loving and comforting, yet slightly apart. But now she had said good-bye. And suddenly the carefully trained professional had slipped away to leave behind the son, exposed, unprotected by the doctor's armor. Now there remained a boy crying for a mother who had loved him in a way no one else—not even I—had. There remained a man who had believed that death could come with dignity and had discovered that when death came to ravage his mother it had little regard for man-made slogans. There remained a human being who, in becoming orphaned, was losing one more buffer between himself and mortality. That night my husband cried for the sadnesses of his mother's life, of which there had been many, and he cried for himself, because never again in his life would anyone call him *schatzie*.

I knew, without his saying, what he was thinking and feeling, and he knew that I knew. Arm in arm we left the hospital, driving home silently. After the death we arranged her funeral, made plans for caring for his ailing father, accepted condolences during the seven days in which my husband sat *shiva* in accordance with Jewish law. But we have never discussed that incident in the hospital, have never even talked about the sadness we both carry within us since his mother's death. There has been no need to. Everything that could be said was said without words that night. It was a moment of total honesty, of complete understanding, of intimacy.

Intimacy is one of those words, like commitment, communication, or relationship, that has been so overused in recent years that one would like to avoid it altogether. Unfortunately, all these words are hard to avoid, if only because they are so popular and quickly grasped. Even if we were to find adequate substitutes for them, the new terms would quickly become equally hackneyed. The best I can hope for, then, is to use these words carefully and as I mean them to be understood in the context of this discussion.

Of all the components of marriage, intimacy is probably the quality most longed for, and often the most elusive. Sexual intimacy is major, of course, but intimacy in terms of closeness and affection between partners goes beyond the sexual aspects of marriage. With that closeness many things become possible. Without it, inside as well as outside marriage, there is loneliness. For all that has been written about intimacy, I still prefer the definition composed more than thirty years ago by psychoanalyst Erik Erikson, not in connection with marriage, although that is implied, but in connection with maturation. In *Childhood and Society*, a book that would become a classic in the field of human development, Erikson speaks about the move from adolescence to adulthood as a time when a young person becomes ready for intimacy. And he defines intimacy as the "capacity to commit himself to concrete affiliations and partnerships and to develop the ethical strength to abide by such commitments, even though they may call for significant sacrifices and compromises."

Unlike intimacy, the words sacrifice and compromise have become less popular with time. Writing some twenty years after Erikson, in her book *Passages*, Gail Sheehy criticized his definition of intimacy as one that demands a "selfless devotion" to the other. From her vantage point in the 1970s, to speak about sacrifice was to blur the concept of the self, and in those years the self and its fulfillment were more important than anything.

More recently we have moved away from 1970s-type thinking and are able to consider once again Erikson's approach to intimacy as a commitment to another person that may demand sacrifice and compromise. Rather than a loss of self, such a commitment requires an expansion of self, an ability to feel what someone else feels, know what someone else needs and put oneself out, when necessary, to satisfy the other person's feelings and needs. Stretching oneself in this way doesn't mean losing oneself or, to use psychological jargon, fusing oneself with the other person. It does mean maintaining a constant awareness of the other person and that person's desires, even as the other maintains an awareness of you and your wishes.

This exchange of knowledge, and with it, the ability to give to another without resentment and in turn receive from that other without embarrassment is what intimacy is all about.

One of the couples who delighted me most, of all the couples I visited and interviewed, were Calvin and Nancy Hart of New Jersey. Calvin works as a horse breeder and trainer at a farm about ten miles from their home in Morristown, and Nancy, who spends most of her time caring for the couple's two children, has become quite adept at making silver jewelry. I liked them because they were straight and honest, with no pretenses. And I liked them because they had a way of phrasing ideas about such complicated subjects as intimacy and commitment in no-nonsense terms that sometimes made me laugh because they sounded so corny but often had a ring of truth that made good sense.

The first thing they told me about themselves was that they had met in bed. It was back in the late 1960s. Both were raised in middle-class families and both had rebelled. Calvin had quit school to join the merchant marine and was stationed in Hawaii. Nancy was hitchhiking around the country and had left California for Hawaii to visit friends. She arrived with fifty cents in her pocket to discover that her friends had no room for her in their apartment. But they knew friends who knew friends who knew of an empty bed in a rooming house, the bed of a sailor who had gone out on some kind of mission. Nancy took the bed. Calvin came home from sea to find a strange young woman in his bed and no place to sleep except for the floor. That arrangement lasted three nights. On the fourth night, Calvin said, "Enough." She was welcome to share his bed if she wanted, but it was, after all, his bed.

She shared it, and has been doing so ever since, for the past fifteen years as his wife. "I guess we woke up one morning and we were making love," said Calvin, "and from then on it just took off."

Not the most propitious beginning for the development of love and intimacy, sacrifice and commitment, and it took a while for these qualities to become part of their marriage. They were "sixties kids," after all, adventuresome, daring, into the drug scene, out partying from "Friday night to Monday morning," in Calvin's words. It was a time of "intellectualism," he explained, a time when "we talked everything to death." Eventually the partying, the smoking, the intellectualism ended, and Nancy and Calvin were left with themselves and their marriage. They moved from Hawaii to New Jersey, where Calvin had been born, and he began working with horses, a lifelong passion. Their marriage took on some of the trappings of the middle class they had tried so hard to escape. It also began to suffer the tensions of an established marriage. Calvin became increasingly more involved in his work, and in his free time thought nothing of riding off alone for hours as if he had not a responsibility in the world. One day, three years into their marriage, Calvin took off on a camping trip with some buddies. When he came home, Nancy and their infant daughter were gone.

Neither of them remembers the precipitating incident nor how they got together again. All they remember is that they "sat down and talked." Said Nancy: "You don't know why the hell you're staying around. Then you look at it later and you say, 'Oh yes, commitment.'" Commitment is a word they both use often.

"But what does commitment mean to you?" I asked them.

Calvin thought for a moment. "I think deep down inside, for me, it means who else is going to put up with my shit? And she's got her shit that I put up with. It's not that we sit and think of it that way. We just live life. But if I think of it, what I think is that each of us gives up a piece of ourselves for the other one. Yet we don't really lose those pieces—they just connect with each other and pull us back closer together."

It struck me as not a bad way to explain Erikson's concept of sacrifice as an element in intimacy.

There is, however, another aspect of sacrifice in an intimate relationship, and one that is far more difficult than giving up something of yourself to understand or help your partner. That is, giving up your own protection and covering, your shell, your safeguard against hurt, and exposing your innermost self. The hardest part of being close to someone is taking that step of uncovering yourself. The risks are enormous, breathtaking, fearsome. When you open yourself to someone else, you make yourself vulnerable, and because of that vulnerability you can be crushed by the other's anger or destroyed by the other's laughter. Yet without that exposure and that honesty between partners, intimacy cannot exist.

Said my philosopher friend Calvin: "You want to know what intimacy is? You want to know what it means to me to be married? It means I got someone I'm pretty damned close to, closer to than to anyone else. She's there to listen to my good times and my bad times. She's in there pulling along with me. Because of her, I'm not lonely—at least not most of the time." It is to achieve this kind of closeness, this ability to be yourself and still be loved, that people marry, because when it works, marriage offers the safest arena for being free.

But even in marriage it is a risky business, letting yourself be known. One of the reasons is that deep within us, at least in many of us, lies a gnawing doubt about ourselves and about whether we are worthy of being loved and nurtured by another. We're afraid to open ourselves up because we're afraid that what will be seen and known will be disappointing. "All the time I was dating my husband-to-be," one woman told me, "I used to ask him why he loved me. I mean I wasn't being coy. I knew there were qualities I had that he responded to, but I always thought also that I was fooling him. It was all pretense, and what would happen when he discovered all the bad qualities?" Calvin Hart put it this way: "Sometimes it's very difficult to accept the support and love your partner gives you, because when you look at yourself in the mirror you always see a creep. No matter what you do, you could have done it better."

Feelings of being unworthy make us fearful of intimacy; they also make us question the worth of the person who loves us. Before I married, I invariably fell in love with men who lorded over me, who acted superior, who expected me to comfort and cater to them. I was not the only young woman of my generation who chose those kinds of men to love and idolize. Our images of ourselves

stemmed in large part from our society's image of women.
We saw ourselves as playthings—intelligent, perhaps, but
inferior to the men around us. Our role, as many of us
perceived it, was to understand men, to delve beyond the
surface of their indifference or self-centeredness and bring
out the good and true hidden within. Those of us who
had an intellectual or artistic bent fell for writers or musi-
cians, artists whose sensitive souls we thought we could
reach through our love and encouragement—even though
they treated us like dirt. When I met my husband and
became romantically involved with him, my greatest res-
ervations came from the fact that he was kind and good
and as caring of me as I was of him. How could I respect
someone who loved me? (The old Groucho Marx line: "I
wouldn't want to join a club that would have me as a
member.") How could he love me if he really knew me?
Either he was flawed or he didn't know me. If the former,
should I marry him? And if the latter, could I risk that
knowledge?

The intimacy that develops in the course of marriage,
when it develops, takes into account the suspicion both
partners have about themselves that underneath they are
really "creeps." Each can expose the creep to the other,
knowing that it will be accepted along with the rest.

Acceptance is a prerequisite for intimacy, and from
acceptance grows trust. You trust one another to accept
you for yourself and, once accepting, not to betray that
trust. That moment in the hospital when my husband
cried was a moment of intense intimacy because it was a
moment of honesty and trust. He let down all his de-
fenses, knowing that he was safe with me, that I understood. I trusted him, also, to recognize the sadness I felt.
It was a matter of trust for me because he knew of other
feelings I had had toward his mother over the years.
There were the early years when I resented over that mother
love that enveloped my husband. I resented the adulation
that shone on her face at his every word, and I grew
irritated at the excessive joy that greeted even his minor
accomplishments. Over time as we became closer, I could
tease her about her "Jewish motherhood," but a touch of
resentment (or was it jealousy?) remained with me, always. My husband knew that, but he also knew that even

when I criticized her, I admired her ability to be so accepting of her child, an ability parents talk about but not many
of us have. All that history and knowledge were with us
at the hospital when we sorrowed together over his mother's dying.

Acceptance and trust in marriage presuppose exclusivity. The reason marriage provides the greatest possibilities for intimacy is because marriage is predicated on the
idea of exclusivity. And one of the differences between
marriage and other friendships is the importance of exclusivity. Most people have more than one friend to whom
they may reveal parts of themselves. But when married
couples speak of themselves as "best friends," as so many
do, they are speaking of having created a kind of club-
house of their own, a secret society that exists in the
larger society but excludes all others from its innermost
core. During my interviews with people whose marriages
had broken up, I was surprised by how many of them
said to me, "The problem was, he never made me feel
special, as if I were different to him than anybody else."
The rival for that position of specialness may not have
been another woman or man; it may have been a relative,
a friend or in many cases a job or career. In marriage the
degree of closeness that develops depends to a great extent on how special each partner feels, how unique and
important in a way that nothing else is.

A friend, recently widowed, told me of being stranded
in an airport on a snowy Sunday. "I knew I would be
hours late coming home," she said. "I waited my turn at
the pay phone—everybody was pushing for the phones to
call home—and when I finally got a phone I suddenly
stopped. Whom would I call? Sure, my parents knew I
was due home that night, but they weren't holding dinner
for me; I had never even given them my schedule. Suddenly I felt an overwhelming sense of loneliness. There
was nobody to whom I was the most important person in
the world, nobody who would worry, when I didn't get
home on time, that the plane had crashed or I had been
hit by a car. I felt more alone that night than I had any
time since Steve died."

One of the reasons the open marriage movement of

the 1970s came and went within a flicker of an eye, I believe, is because it disregarded the need partners have for exclusivity in marriage, for being the most important person in the other's life. Once others are brought in, the trust is diluted and the old fears of revealing oneself take hold again.

As I came to know more and more couples in the course of writing this book, I came to believe that every marriage has its secret, some reality that is exclusive to the couple. The stronger the marriage and the closer the partners are to each other, the more likely it is for that secret to be kept within the marriage than to be opened to the outside. The secret might be that he's lousy in bed or that she sucks her thumb at night. The secret might be that she is five years older than he is, or that he's afraid of heights. The secret might be that while to all the world he is the epitome of confidence, he paces the floor night after night unable to sleep for worrying about his abilities and his accomplishments. The secret might be that while her beauty is the envy of her friends, she is distraught about aging, obsessed with anxiety about every wrinkle or line.

Sometimes, sitting with a couple and talking for several hours, or alone with a wife or a husband, asking questions or listening hard, I would have the feeling that our meeting was turning into something more than an interview. The air would become heavy with emotion, and I would sit back, barely breathing, as the interviewees searched into themselves and spoke about things they had hidden or put aside long ago. That's how it was that I learned the secret in the marriage of Manny Battista and his wife, Bernice.

The marriage had puzzled me. Twenty years older than Bernice, Manny had come to America from Argentina about sixteen years ago, shortly before the two met and married. He works as a bookkeeper, and in his free time loves to "play the numbers," with few regrets about the money he might lose on a gambling venture. Handsome and urbane, he has an easy charm and a wry sense of humor that wins strangers over quickly. Bernice is just the opposite. Plump, somewhat disheveled, she worries every issue to death. In the course of our meetings, both described the severe depressive states she sometimes falls into, a depression that seems to have a biological component. She, too, is a bookkeeper, working for the same firm as Manny, although in a different office. Because of Bernice's depressions, Manny has taken over almost all household chores, and especially the responsibility for their three children, who are cared for by Bernice's mother while the two are at work.

But Manny has few complaints about the division of labor or anything else about his family life. When he speaks of Bernice, it is with warm devotion, in deeply loving tones, always protective and admiring of her. "We complement one another in so many ways," he told me, "like a left shoe and a right shoe." I believed he meant what he said, but I wasn't sure why he felt the way he did.

Bernice spoke at great length in my meeting with her about her parents, her brothers, her differences with her mother in matters of childrearing and household care. When I asked about Manny's family, she was vague. She knew little about them, she said, because he had lost track of them in the years since he had been in the States. Instead he had become closely attached to her family. One of the few differences between them, in fact, was his friendship with her parents and his refusal to join Bernice in criticizing them.

Manny had little to add to their story when I met with him by himself. It was a warm summer evening. He had stayed after work to see me in his office after everyone had left. Alone with me he appeared more tense and withdrawn than he had been when I met with the two of them together. He gradually began to relax in the hour that we spoke, but by the end of the hour I felt I had little more to learn from him. Tired and hungry myself, I turned off my tape recorder, put down my pad and pencil and thanked him for his time. He lit up a cigarette and leaned back in his chair, deep in thought.

"Did Bernice tell you anything about my background?" he asked.

"No," I said, gathering my belongings. "Only that you weren't close to your family."

"I knew she wouldn't." He smiled. "I'm glad. But I will tell you something nobody knows except Bernice."

"What's that?" I reached for my tape recorder.

He paused. Then: "I was married once before."

"In Argentina?"

"Yes, in Argentina."

"Why is that such a secret? Many people are divorced and remarried."

He looked away. "It was a horrible marriage. Eleven years of misery. My wife had been a beauty quèen, a runner up for a Miss Universe contest. She continued the role into our marriage. She acted like a queen, with no respect for me. She treated me shabbily, viciously."

"Were there any children?"

Silence draped the room. The air thickened. His voice became hoarse.

"Two. A girl and a boy."

"Have you ever seen them again?"

"Never. I left Argentina and that life behind me. I haven't kept in touch with anyone in my family. But the children . . ." I had to lean forward to hear him now. "You remember when the British invaded the Falklands? I was glued to the TV set. My son would have been old enough to fight in the Argentinian army. I kept watching and wondering whether I would see him. I never stop thinking about the children."

"And Bernice?" I asked. "What does she say about that marriage?"

"Bernice understands completely. She knows how horrendous it was. Our children don't know, and I'm not sure I'll ever tell them. But Bernice understands about the other children, about everything. She's made my life worth living."

Now this marriage made sense to me. Smooth, sophisticated Manny still smarts from the humiliations suffered at the hands of a wife who saw herself as the eternal beauty queen. He still agonizes over the children he left behind as the condition for escaping the degradations of that marriage. Bernice knows all that. Bernice might become depressed or angry, demanding or petulant. But she will never humiliate her husband. She needs him and depends on him, and that need balances his own enormous need to have her respect. Bernice loves her husband, and in that love Manny has been able to regain his confidence and love for himself. Nothing she asks of him, then, is too much. Bernice never told me her husband's secret, and I never told her I knew it. It remains an undercurrent that ripples through the rest of their marriage.

It takes time to feel the trust and acceptance that allow for the sharing of secrets, and time is another major element in the intimacy of marriage. Many couples told me that they fell in love with one another instantly, and I believed them. I believe that love at first sight does happen, and that for a variety of reasons people can feel immediate attractions for one another, can even know instantly in some ineffable way that someday they may marry. What I do not believe in, however, is instant intimacy. The deeper love that grows from that first attraction needs time in which to take root and then expand. Over time, couples build up a history of their own, chapter by chapter. For those in enduring marriages, each new segment strengthens the bonds between them. "Who else could ever understand what it felt like when my son died?" asked a mother of a child who had died of Tay-Sachs disease. Sharing the suffering through the boy's illness and death had brought her and her husband as close as any two people could be, and nothing in the future would eradicate the history they shared.

Over time, also, partners realize and accept the fact that intimacy is not a steady, unchanging phenomenon in marriage but that closeness comes and goes. There are times when you are both so involved with your work or your family that you have little energy for each other. You go through days, sometimes weeks, of anger, even hatred, in which you wonder how you will ever get connected again. You go through periods of such distancing that you question what you are doing together in the first place, no matter how long you have been married.

At a luncheon I attended, the hostess asked all her guests, "What would you have liked to know before you married that nobody ever told you?" One woman answered immediately: "I would have liked to know that one day, after years of marriage, I could sit across a room from my husband and look up and think, 'Who is this man I'm married to? I feel nothing for him. I don't belong with him or his family who are so different from me.' And then, the next day, feel the same closeness I've always felt."

People who have been married for some time recognize that these periods of distancing break into the periods of closeness and that with time the closeness returns. Said one man: "You go through phases when the marriage seems to sour for a little while. It's because . . . who knows why? It just doesn't seem to be working the way it should—no special reason, just the old everyday living." His wife added: "You think, 'Gee, something's wrong here,' but you don't think of having an affair or running away, or splitting. You just sort of keep going and know it will get better."

One difference between new marriages and those that have lasted for some time is that in enduring marriages you know time is on your side and somehow you will get close again.

Time also allows you the security of taking each other for granted. Security and taking-for-granted are terms we often hear used to connote marital boredom or neglect. Certainly when spouses show little interest in each other and make little effort to enjoy one another they are taking each other for granted in the most negative sense of that phrase. And in such situations security becomes a euphemism for dreariness. But in its best sense, taking for granted means that with time partners come to count on mutual love and care, and security means that their energies are not tied up in having to impress each other or prove themselves. Although advice books emphasize the need for excitement in marriage, married people emphasize the comfort and security that come with feeling wanted and valued.

"Carl used to say to me after we were married," a woman married sixteen years told me, " 'I wanted to get married because I wanted to take you for granted.' It sounds horrendous but I understood what he meant. What he was thinking was, 'I want to know that I can have you all the time, that I don't always have to put in the effort and bring you flowers and so on.' " And, this woman went on, "I could accept that. There's an underlying knowledge that you care about each other. It's nice when you *want* to show the other person that you care. But the fact that you don't *have* to frees you to enjoy each other." Over the years, couples can become close enough to enjoy the freedom of taking each other for granted yet caring enough not to do so all the time.

But every marriage that lasts is not necessarily a close one. As everyone knows, in many marriages the steadfastness of security replaces love, and being taken for granted becomes a substitute for intimacy. How do couples achieve and maintain intimacy and closeness over time?

A study reported by Nina S. Fields in the journal *Social Work* indicates that people in marriages they consider satisfying have a clear-cut knowledge and understanding of each other. In the study, couples married on an average of twenty-four years were asked to describe themselves in terms of personality, interests, emotional feelings and social needs, and then to describe their spouses in the same areas. The researchers found that in satisfying marriages spouses were able to describe their mates in very much the same way that the mates described themselves in appearance, feelings, strengths and weaknesses. They were people who knew each other well, and that knowledge had both grown out of the closeness of their marriage and led to further intimacy.

Getting to know one another and sharing the intimacy that follows involve spending time together, talking to each other, listening to become sensitive to the other's needs—communicating with each other. Everybody knows about communication: A waitress in a coffee shop I frequent, married thirty-eight years, tells me that the reason her marriage is good is that she and her husband, a construction worker, communicate all the time. A lawyer who specializes in divorces calls me from Wisconsin to say that the key factor he finds in divorces he handles is that couples cannot communicate and have not been communicating for years.

Everybody communicates about the importance of communication, yet for many people the ability to communicate remains one of the most difficult skills in life and in marriage—so difficult, in fact, that entire businesses have been built around teaching people how to communicate. In Minneapolis, for example, an organization called Interpersonal Communication Programs, Inc., runs nationwide seminars on communication, with one program devoted especially to "couples communication." And on any given weekend through the country you can probably find a marriage encounter group, where couples are working hard to learn how to communicate their feelings to one another.

In Massachusetts I met with six couples who run marriage encounter weekends. The marriage encounter movement was begun by the Catholic church and grew to great popularity during the 1970s, spreading to other religious groups as well. In recent years the numbers of people who attend these groups have slackened as the encounter movement in general has shrunk. Still, the network is wide, and couples continue to attend encounter weekends to "revitalize" their marriages, as one participant told me.

The group I met with described an encounter weekend as forty-four intensive hours in which partners share their feelings on a variety of topics. One of the first lessons they learn is to distinguish between feelings and opinions. If you say, "I feel you should try harder," you are really stating an opinion. A feeling is expressed in such statements as "I feel sad" or "I feel glad." By making such distinctions couples soon discover hidden ways in which they may have been attacking one another. To get practice stating real feelings, they write each other letters about their feelings after hearing formal presentations on such topics as "self," or "we and our community." The exchange of letters is called "dialoguing." At the end of an encounter weekend, many husbands and wives, brought closer by the experience, renew their marriage vows in a communal ceremony.

The evening I spent with the encounter leaders concluded with a simulation of how an encounter weekend might end, without the marriage ceremony. The lights were dimmed, a candle lit, and each person in the room was invited to say how she or he felt about my visit.

"I was cautious at first," said one woman, "but now I feel hopeful." And she snuggled closer to her husband.

"I feel special," said a man, looking into his wife's eyes, "close to everyone in this room."

"I feel bright yellow," said a woman dressed all in brown.

"And I feel warm, snuggly and happy," said another woman.

I felt puzzled. I could not quite figure out what, in their factual description of "encountering," had led these couples to such feelings of intimacy among themselves or with me. Perhaps speaking about encounter groups had stirred up memories for them of emotions felt at past sessions. Or perhaps—and I suspected this was true of some of the people in the room—speaking about feelings and conveying them to one another is a form of excitement in itself. Did that excitement of the moment have anything to do with their lives? Do people leave encounter meetings or communications sessions and change the way they behave toward one another, or is the process itself also its end result?

It is admirable for couples to undertake these sessions to draw closer, and many claim to have been helped by them. In addition, the technique of writing down feelings is probably an excellent way of learning to express emotions that may be difficult to put into words when face to face with another person, even (or especially) a spouse. Still, the encounter programs make me uneasy. I am not sure that speaking self-consciously about feelings in an intensive weekend or two isn't a kind of burlesque of intimacy. I am not convinced such intensity has much to do with the long haul, with learning to know one another and pulling closer by speaking and listening to what each has to say.

Communication in marriage is a subtler business. It grows out of the everydayness of life, out of comparing experiences at dinner or at the end of the day—what you did and what I did, what the boss said and what the baby said. In the early years of marriage, and especially for busy two-career couples, this swapping of information leads to an involvement of each spouse in the life of the other and a sense of being important and heard. In *Blue Collar Marriages*, sociologist Mirra Komarovsky reported that among working-class marriages she studied, one of every three fell short of the ideals most of us hold for the kind of psychological intimacy that should exist in marriage. Husbands and wives in these nonintimate marriages had little emotional contact primarily because they had little interest in their mate's daily life. One twenty-two-year-old man, married three years and typical of other young men in the study, spoke of his boredom with his wife: "What does she have to talk about? Dirty diaper stuff. I don't care about that." Yet it is exactly this kind of "stuff" that couples in close relationships do talk about, each willing to spend the time and listen to the things that are important to the other. The expressions of feelings don't depend on sessions of soul searching and self-revelation. The ability to speak to a spouse about feelings grows out of being free enough to talk about the little things that hurt or excite, knowing that there is a receptive ear at the other end of the conversation.

The things couples discuss vary, and what is an intimate conversation to one may appear empty to another. In California I met a recently married couple, both professors of art history and both in their early forties. Shy and reserved with me, they seemed equally formal with each other. Much of their courtship, they told me, was conducted through letter writing because they had been teaching in different states when they first met. They wrote dozens of letters back and forth, each carefully numbered, and when either of them wanted to refer to a previous letter they referred to it by number.

When I spoke with them, the husband, James, cautiously brought out letter number 23. It was, he said, the seminal letter in their relationship, the one in which he proposed to his wife, Zelda. Wrote James: "I desire marriage, of course, for carnal reasons, among other things. But also because I believe face-to-face communication is very important. If it makes sense to marry at all, it makes sense to put ourselves in a position to talk. With you I have the feeling that we could go on and on, down ever-widening and branching and illuminating corridors, indefinitely or to an end that we don't yet imagine but which will have been worth it. Only with you do I have the feeling of interests opening up, rather than just playing out what I have already mastered. All this is not, of course, marriage per se. But it would be our marriage, and I'm itching to get going."

"What do you talk about now that you're married?" I asked Zelda.

"Well, we talk about who buys the orange juice and who makes the bed. But, truthfully, our best talks are just what James had envisioned. We talk about art. James favors classicism and I love romantic styles. We've had heated arguments about the virtues of each school. We've really come to know each other well because of those arguments."

My first thought on meeting James and Zelda was that they use their intellectualism to shield them from intimacy. My second and current view is that for them intellectual conversation is a path toward intimacy. When they talk about art, they open themselves to the most passionate interest each holds, and through those discussions each has begun to penetrate the other's inner life.

It is something of a truism in our society that women have been socialized to talk about their feelings and men have great difficulty expressing emotions. Taught as little boys not to cry, to be strong and hide their hurts, men grow up unable to speak about or even to recognize the pain that lurks within them. In my own research among the many couples I interviewed, however, I did *not* find this to be a generalization I could make among men of any social class. I did meet men who were closed off, shielding their emotions like so many playing cards. And I did meet women who fit the stereotypes of emotional or excitable. But I found many of the men to be far more open in revealing themselves than I had expected, and I met a good number of women who shied away from letting anything out.

The men who did fit the image of the traditional strong, silent type were usually older men in their sixties and seventies. It could be that the freer social atmosphere of the past two decades with its emphasis on similarities rather than differences between the sexes has allowed younger men of all classes to be less closed off from themselves. It could also be that in the course of marriage men and women learn how to maneuver around one another's reserves, and what I was seeing among the more open men of all ages was behavior that had started out one way and been changed through coaxing and conditioning.

Nate Murray certainly showed the results of coaxing when I met him. I had spoken with his wife, Sally, first, and she had set up the meeting with Nate. A gardener, he trooped into his home and sat before me, hat in hand, shuffling with the discomfort of a man more at ease with plants than with people.

"So what d'ya wanna know?" he asked.

"Sally told me you've been married forty years," I answered. "That's a long time."

"You call her 'Sally.' I call her 'Peach,' " he said. "So what d'ya wanna know?"

"I guess I want to know whatever you want to tell me about your life together. How you get along, things like that." I was being cautious; he seemed so uncomfortable.

"I don't talk much," he said. "The wife, there, she's the talker."

"Do you listen to what she says?" I smiled.

"Yeah, I do." He was beginning to relax. "Tell you the truth, I tune out most people—I used to tune out the kids, my family. But I won't tune the wife out. Even if there's a conversation going on, the wife says something, I pick that up. So what else d'ya wanna know?"

"How come you don't tune your wife out, even after all these years?"

"I don't know." He twisted his hat. "We got things to say to each other. She asks me a lot of questions."

"Do you answer them?"

"Sure I answer." He laughed. "That's how she gets me to talk. But I don't mind. I kind of like it. We talk a lot. So what else d'ya wanna know?"

Nate was used to answering questions. It was the way he had come to open up to Sally, gradually learning to tell her "what else" she wanted to know. "You have to kind of draw it out of him," she had told me. "But it's okay; there's a lot of warmth inside that man."

I heard similar things from other people with silent partners. They had learned to draw out their mates with questions about themselves, nothing profound, just ordinary questions about things they knew interested the other. And the partner had learned to loosen up, to trust enough to be able to talk not only about interests but also about self. There may be times of agonizing frustration for both partners in such relationships, times when the freer partner wants to or does scream, "Say something, damn it!" and the tighter partner tries but cannot articulate emotions. It helps in those situations to recognize that people who hold things back are not emotionally dead. Their inability to express what is within doesn't mean they don't feel things, perhaps even as deeply as the more expressive partner. Their feelings need to be respected, and so do their silences.

Silence is as important as speech in marriage. Our current obsession with communication makes us forget sometimes that some things need not or should not be said, even in the most intimate relationships. Says Henry Spitz, psychiatrist and family therapist, "Some of the most devastating things I've ever heard have followed the phrase, 'Let me tell you how I honestly feel.' " His modification: "Honesty with some concern for the other person's feelings." Several studies done by psychologists have found that from the very earliest days of marriage couples quarrel about things that are said and that become irrevocable. In one such study, published in 1970 (at the height of the "let it all hang out" movement) in a journal called *The Family Coordinator*, couples were asked, "Does your spouse have a tendency to say things that would be better left unsaid?" Those who seemed to be getting along well in most areas answered, "No." Those who had experienced problems in their marriage answered, "Yes."

A historian told me that his wife likes to talk everything out, and that they do talk out difficulties—"the first round by shouting at each other." Sometimes, however, he says, "No, let's not talk this one out; let's act as if everything is all right even if it isn't." And that is useful in calming them both down.

Too much talk clutters the mind, pushing the other person away rather than pulling partners closer. Over the years in marriage, many couples find that they can convey their feelings with a quickly understood glance, a touch, a tone of voice. Things that needed to be said earlier no longer have to be spelled out. They can laugh together at secret jokes or cry together, silently. That is not to say that conversation ends as marriage goes on. Couples who have warm, intimate relationships continue to find each other interesting and enjoy talking together. But they also enjoy sitting together quietly, "comfortable in our quietness," as one man put it.

Communication takes many forms and so does intimacy. We are a society so in love with numbers and hard facts that we try to quantify everything. I have seen innumerable charts purportedly measuring the degree of intimacy in marriages. One, often used by marital therapists and reproduced in textbooks, is a classification of intimacy and marriage itself constructed by two sociologists, John F. Cuber and Peggy B. Harroff. It categorizes marriages into five types. At one end is the "total marriage," in which the partners share all activities and place their own relationship above all others. At the other end is the "conflict-habituated marriage," filled with tensions and continual fighting. In between are the others: the "vital marriage," whose spouses are close but less so than those in a "total marriage"; the "passive-congenial marriage," whose partners get along well but are somewhat uninvolved; and the "devitalized marriage," in which partners started out with a strong sense of intimacy but lost it over the years.

The impression one gets from this and other classification systems is that marriages fit into one or the other category, and remain true to type throughout their existence. Yet I could not categorize the marriages I examined in this way. What I found, instead, is that degrees of intimacy shift and change within any given marriage at different times. Moreover, what is a "total marriage" for one couple might be regarded as a stifling marriage for another, who need to keep something of themselves in reserve for themselves no matter how loving their feelings for one another. Couples have individual styles of intimacy and individual ways of being close that may not conform to an ideal, but that satisfy them.

I think of an Indiana nurse whose marriage, she told

me, was "blocked" emotionally until she and her husband became "born-again" Christians. Together they began studying religion, going to meetings and attending prayer groups. The more deeply enmeshed they became in religion, the closer they moved toward one another. The time they spent praying together became the highlight of their day. "We are as intimate during those moments of prayer as we are during sex," she said. Not exactly everybody's cup of tea, nor is the intimacy in this marriage "total." But the connection and trust that have developed mean a great deal to the two people involved.

And I think of my mother-in-law's marriage. Its beginnings were certainly not conducive to intimacy as we know it. The marriage was arranged by a matchmaker. That was the custom among Orthodox Jews in Belgium before World War II, and as a dutiful daughter, she would not deviate from custom. The only consideration her parents gave to modernity was to allow her a bit of a choice.

"They brought me three men to choose from," she told me some time before her illness. "The first one was such a tiny shrimp of a thing. He was very wealthy, and my parents thought it would be a good match for the family. But I couldn't stand him. He looked like a little mouse, strutting around.

"The second man was nice enough," she went on, "but there was something about his family my parents didn't approve of. Then they brought Papa."

Although my father-in-law was not much taller than the first hopeful, he was a handsomer man. And while he came from a poor family, he brought with him the prestige of having been descended from thirty-three generations of rabbis. She could find no serious reason not to consider him. They had three dates, each chaperoned by an aunt or a cousin. On the third date, the young suitor turned to her and said, "I think it's time we address one another as *tu*." That is the familiar form of "you" in French, and more personal than the formal *vous*. Then he gave her his arm, and with that gesture the engagement was sealed.

And love?

"That," she said, "was not something we thought about."

The marriage lasted for fifty years, until her death. Throughout, they suffered difficulties: the war, business failures, his chronic heart illnesses. They had times of conflict and times of "passive congeniality" that were not intensely close. But they had other times in which they shared a devotion and loyalty to one another that few love matches could rival.

Once, after she had become ill, she said to me, "No one will ever know the things Papa does for me, the way he takes care of me. There aren't many men who would do what he does for their wives."

"And haven't you done much for him?" I asked.

Yes." She looked serious. "Yes, I have. Isn't it funny? If I had been free to choose someone to marry the way you were, I don't know whether he is the man I would have chosen. But I can't imagine ever feeling closer to another man. I don't know if you can understand this; things are so different now. We—how shall I say it?—we always felt safe with each other."

I could understand.

CHAPTER THREE

~·~

Power and Dependencies
The 99%-1% Formula

The Christens' apartment said it all. A duplex overlooking New York City's East River, it opened on its second floor to a terrace whose views swept all the way to LaGuardia Airport. Enclosed in a glass case at one corner of the terrace stood a canoe, big enough for one, carved in the late nineteenth century by an unknown Indonesian craftsman. At another end a big-bellied sculpture of a woman, this one a product of a New Guinean tribe, gazed serenely out at the flowing river. Inside, African masks and shields decorated the walls, and primitive sculptures of male and female nudes cast dramatic shadows over the pristine modern furniture. A Freudian, I thought, could have a field day with the phallic symbols incorporated into this room and its adornments. All of it—the apartment, the rare primitive art, the terrace with the "best view in town"— were, in fact, symbols of Jason Christen's manliness, his energy, his determination and success.

Jason is a plastic surgeon, one of the best known in New York. Into his skilled hands are placed the bulges and bumps, the double chins, "wrong" noses and baggy eyes of society women and actors, television newscasters, politicians and ordinary people with a bundle of money.

And under his meticulous knife his clients emerge look-ing, or at least believing they look, younger, healthier, happier. His ability to bestow the accoutrements of eternal youth on the not-so-young has given Jason a degree of power among the influential of New York that few other physicians enjoy.

Power was what I had come to this apartment to speak about. The subject of power in marriage has be-come unusually popular lately. Whereas in earlier times matters such as the importance of love, economic ques-tions or family pressures might have been the central themes in writing about marriage, today psychologists, feminists and even literary critics often depict marriage as a power struggle between partners. From my vantage point, isolating issues of power as the main element in marriage is no more valid than declaring intimacy or sex to be the only important components of marriage. What is valid, however, is to explore the ways couples come to terms with questions of power and to recognize that those questions are one more aspect of the many complexities that make up a marriage.

Generally, to speak of power in marriage is to speak of the ability of one partner to influence or change the behavior of the other. The person with the greatest power is usually the partner who makes most of the decisions in the family and in one way or another controls the actions of the others. For many couples marital power stems from economic power: the person who brings home the bacon gets to become boss. In most cultures today, the man is that person.

One of the reasons I had chosen to interview the Christens was that Jason is a man who openly enjoys his money and position in society. I wanted to learn how the power he exerts in his professional life manifests itself in his marriage. Have his enormous success and wealth tipped the marital scales in his favor? I also knew that his wife, Lila, had recently begun working as a real estate broker. What did that job mean to her, and how did it affect her marriage?

When I called Lila and asked to set up an appoint-ment, she suggested an alternative. The Christens would be having dinner one night soon with old friends of theirs,

Audrey and Stanley Lowe, and she wondered if I might not like to meet with all four of them after dinner and spend some hours talking together. Financially the Lowes were no place near the bracket the Christens had climbed to, but, Lila said mysteriously, there were things going on in their marriage that were similar to issues she and Jason had been dealing with. Audrey, too, had gone back to work after years of staying home raising the couple's two children.

I accepted the invitation, and that was how I found myself on an unusually warm November evening gazing out over the East River from the terrace of the Christens' magnificent duplex apartment. Jason was taking me on a personal tour, and explaining in great detail the value of every art object he owned.

"I really made a killing with that *bis* pole," he said, pointing to a memorial pole from New Guinea, as we moved from the terrace into the living room. "Nobody was interested in this primitive stuff years ago. I bought it for a song. Now it's worth many thousands." He sounded like other wealthy art collectors I have met who can't resist talking about the price of their treasures no matter how much they love the art objects themselves.

"Does Lila share your interest in collecting primitives?" I asked.

"No, I don't," Lila called over to where we were standing. "I'm not an acquisitive person. I've never collected anything in my life, not even jewelry. There are times when I don't give a damn about all this art; it's just a bunch of stone and wood and pigments. I don't care if they are good investments. I'd rather spend the money on a new kitchen."

Her words sounded harsh, but the smile that accompanied them took the edge off their sharpness. What a knockout of a woman, I thought as I looked at her. Tall and thin, she still had a model's figure at age forty-eight. She was taller than Jason, and her physical stature seemed to balance his aggressiveness and self-assurance.

"Is Jason's collecting passion an issue between you?" I asked both of them.

"Oh, only partly," Lila answered. "After all, it's his

money, and he has a right to spend it the way he wants to."

"Come on, Lila," Stanley Lowe interrupted. "I can't believe you really mean that. You're not exactly the submissive type."

"No, I'm not anymore." Lila looked at her husband. This was clearly not a new topic of discussion for them. "I'm not as submissive as I once was. But believe me, I still have trouble asserting myself in money matters."

"Why?" Stanley persisted.

"Truthfully, I've always felt that he has the power in this household. First, because he makes so much money, and second, because he handles all our investments and finances. How can I tell him what to do with his money? I don't even know how much money he earns."

"Really?" Stanley was shocked. "Jason, you don't tell Lila how much you earn?"

"If she'd ask me, I'd tell her." Jason fiddled with a little statuette on the coffee table. "But I don't volunteer information."

"Then why don't you ask him?" This time Audrey looked at Lila incredulously. I glanced over at her. A tiny woman, dressed somewhat drably, physically she was no match for Lila. But she had a determination in her voice that led me to make a mental note to draw her out later.

"Why should I ask him?" Lila answered slowly. "There's a kind of protection in not knowing. Anyway, I know we have plenty, so what difference does it make how much? The issue is, how do we spend it? Do we spend it on more art, or do we spend it on a new kitchen, or on the roofing we desperately need in our summer home?"

"Isn't it funny—" Stanley broke in. "Here you are with all this money, and you're still fighting about money. One way or another, everybody always argues about money."

About money or what money represents, I thought. Impoverished people fight for survival, but in middle-class homes fights about money are often really fights about who makes big decisions and who controls the direction the family moves in. Although I was eager to hear more about the money-power connection in both these couples' lives, I didn't want to push too hard. I had not told them beforehand that that was the secret agenda of our meeting.

As if he were reading my mind, Jason said, "I'll be honest. Money represents my ego and my narcissism. You know where I came from? I came from nothing, from a poor family of Greek immigrants. We lived in Queens. My father owned one of those small, twenty-four-hour grocery stores, and we lived over the store. I won a scholarship to go to college and got a fellowship for medical school."

"Yeah." Lila continued the story. "We got married right after he finished medical school. Then he went into the army. We had a steady income of eighty dollars a week, but I think we fought less about money then than we do now. It had to be spent on necessities. But even then Jason had a lot of confidence in his ability to earn money. He never thought of socking it away. It was so different from my family. They were better off than Jason's parents, but they were very conservative in dealing with their money. I liked it that Jason didn't worry about saving money, that we lived up to what he made. I never knew how much he was making, even in those early days when he was just opening a practice. I kept myself a little ignorant so I didn't have to worry about the future. I could go ahead and spend what he gave me."

"But now you've come to resent that?" I asked.

"I resent it, because, as Jason said, money has become his ego. He fills up the apartment with art because that's a statement about him. It says, 'Jason Christen is successful; he's cultured.' It has nothing to do with me. He controls the money so he makes the decisions about how to spend it. If I were earning what he is earning and he were earning what I am earning, our lives would be completely different. I would have the power to make the decisions about how we use our money.

"But," Lila went on, "things are changing now. I have my own bank account and my own money, and I tell you, it's a very important thing for me even though I make so much less than Jason. I just don't feel so powerless anymore."

"Was there any one thing that led you to go to work

after all these years?" I asked. "Was it the women's movement?"

"I'll answer that," Jason rushed in. "It was very clear that what she had to avoid at all costs was ending up like her grandmother, who sat into her eighties twiddling her thumbs with nothing to do. That was a nightmare that had to be prevented no matter what. I encouraged her to find a career once the kids were on their way. What she decided to do was her own business." He seemed pleased with himself, the benevolent ruler who had moved aside to allow his subject a bit of independence. Lila picked up on his tone immediately.

"It wasn't Jason's decision for me to work. It was my own," she said with a slight edge in her voice. "And it hasn't been so easy for anyone. Even though my children are older now, I still have to spend time with them. I'm trying to make things nice for everybody—my kids, my husband and as much as possible for me, too. I don't have the answer yet. I'm just at the beginning. I don't know how far I'm going to want to go and how far I'm going to be able to go."

"How about you, Jason?" I asked. "How has Lila's working affected you?" He had seemed so nonchalant about her going to work, but as she spoke, he began to look uncomfortable.

"Well, at the moment I might find it a bit difficult." He smiled weakly. "But I'm a very adjustable guy. I'll bitch and moan about something, but I can accept it if I have to. I mean, I did think she should go to work."

Audrey laughed. "I guess you're just more easygoing than any of us thought, Jason," she said sarcastically.

"Okay, okay," Jason said, putting his hands up. "I can get angry about her working. Sometimes it creates a burden on me that I find difficult. It causes me inconveniences. Like sometimes she takes the car when I need the car, or she comes home late and I can't keep a tennis appointment I've made. But honestly, for me to say that that kind of inconvenience outweighs the necessity of her working is ridiculous. On the other hand, for me not to be angry about being inconvenienced would be for me to be a saint, and I'm not ready to be canonized."

At least it was an honest statement. I have known

men who have only praiseworthy things to say about
their wife's new occupation or career, yet find every occasion they can, both privately and publicly, to undermine
the work. The Christens were still in a tug-of-war over
money, work and power, but it was nice that they could
acknowledge it. Lila must have felt the same way I did.
She got up, put her arms around Jason and laughed. "He
just wants me to be here slaving for him all the time," she
said. "But in spite of all his bitching, he is proud of me.
He complains because he suddenly has to do a lot of
things he never did before."

Jason could not let that one go by. "I don't complain," he said, "about doing things. I complain because
when I do them you don't like what I do. For example,
we're giving a fancy Sweet Sixteen party for our daughter.
Lila didn't want to have it at home, but she also didn't
have time to look for a place in which to hold it. So I just
went out one day during lunchtime, took a quick spin
around all the hotels in the area and chose the one that
looked best to me. It also happened to be the most expensive. Well, Lila got furious. She hasn't stopped complaining about how much money this affair is going to cost us.
My feeling is, the place is beautiful, we can afford it, and
why not? If Lila doesn't have the time to shop around,
why can't she just accept my judgment without debating
me on it?"

What a delicate business this issue of power is, I
thought. We women want more power in so many areas,
and we should have it, yet it is still hard for us to give up
power in the realms that have traditionally been ours,
even when relinquishing that power is to our own benefit.
Lila knew that it was useful to have Jason get rid of the
chore of choosing a place for their daughter's party, but
she hated to give up control over an area that had always
been her own, even though she was gaining control in
other areas now.

I turned to the Lowes. They appeared so different
from the showy, loquacious Christens. Big, chunky, bear-
ish Stanley is a free-lance filmmaker. Audrey, half his
size, laughs quickly at her husband's wisecracks, but maintains, always, a quiet strength. He had told me earlier in
the evening that the two were introduced twenty-seven

years before by mutual friends. As soon as he'd looked at Audrey, he knew he wanted to marry her. Mustering all his courage, he asked her for her hand on their second date. She agreed immediately.

"Has there been a struggle in your family over money and power?" I asked.

"There sure has," Audrey answered. "But boy, is it different when you don't have money. Neither of us knows anything about money, but we still fight over it and what it represents. In fact, we've just been through a money-power struggle that in some ways is still going on." She looked straight ahead now, as if to avoid Stanley's eyes. "I was very unhappy," she said softly. "I have never had such unhappiness in all our marriage."

The atmosphere in the room changed. The Christens' bravado, their sparring, quieted down. We all looked at Audrey, but it was Stanley who spoke.

"I had been feeling some financial pressure for a long time. I'm a damn good filmmaker, you know that, Jason, but if you're not twenty years old and into weird things, you're no good anymore. In our society you're not venerated as you get older; you become an outcast, and it gets harder and harder for you to find work." He was bitter now, his voice breaking with emotion. "I wanted Audrey to go back to work. As you know, she had worked a little after we married as a science writer, and she had done some free-lance work over the years when the kids were growing up. I felt we needed the extra money and that she could probably get a good job with a pharmaceutical house. But in addition, I felt the way Jason did, that Audrey is more than a housewife. She could feel her own worth as a person if she could get back out there and do something for money."

"More than a housewife!" Audrey's face was flushed. "I was a mother; I was a housekeeper; I was a companion. All those roles were all right for me at the time, right? He would have been furious if I left the boys and went to work when they were young. But now that he wants me to work again, there's something wrong with being 'just a housewife.' "

"That's not what I meant." Stanley looked pained and sad. "You know how much I appreciate what you've

done for the boys and for me. It's just that I felt you were
ready for something else now, but you were afraid to take
that first step to test yourself."

"I know," said Audrey, relaxing for a moment. "And
I really was ready. I knew we needed the money and I
knew this was the right career for me. That wasn't the
issue. But what happened is that Stanley kept pushing me
to go out and look for a job. I wanted to prepare some
samples and to practice for a while so that I could present
myself and my credentials well. I felt I wasn't ready." Her
voice became strained again. "He kept pushing me and
pushing me. I kept saying to him, 'You're not helping me;
you're belittling me by acting as if you know what I can
do better than I do.' But he wouldn't stop."

"I couldn't stop myself," Stanley said. He looked at
us as if we were the jury at a trial. "I knew I was right.
But still, I'd promise myself that I wouldn't say anything
to her. And so help me, I tried not to, but then more time
passed, and wham! in the middle of a discussion I'd bring
it up again. And every time I did, I'd think, 'Oh God, I
made her cry, I made her so unhappy.' I would feel so
guilty even though I knew I was doing the right thing by
urging her to go back to work."

"Don't you see," Audrey began. It was her turn to
face the jury. Instead she faced her husband. "Why couldn't
you trust me to know what was right for me?"

Stanley hesitated. A smile began to break up the tight
line of his mouth. "It turned out I was right, didn't it?
When you went for it, you got yourself a good job as a
science writer. So I guess I was justified."

"Do you believe this?" Audrey shouted. "He won't
give up."

It was time for me to interrupt. "And where do you
stand today?" I asked Audrey.

"Well, I'm working for a big pharmaceutical company, and—guess what—Stanley is pushing me now to
ask for a raise."

We all laughed, and turned to other matters.

Later, after I had left the Christens and the Lowes, I
tried to sort out what we had discussed. For both these
couples power and money were closely connected, and

both were struggling to deal with that connection in new ways. In the Christen household, Jason had clearly been the power holder since the earliest days of their marriage. Later in the conversation Lila said that she had often given in to him even in matters relating to their children, although that is supposedly her domain, because at times she simply doesn't feel strong enough to fight him. Lila probably will never have equal power with Jason, in large part because dominance and assertiveness are essential elements in his character, to a lesser extent because she still wants him to take on the responsibilities that go with making decisions. She is comfortable not knowing how much money he makes, not having to make investment decisions, and he is delighted to keep her out of those business matters. Still, things are beginning to change. She is getting stronger in other ways, and he is stretching himself to accommodate her strengths. As she earns money of her own and gains confidence in knowing that she could support herself if she had to, she is getting more clout in the family. And he is learning to give in to what she wants. He may be kicking and screaming all the way, but he is willing to change his routines and put himself out to fit her schedules.

For the Lowes, the power shake-up is somewhat different. Although their marriage has been organized around traditional lines, Stanley has never been as authoritarian as has Jason, and power has not been an ongoing issue as it has been with the Christens. But the need for a second income polarized Stanley and Audrey into male-female power corners. He, playing the role of the strong, knowledgeable male breadwinner, pushed her into doing what he wanted her to do, on the assumption that he knew her better than she knew herself. She held off, probably longer than she needed to, as her only way of combating his badgering, a power play of her own. But she also held back because of her own insecurity and fear of acknowledging that she could no longer depend on him to support the family. She told me when we had a moment of conversation alone, that after she started working she would hand Stanley her paycheck, even though she had always managed the money in the family. When he asked her why she was doing that, she replied, "I guess I still

see it as your money, regardless of who is making it."
Audrey had felt comfortable as "just a housewife," as she
said. For her, the idea of building a career did not come
from inner pressure, as it did for Lila. The pressure came
from the outside, from Stanley, and she felt threatened by
the role being foisted on her. There was security in keeping things as they always had been, in remaining the
economically dependent housewife even after she began
working, rather than facing up to the fact that her position
was changing.

Audrey's revelation reminded me of the early years of
my marriage, when my husband was in medical school
and I was our sole support. I gave my paycheck to him
every week and avoided being involved in any financial
decisions we had to make. I was somewhat embarrassed
about being different from all my friends, whose husbands earned their livelihood and expected their wives to
keep budgets within the limits they had set. I wanted to
normalize our marriage by turning over my money to him
so that he could be the official head of our household and
I could pretend to myself that I was a good housewife,
like my friends, even though I was working.

My attitude reflected that of my society. During those
same years, I applied for a charge account at Marshall
Field's, the largest department store in Chicago, where we
lived then. Although I was earning a substantial salary,
the store denied my application. The income of the head
of the household, namely the husband, determined the
issuance of charge accounts, and since the head of our
household earned no salary, it made no difference how
much money his wife brought in.

The social pressures and the expectations for men
and women have changed drastically, and women like
Audrey, reared in those earlier times, are having trouble
adjusting to the changes. Because so many of my viewpoints today have been fashioned by the women's movement, I was surprised by how many couples I met whose
marriages follow traditional patterns, and especially, by
the numbers of women in those marriages who claim to
be satisfied with their lot. When we hear statistics about
the increasing numbers of women who work outside their
homes, we tend to forget that nearly half of married

women are not in the labor force. Many of these women still consider their work at home to be the only important work they should be doing. "This business of mixed roles—male and female sharing everything—is making life harder for young people," one woman said. "Men and women are supposed to be different. I know what I'm supposed to do and my husband knows what he's supposed to do, and that works out just fine for us."

These women have felt stressed by the changing expectations of our society toward women. Some are sad and angered by the derision voiced by their own children. "My daughter once asked me," a mother reported, "how I could stand spending my life as an appendage of my husband. I was so hurt, but I simply told her that when I was keeping house and raising kids and watching every penny so that she and her sister could go to college and develop careers, I didn't see myself an 'appendage' of her father. I thought what I was doing was mighty important. And so did my husband."

In a well-known and often quoted book, *The Future of Marriage*, first published in 1972, sociologist Jessie Bernard concluded that based on statistics of health and illness, marriage is good for men and bad for women. Married men, she pointed out, are generally healthier than unmarried men, but married women have a higher incidence of depression and mental illness than single women. A later and less well-known book, *The Inner American*, showed a different perspective. The authors, three social scientists, surveyed the attitudes of Americans toward themselves and their lives in 1957 and again in 1976. Although they agreed that marriage may be "felicitously arranged" for men, they were impressed with the similarities of men's and women's positive responses to questions about their marriages, even in 1976, when so many changes in attitudes were taking place. A majority of both men and women, they found, saw their marriages as fulfilling to themselves and important to their social validity. And 86 percent of the couples surveyed perceived their marriages as equitable.

Viewed objectively, women who have no source of income of their own often do not have equal power in their marriages. But many women in traditional roles, who are satisfied with their marriages, weigh the influence they carry in such spheres as child care, household management or social life as equivalent to the economic influence their husbands exert.

Peggy Flaherty seems such a woman, and her husband Tom speaks with conviction about the equality of their marriage. The Flahertys have been married for thirty-eight years. For twenty-five of those years, Tom has worked in various capacities for a large steel company; before that he was a dock worker.

"We got an apartment on the same block as my parents right after we married," Tom said. "Peggy worked in a clearinghouse, from about 7:30 in the morning right through until 2:00. She was working about two weeks when my father called us up to come over for a pick—that's an Irish snack of deli foods and tea, you know. So we came over, and Peggy was sitting next to me, and my father leaned over and talked around her. 'Tom,' he said, 'when is she going to quit working?'

"I could see Peggy stiffen. I said, 'Gee. I don't know, Pop, we've never even talked about her quitting.' So he said, 'You make enough to support her, don't you?' I said, 'Sure.' 'Well,' said he, 'the whole neighborhood is talking about you. They haven't said it yet, but you're almost like a gigolo.' So then I spoke to Peggy. I said, 'We don't need your income.' She said, 'What am I going to do with myself?' and I said, 'Go visit your mother, and get friendly with some of the girls in the neighborhood. From now on I'm acting like a man. I'm supporting you.' "

Peggy quit her job. She went back to work once years later, but that job lasted only a few weeks. She left at Tom's insistence, because she had to work on his days off, and he preferred to be able to spend time with her at home. In spite of her lack of income, however, they both maintain that she controls the purse strings in the family.

That control began when the Flahertys first married. Tom brought home his first paycheck in cash, in a brown envelope. He put the envelope on the table, and they sat down to dinner. They managed to ignore the envelope throughout the meal. Finally, Tom said, "Honey, don't you think we should talk about that?"

"I won't touch it," Peggy said. "My father always handled the money in my house."

"My mother always handled it in my house," Tom answered. "But I'll tell you what we'll do. For six months I'll bring it home and you'll handle it. If you bomb out and get in trouble, I'll step in."

Peggy agreed. Six months later, she had managed to save $100, and clear them of all debts. From then on she had charge of the money. "I haven't the slightest interest in it," says Tom. "All I know is I can make as much as we need. She does all the investments. She makes the big purchases. She's a comparison shopper. She'll pick out a car or a TV set, and then I might come in and do a little bargaining with the owner. But basically, after she does the work, all I have to do is rubber-stamp it."

The "rubber stamp," of course, is the true indication of the nature of the economic power Peggy has. That is, it is power relegated to her by Tom. She does the research, lines up investments, makes purchases. But all her suggestions need Tom's approval because he is the source of the money and the final arbiter of how it will be spent. He is, in truth, the boss.

The arrangement they have pleases Peggy as well as Tom. She likes being in charge of the money for him, just as she likes choosing his clothes and laying out what he will wear every day. Tom describes that responsibility as an indication of her great influence in their marriage. Although Peggy agrees that she has that influence, she also knows that in her responsibilities she caters to Tom. That doesn't bother her; they divided the labor as they saw fit a long time ago, and she is content to continue that way.

Unfortunately in some marriages very little power is relegated. Some men keep tight check over their money, doling it out or withholding it as they see fit, and leaving their wives in a position of utter dependency, not unlike the dependency children experience. Much worse, there are women trapped in miserable marriages, women dominated by their husbands, who want to but cannot escape because they have no means of support. For these women, lack of economic power is lack of all control in the marriage, a helplessness that puts them at their husband's mercy.

Many other women, like Lila Christen, are not unhappy in their marriages, but they are no longer satisfied with relegated power or with traditional places. The marriages of these women, who have gone back to school or taken jobs outside their homes for the first time, are in the greatest flux and under the greatest stress today. These marriages began in other times—in the 1950s, 1960s, or even early 1970s—under another system, with a different unspoken contract. It is not easy for both partners to turn their thinking around and look at one another from a perspective that didn't exist before.

Said a fifty-year-old Ph.D. candidate in political science: "My husband is as understanding, I think, as a man can be. But men in his age group can't actually know what it feels like to be a woman and to have put your competitive and intellectual desires on the backburner for years in order to pay attention to things like broken toes."

Presenting the male point of view, a businessman discussed his conflicts about his wife's recently acquired profession as a buyer for a department store. "We men have had to reeducate ourselves," he said. "After all, the image of a wife I grew up with was my mother, a loving woman who was always home and always wore an apron." Because of her work, his wife travels to Europe several times a year, leaving him in charge of their home and twin teenage daughters. "It took me a long time to get used to her traveling, and I'm still not completely accepting," he admitted. "I keep thinking, I'm the boss in the family; I should be traveling to Spain, Portugal, Morocco and all those places she goes to. To pretend that this hasn't put a strain on our marriage is to lie. I've had to adjust to her career and she's had to adjust to my adjusting."

The adjusting may be especially hard for remarried couples. Women who have learned to get along on their own after a divorce or death of a spouse may expect more economic equality and independence than their new spouses are prepared for, especially those men who had previously been in traditional marriages themselves.

What struck me about the couples in first or second

marriages who manage to keep their unions strong in spite of economic power pulls was the kind of step-by-step adjustment each partner made to the new circumstance of a wife working or seeking a career. Each gave the other time to get used to a way of living that undid what had come before. And in spite of angers and arguments, each seemed willing to wait it out while the other caught up. Time and again, in fact, as I spoke with couples, I found myself thinking that the old angers—the angers with which the women's movement began, the angers that made it possible for women to break out of long-established modes and find power centers outside the home—have cooled. Now wives and husbands are coping with the new realities, struggling to pick their way around the rubble of fallen traditions, with no field guide to chart the path. So instead of being angry, they are trying to be patient with one another. And as they renegotiate their underlying contract, they are discovering that at this stage forbearance can be more useful and far less destructive than rage.

A social worker explained it this way: "In principle I believe that I should be as free as he is to pursue whatever goals I want in life, and that is certainly what I'm telling my daughter. She's going to have many more options than I had. But my husband and I didn't start out this way. How can he know how to react and how to treat me differently? It takes time and training."

I heard anecdotes from everyone. One wife told about the day she went on a business trip and forgot to call to say she could not get home in time for dinner. When she finally did call, her husband became furious, screaming at her about her irresponsibility, about her devotion to a "miserable" job instead of to her family, about how things were going to be different in the future. "I absolutely curled up on the phone," she said. "It was as if we were back to square one, as if all I had been through—we had been through—to get me where I am had never happened." A week later, however, this same husband helped his wife host a company party at their home. He played the role of a perfect "company wife," charming her boss, engaging her coworkers in conversation, making it clear to everyone that he supported his wife all the way in her career. Another woman spoke of her husband's impatience when she talks "feminist talk," of his need to have her think of him as a "macho" man. Yet this man wakes up at six every morning to drive forty-five minutes out of his way to take her to her job (because she hasn't learned to drive herself), then circles back to his own office. These are not perfect situations, but they are not sellouts, either. They are just attempts by people to find their balance on slippery terrain.

Ours is not the first generation in which wives have worked. There have always been women who worked outside their homes, because their families needed the extra income or because they wanted to. Nate Murray, the gardener who calls his wife Sally "Peach" and talks only when probed, spoke about Sally's insistence on working when they married forty years ago. "We had two conditions when we married," Nate told me. "One was that I go hunting with the boys for a week every year, and that was not going to change. The other was that she not work after we married—I was the sole support and *that* was that, no ifs, ands or buts. Well, we kept to the first agreement, but we discussed, fought and had many back and forths on the second. Finally I gave in. I said, 'If that's what you really want, go ahead.' " Among all the married women they knew, Sally was the only one who worked.

And that is the difference between other generations of working women and the current one. Now that working wives and mothers have become part of our social structure, women are insisting that the equality and power they are winning in the marketplace be extended to their homes, that the lines between women's work and men's work be eliminated. This group insistence that power be wrested from the hands of men and divided equally between men and women has been at the root of many of today's marital struggles about working women.

Adding to the difficulties of having two careers or two occupations in a family and the juggling of power that accompanies them is a new sense of competition that crops up. Competition can be a dirty word in marital circles. Few husbands and wives would admit to competing with one another. When I asked a young couple, both lawyers in large prestigious firms, whether they ever felt competitive about their work or progress in their respective firms, they gave me all the right answers at first.

"Oh no," said the wife, "I feel so connected to him, like whatever he does reflects on me, too."

"Oh no," said the husband, "I couldn't be the least bit jealous. Anything she accomplishes gives me great pleasure."

"Even if she begins to make more money than you?"

"Oh, I don't think I would mind that. But . . . well, if she gets to be famous, like gets her picture in the paper or something like that, I don't think I could stand it."

Every couple has its own tolerance for where the competition begins, but it is hard to remain neutral when you are both striving for recognition or money in a realm outside the marriage. A psychiatrist and sex therapist with whom I spoke, Alexander Levay, described competition as one of the most common sources of problems in two-career marriages. "People who are sophisticated and intelligent, who have succeeded in their professions," he said, "really know how to do a job on each other. Their desire for excellence stimulates them to compete in all areas, including home life. What they need to learn—and they don't in their work—is how to be compatible rather than combative."

It is easier in traditional marriages, where the family pulls together as a unit for the husband's accomplishments. He works hard to provide economic security for his family, and she basks vicariously in his successes. Competition is less keen, also, when a wife who works regards her work as a job rather than a career, so that her husband's work is still central to the family and her responsibilities remain in the domestic sphere (even if she earns a substantial salary).

In all these supposedly noncompetitive marriages, however, competition may take different, less obvious forms. A woman might compete subtly by trying to make it obvious that she is the power behind the throne, deserving of recognition for her husband's success. Or the competition might center on who is the better parent, who is more attractive, who is more desirable to friends, who is more loyal and faithful.

Competitive feelings in marriage need not negate the love partners feel or the sense of joy and pride in each other's accomplishments. Couples who acknowledge these feelings can help diffuse them and make them less destructive. An artist whose wife is an actress still in the struggling stages of her career recently won an award for a series of etchings he made. Within their circle of friends he was widely acclaimed, and even became something of a celebrity. His wife happily shared his excitement when the award was first announced and then dutifully attended all the parties in his honor and toasted him along with everyone else. But at home she became moody and withdrawn. "Are you jealous of my reputation?" he finally asked her timidly. "I'm only human" was her reply. Her admission drew them closer: both could speak more openly of their own ambitions and at the same time recognize the other's fragility and ongoing need for support.

Competition becomes more threatening to a marriage when a wife moves ahead of her husband in the workplace. For all the sweeping changes we have undergone recently, our society still regards the husband as the provider, his wife's work as secondary. People are still inclined not to comment about a woman who is out of work, but to speak in whispers about a man who is. Among the more difficult marriages I investigated were those that had begun on the assumption that the husband was the breadwinner in the family, no matter what work the wife did, and got turned around so that she either surpassed him professionally or became his financial equal.

A man who has made peace with his wife's success described his anger and unhappiness in earlier years, when she began passing him by both in terms of finances and prestige: "I didn't like my work and I was unsure of myself. I was jealous of Sophia because everything she did turned out right, but I was also anxious to appear worthwhile in her eyes and in the world's eyes. I felt frightened and threatened by her achievement, and part of that had to do with my perception of success on my own terms. I have achieved that now and feel secure in what I do. Because I like my work, I'm at ease with myself, although she still earns more than I do. Sometimes I wonder whether the same thing could happen to me again—that kind of anger and resentment I felt—if I lost my position. I would have such mixed feelings. I would need her strength and support on the one hand; on the other hand I might become irrational and enraged again. Your own view of your work is terribly important to your marriage."

A woman, divorced after twelve years of marriage, told the reverse of this man's story. She had done fairly routine work as a copy editor in a book publishing house to support her husband through medical school and specialized training. In the course of her work she presented the editors of the house with ideas for marketing their books, and the ideas inevitably paid off in higher sales. The woman began to move rapidly through the ranks of the editorial department until she was made vice president in charge of subsidiary rights. The lucrative paperback sales she arranged brought her fame within her company and throughout the publishing world. Meanwhile her husband, finished with his training, was establishing himself in his medical practice. Although he liked his work, he began to hate hers, especially her successes and the recognition she received in a realm far wider than any he could hope to reach. Now he insisted that she leave that work so that they could have a child, refusing to listen to the many possibilities she presented for both work and children. Torn with guilt, she developed a slew of physical symptoms—backaches, headaches, sleeplessness—all of which he diagnosed as the results of stress in her job.

After a year of anger and quarreling, she left the marriage. The sad thing, she said, was that they had everything going for them, and they could both have been happy in their work and their marriage. The problem was that he didn't respect himself enough or feel strong enough to live with a successful wife. Eventually she lost respect for him, not because he had achieved less than she, but because he couldn't handle her achievements.

A strong sense of self for both partners and mutual respect do seem to be prime ingredients in lasting marriages in which a woman earns more or achieves more than her husband. In the best of these marriages the husbands recognize their importance to their wives well beyond the economic or social sphere and the wives respect their husbands as they are, often turning to them for nurturing and support, or for artistic or romantic qualities they themselves might lack. A well-known journalist spoke of the closeness and love in her marriage to an unknown physicist. "He's quite a bit older than I am," she said, "and in many ways he has always been my mentor and protector. But it's more than that. He's the only person with whom I'm completely myself, the only person who's not afraid of me—he sees right through my toughness; he'll laugh at me when I start thinking I'm important, and I'll take it from him because I respect his opinion more than anybody's."

Alone with me, her husband said, "I do hate it when people introduce me as 'the husband of . . .' rather than by my own name, but that's a minor price to pay for the excitement of living with this woman. I'm so proud of her. I get such a kick out of her achievements, and her financial success has made both our lives easier. Why should I complain?"

The most problematic of the reverse-role marriages are those in which the reversal is total: the wife earns the money and the husband keeps house. During the early 1980s when many blue-collar workers lost their jobs because of poor economic conditions, an in-depth report in *The Wall Street Journal* described the anger and frustration many of the men felt as their wives became the family's main support. They complained that their children no longer respected them and turned to their mothers for unilateral decisions. While some wives enjoyed their newfound power, others felt resentful that now they had no choice but to work. Although these women knew they could not blame their husbands, some said they had lost respect for them.

Supporting these reports, sociologists Philip Blumstein and Pepper Schwartz found similar reactions among middle-class couples, as they reported in their book *American Couples*. In marriages in which the partners have changed places, there was great unhappiness on the part of both spouses.

I did meet a few couples who seemed very much at

ease with reversed roles. In one marriage in which the couple had a three-year-old child, the wife was a computer programmer, the husband an occasional student. Drivingly ambitious, she signed up for one course after another to elevate her position at her company. He dabbled in economic studies at a local college. We corresponded for a while after ending our interviews. In one letter, she described her busy life and the many consulting jobs she was adding to her regular work. About her husband she wrote, "He's working hard at his studies, but he can't take on too much, and his studenthood is complicated by the fact that he has an active three-year-old to care for." I wondered whether he would come to resent having his "studenthood" interrupted to care for his child, and whether he would not eventually want more equality in his marriage, as so many women in similar positions have argued for in theirs.

A more typical attitude toward househusbanding is that of Tammy Johnson. Her husband Bart comes from a well-to-do industrial family. For eleven years of their marriage, Bart worked as a stockbroker, supporting his wife and children in fine comfort. In the twelfth year, Tammy decided to pursue a career of her own. "I wanted to prove that I could support myself," she explained to me. "I wanted to know that I wasn't powerless, that I could walk out if I ever had to and not be afraid." Bart did not object to her push for independence. In fact, as she became more involved in her work in a bank, he willingly assumed many household obligations, leaving his office early to shop and cook or to chauffeur their children to various appointments. Gradually, Bart spent more and more time at home and less at his work.

One day he announced that he was giving up his work. He had made a number of good financial investments, and those, together with Tammy's salary, would allow the family to live nicely. As for him, he would now spend his time doing what he really wanted to do—study music. Tammy hit the roof. "I did not marry in order to support a man," she told me, long after Bart had left his job. "Luckily Bart doesn't depend on me for money because I don't know how I would have stayed in this marriage if he did."

"But why?" I asked.

"Because that was not the way I was raised, and that's not the way it's supposed to be. I couldn't respect myself and I couldn't face the rest of the world with that kind of husband. Even though I'm not supporting Bart, I'm not comfortable with his not working, and it's been three years now. I still hold the idea that a man should be a self-sufficient creature who provides for his family by going out and working. In spite of my own success, I feel he should be caring for me."

Tammy, it seems, wants it both ways. She wants to be free to spread her wings and assert her own power, but she doesn't want to free Bart from the role of powermonger, which he is not in the least bit interested in keeping. She may be more outspoken in this respect than other women, but her attitude is one I heard in various ways from others ("I would certainly find it difficult to have my husband at home being a wife," said a recent bride).

This persistent attitude toward the proper function for each sex, among women as well as men, is one of the major stumbling blocks to balancing economic power in marriage. Is it a sign in women of a deeply bred and unshakable dependency, as some observers argue? I don't believe so. Tammy is not afraid of breaking out of her old dependency mold—she fought hard to create a successful career for herself in what was once a man's world. What she is afraid of is acknowledging her independence and living with the consequences.

Tammy doesn't want to let go, either, of areas of control that had always been hers. Her reaction can be compared to Lila Christen's crankiness when Jason found a hotel room for their daughter's Sweet Sixteen party. Women have difficulty giving up the arenas of power they once had when they are still on shaky grounds about what new powers they do have. So we hold fast, even when that holds us back, insisting that only we know how to cook what the children like, make beds that aren't lumpy, organize the kitchen or the linen closet. We insist on doing those things that customarily fell into our domain and—God knows—most men are only too happy to let us do them.

In spite of all the women at work today, survey after survey has shown what every working woman knows—that few men take an equal share in housekeeping. They may "help"—yes, more than they ever did before—but share the work equally? No, not yet. In most families the wife, not the husband, carries the domestic burden, no matter how many hours she works or how important her job. Even when a family has hired help, the woman is the partner who stays home if necessary when a child is sick, makes the doctor and dentist appointments and generally feels accountable for the housework. The weight of responsibility that women carry frees men to attain greater economic power: a father can work later or travel on a business trip; a mother must be sure to make arrangements for the children if she is going to be absent. And it's this ultimate responsibility, no matter what, that young women fear when they speak of combining careers and families. "It's all we talk about," one female medical student told me. "We have the feeling that if we marry and have children, instead of equality what we'll be getting is two jobs."

So we have a way to go in shifting power zones. And we have a way to go in changing our thinking about economic power in marriage. Meanwhile, within individual marriages, couples like the Christens and Lowes and many others are working out their own strategies, and, in spite of frustrations, trying to give themselves time to get used to new ways. Other couples are continuing in traditional patterns that seem comfortable to them. And a few younger couples are following tradition, but with a twist. As reported in *The New York Times*, several women who appeared at the tenth reunion of the first coeducational graduating class of Princeton University announced that they were not continuing their careers once they had children. These women saw themselves as pioneers going against the social trend of women working even when they have young children. What set them apart from traditional housewives, they maintained, was the knowledge, shared with their husbands, that not working was a *choice* they had made, that they could work if they wanted to. Such women are banking on the idea that their marriages will be egalitarian ones even if economic strength is concentrated in their husbands' hands. Because they began with a different contract, they expect that when they move into the marketplace later, they will not have to go through the struggles of couples like the Christens and the Lowes. I like to think they will be right.

I have dwelled at some length on economic power in marriage because it is a subject much talked about and the source of many conflicts. Yet to make economic power the only focus of a discussion on power in marriages is to omit an equally crucial area: emotional power. By that I mean the balance or imbalance of dependencies within a marriage, the psychic need one partner has for another and the power that neediness gives the other. If economic power is the more obvious form of power in marriage, emotional power is the more visceral, and potentially the more serious.

When we consider emotional dependency along with economic dependency, it becomes harder to say who is the dominant partner in a marriage. Often it remains the man. For some women economic dependency leads to emotional dependency. These women grow used to being told what to do, to having decisions made for them, to looking up to their husbands as the authority figures on whom they depend for everything. (But even in the most autocratic marriages, men have dependencies of their own. They turn to their wives for nurturing. They turn to them for emotional support, for ego strength, as an outlet through which to express their fears or frustrations. I think of Menachem Begin, former prime minister of Israel, and during his tenure in office one of the most powerful men in the world. Begin resigned his position several months after the death of his wife of forty-three years, Aliza. With her death, he became a shadow of himself, morose, withdrawn, uncommunicative. For Begin, Aliza provided the emotional balance in life. Only to her could he speak of his doubts and insecurities, only to her reveal his weaknesses. From the viewpoint of the outside world, she was very much in the background, the devoted wife following him wherever his career took him, backing him no matter what he did. Yet he needed her and depended on her to sustain his life as he wanted to live it.)

In other marriages the positions have become reversed, and no matter what the financial breakdown, it is the woman who dominates. So strong are traditional forms, however, that when a woman does provide the emotional backbone to a marriage, she often pretends she doesn't. That's certainly how it is with the Newmans of Florida.

Zach Newman is a retired shoe salesman, living with his wife Sylvia in a garden apartment in Miami Beach. Seventy-ish-year-old Zach towers over Sylvia, who looks shorter than she is because of the arthritic bend in her back. What I first noticed about Sylvia was how quickly she spoke, words falling upon words. What she spoke about mostly was her love for Zach, to whom she has been married for forty-one years:

"He's so good to me, I don't know how I could have managed in life without him. I mean he's everything. I simply can't get along when he's not with me. You know, when I was going through the 'change'—you know what I mean—he never made big demands on me the way some men do. He was so understanding and considerate, and I'm so grateful to him. I get tears in my eyes when I talk about him."

And all the while, Zach sat quietly, smiling warmly, clearly the hero, the master of his realm, who wisely dispenses his love and devotion to his wife, his second-in-command. Except that the longer the conversation went on and the more deeply I probed, the clearer it became that Sylvia is the center of this marriage. It is he who depends on her, for everything. She taught him "manners"—to open the car door for her, for example, not just to get out and leave her behind to open the door herself. She knew when it was time for him to retire ("you can't go on squeezing big feet into small shoes forever, you know"). She chose their apartment; she organizes their lives.

At the end of our meeting, Zach, who had spoken softly and sparsely all evening, turned to me while his wife was in the washroom. "She's really the boss in the family." He half-smiled. "I couldn't manage without her to make up my mind for me. It doesn't bother me at all.

But don't say anything to her about it. She likes to act as though I'm the bigshot."

Sylvia is not alone among women in pretending to be weak, incompetent or meltingly helpless to cover for the neediness and dependency of a husband. Inside she knows, as do other women like her—and their husbands—who really calls the shots in the family.

Most marriages, however, cannot be categorized as clearly as Sylvia and Zach's, nor are they as one-sidedly male-oriented as tradition would make them out to be. There are marriages in which one partner seems hopelessly dependent on the other and in spite of that dependency—or really because of it—wields the greatest power. The "power of the powerless," experts call it. The weaker person may manipulate the other by arousing such feelings of guilt that the other gives in to everything simply to relieve those tormenting feelings. Or the weaker and more dependent one may make so many demands that the other agrees to them in order to keep peace in the family or to keep from being miserable. Then, sometimes, the person who loves the least wields the greatest power. I think it was Voltaire who spoke of the person who kisses and the person who holds out a cheek to be kissed. The one who kisses, the one whose love is greater than the other's, is more willing to back down because that person is more invested in keeping the marriage going, more fearful of losing the other.

In some marriages, too, there is a kind of power one partner holds that comes simply from the person's own inner confidence. This person may yield on issues, not out of weakness but from a deep personal knowledge that he or she can tolerate yielding, while the partner has difficulty with ambiguity and with compromise. In such situations, the weaker partner needs to hold on tightly, to maintain strict control, while the stronger one is able to accommodate without losing strength.

Sometimes I had to meet with a couple several times before I could understand the power structure between them, and even then I was not sure. One of the main reasons it is more difficult to analyze emotional power than economic power in a marriage is that when asked about dependencies, about who relies on whom and who gives in more to whom, most couples insist that the situation is about equal between them. They do this partly because equality in all forms is so highly regarded in our society, and nobody likes to admit inequalities in his or her own marriage. But more important, they do it because they perceive themselves as equal. That is, they recognize that each has dependencies and that there are times, maybe years, of great inequality, when one depends more on the other. But they also know that, no matter what it looks like from the outside, over time the dependencies in their marriage usually offset one another. They know that the partner who loved less yesterday may love more today, that the one who was weak in the early years may become strong in the later ones. What I came to realize was that in marriages that work well, "equal" means that each partner supports the dependencies of the other when necessary, and that in the process they establish a balance of power that is never static yet is steady enough to allow for the intimacy and security that form the heart of a marriage.

Dependency is a loaded word. It conjures up visions of leaning bodies, of oppressive demands, of a narrowing of the self as it slides into another's being. We have put so much value on independence in our society, that we don't want to admit to dependencies or recognize their validity. Yet every person, no matter how independent, has areas of dependency and need. Although self-reliant people may be more adept at finding ways of meeting those dependencies, everyone struggles with some emotional needs that cannot be satisfied alone, and most people struggle with many. Marriage is not the only way to fill in the lacks, to shore up the longings, but it is the way that provides the most enduring support, the way that comes closest to offering the securities of childhood, but in an unchildlike way.

Childhood is when the seesaw of dependence and independence begins for everyone. According to child development theory an infant is connected to its mother in what is known as a symbiotic relationship; that is, the child barely distinguishes between its mother and itself, so tied is it to the mother, so dependent on her for nourishment, for care, for life. As the baby grows into childhood, it begins to discover a self that exists apart from its mother—begins, then, to develop an identity of its own. This process continues well into adolescence and beyond. During the teen years young people separate themselves as completely as possible from their parents, sometimes only with great angst and rebelliousness. The process of separating is also a process of maturing, of finding out who I am as opposed to who my parents are or who they want me to be. The more mature and self-knowing a person is, the more prepared that person is for marriage.

The theory makes sense. Youngsters who enter marriage as a way of avoiding the difficult process of breaking their dependence on parents and forming their own identities enter with a handicap. They are placing the burden of growing up on marriage, a burden it was not meant to bear. And if neither partner has formed a strong sense of self, the task is even harder, because each looks to the other for fulfillment and completion. With both making the same kinds of demands, neither has much chance of being satisfied. Marriages work best when both spouses have a grasp of who they are as individuals, apart from their families or their friends.

Unfortunately, life is rarely as clear-cut as theory would have it. While it is true that each stage of development is a move away from what came before, each also pulls something of the past along with it. Very few of us, if any, make a clean break with the past at each step. Very few—I doubt any of us—had parents who were unqualifiedly adept at helping us pull away from them while maintaining their closeness to us. In the long process of growing up, children are constantly torn between wanting to be held close and wanting to be let free, and sometimes they want both things at the same time. Parents cope with these needs as best they can. Some push their children away before the young ones are ready; some hold on long after they should have let go. Whatever their shortcomings, parents produce children who are less than perfect. And every one of us reaches adulthood with a less than perfect sense of self, with some needs unfulfilled, some dependencies unsatisfied, some fears unabated.

When people marry, even the strongest ones turn to

their partners to fill unmet needs and dependencies. When necessary, we make parents of our partners because those old needs come up again and again. A man with a reputation for being a tough boss in the business world may actually be torn by self-doubt. He feels safe in voicing those doubts only to his wife, on whom he depends to reassure him, to advise him, sometimes simply to listen to him. His wife plays the role of all-accepting, all-forgiving mother in this regard (a role Mother probably never filled that well), offering consolation and confidence to help him handle uncertainties and anxieties his colleagues in the business world would never tolerate. A talented woman, determined to pursue an acting career, is terrified of each audition, barely able to get herself out of the house in time. Her husband bolsters her, encourages her, accompanies her to studios as she makes the rounds. He plays the role of father, the supporter, the protector, the omnipotent. In these situations that is the role for which she needs him.

At different times, each spouse in a marriage parents the other, which means that by acting like a loving parent each comforts and aids the other. And that is fine. More than fine. I believe that one of the great strengths of marriage is its ability to offer this kind of security and protection against the outside.

Being parents to each other stops being fine, however, if partners become so dependent on one another that they lose all perception of their own identity—if, in the words of Swiss novelist Max Frisch, you lose "your self-integrity (meaning that you no longer venture even in secret to hold views that could shock your partner)." It stops being fine, also, if the dependency of one partner is so childlike and clinging that the other must constantly play Mommy or Daddy. I have a second cousin, a widow, who languishes in a condominium in California. Through thirty-six years of marriage, she was "Baby" to her husband, who pampered and indulged her. She never worked outside her home, and did almost nothing inside either. She slept until noon, and when she awoke, she spent the day at the hairdresser or playing cards. Her activity began only when her husband returned from work each day. Then they would go out to dine or to dance, and she would confide to him all the little discomforts of her day, the slights of neighbors, the arguments with her mother. He listened and sympathized with her, always assuring her of his love. He enjoyed her utter dependency, which made him feel strong, masculine and important. The price he paid for it was a profound loneliness, an inability to turn to her for any of his own needs. She loved being constantly coddled and cared for. The price she paid came after his sudden death. Alone, she did not know how to manage her life, how to sustain herself, how to deal with the smallest frustrations. She lies in her beautifully furnished condominium (which he had bought and decorated before his death), sleeping or crying away most of the day, wondering who she is and what she should be.

In mature marriages, each person is able to lean on the other when necessary, and in turn be leaned on when that is called for, to play child sometimes and parent other times. The Winterses, a couple who live in Augusta, Maine, epitomize to me the interdependence that makes for a balance of emotional power in marriage.

I could not take my eyes off Jeff Winters the first time I met him. He looks like every picture I have ever seen of Abraham Lincoln as a young man—Honest Abe without a beard. And when he draped his long legs over the arms of a living room chair, leaned back and spoke in a twangy New England drawl, I had visions of apple pies and American flags, and an uncluttered life far from the buzzing city.

Jeff and his wife, Claudia, live on a small farm that had belonged to Jeff's father in the house that his grandfather built. Jeff's father had been a gentleman farmer, hiring others to care for his land, and his three brothers had gone into various professions. But Jeff returned to the farm, where he raises chickens and pigs, and in off periods, does bulldozing and lawn maintenance for the folks in the area. Jeff and Claudia have known one another since kindergarten days.

Claudia's strong New England face is bluntly framed by short, sand-colored hair. She speaks in unadorned terms that match her straightforward appearance, yet when she spoke of Jeff, her voice took on a huskier tone and her face softened, almost into beauty. They were married in

1959, when they were both twenty-two. That was the year Jeff dropped out of college, Claudia told me. She had continued her studies, while setting up house as a bride.

Ten years into their marriage, Claudia became an alcoholic. Neither could explain exactly how it had happened.

"It was a kind of gradual thing," Jeff said. "Our friends were all pretty heavy drinkers."

Claudia disagreed. "I think if we want to be honest, we can't blame it on our friends. It was something in me. Everyone always knew me as 'happy-go-lucky Claudia,' and I worked at keeping that image. But nobody is happy all the time, and I never allowed myself to be sad, to admit to frustration or disappointment. I think my parents had wanted me to be a perfect child, and I had tried too hard to live up to their expectations. Then, being married, having young children [there had been three born during the first five years], and watching a couple we were very close to split up—I don't know, I guess a lot of things came together."

Claudia, I soon discovered, was not comfortable with introspection. She resisted looking for deeper motives for her drinking, yet she would not be dishonest and blame others or gloss over that period of their life. Nor did Jeff hesitate to speak about the years of her drinking; for both it seemed as though describing those years put them firmly into the past, a part of ancient history.

"I was heartsick over it," Jeff said. "I can't . . . well, I can't begin to express the kind of burden you carry in that situation. I mean, you know, when you deeply love someone, to have that between you. It has such an effect on your whole relationship in every way."

The irony of Claudia's drinking for Jeff was that his father, too, had been an alcoholic. Jeff winced when he talked about that and about how his mother finally left her husband after years of suffering his drinking. After she left him, he lived alone in a "grungy little apartment," which Jeff and his brothers visited from time to time and where they sent him money to keep him in his half-existence. And after all that, Claudia, the person Jeff thought he knew as well as he knew himself, turned into an alcoholic. It was a trick of fate he could not fathom. "Having lived through it twice," he said, "you feel such a helplessness about it. You kind of live from day to day, thinking maybe something will happen and it will go away, but it doesn't."

Actually, for Claudia, it did go away, but not without great effort. For years Jeff pleaded with her to join Alcoholics Anonymous. Like other drinkers, she resisted, arguing that she could stop any time she wanted to. Finally she gave in. "I went to the first meeting of AA for Jeff. They teach you there that whatever you do you should do for yourself, but I know I went for him." She looked at him, with that softness in her eyes. "I went for our marriage and for you."

The remarkable thing about Claudia's drinking was that after only three meetings of AA, she was able to stop, and has not touched a drop since. She discovered, among other things, that she is extremely susceptible to alcohol; just a little can make her very drunk. Now, seven years later, she was able to look back at those days as some nightmare from another life. There has been another, more horrible, nightmare since then that is discussed later, the death of their son Todd. But Claudia has not forgotten the darkness of those alcoholic days when she neglected her home, her children and her husband because of her romance with the bottle. And she credits Jeff both with her success in breaking the habit and with her ability to remain dry. "When I stopped drinking," she said, "Jeff told me that he was absolutely sure I would never slip again. And I never have."

From the way Claudia described him, Jeff, it seemed, was the strength in this relationship. But I wasn't so sure. Did he depend on Claudia in any way? I asked her. "I don't know, maybe on my sense of humor," she laughed.

I turned to Jeff. "What do you think?"

The seriousness of his answer surprised me. "She's the most supportive woman on earth, in any situation," he said simply.

"In what way supportive?" I nudged.

"You know, business, whatever." He looked down. Then he looked up again, straight at me, with his Honest Abe eyes. "It hasn't been easy for me, being the black sheep in my family."

And there it was. Calm, self-controlled Jeff is torn by

feelings of inadequacy and of betrayal of his family. The "dropping out of college" that Claudia had mentioned so casually early in our conversation was actually a major trauma of Jeff's life and a culmination of years of school failures. His family had not meant for Jeff to be a farmer or a glorified handyman. Each of his brothers had graduated from fine universities. Jeff had gone to a small, less prestigious college, but even then he couldn't make it. "I hated it," he said. "My brothers are very bright. They just breezed through. I struggled and struggled and got nowhere."

Almost before he finished the sentence, Claudia rushed in. "The thing that's so difficult about Jeff is that he equates brightness with high marks. He's much brighter than his brothers. I suspect he was dyslexic in school and nobody picked it up."

"So," Jeff continued, "I decided to give up on schooling and do the kind of work I like to do: physical work. But it's not so easy to work for people you also socialize with."

Claudia again: "Who cares? They all respect you." She understands very well how he feels. She hasn't forgotten her father's objections to her marrying Jeff because he was "nothing more" than a farmer, a laborer. To me she said, "In terms of the type of work Jeff does, it's been complicated. In a town where his family had been white-collar workers, professionals really, he became a blue-collar worker. We were a mixed bag at first. We were invited to cocktail parties with both our parents' friends, who were all upper crust. And Jeff would be ashamed, embarrassed to face people socially when he had tended their lawns."

"But it never bothered Claudia," Jeff added. "As I said, there's no doubt in my mind that she's the most supportive woman in the world."

"Well, if I've done anything," she said, as though thinking out loud, "it's to give him back the confidence that somewhere along the way he may have lost."

They are a team, Claudia and Jeff Winters, bolstering one another, succoring one another, exchanging pep talks and inspirations. Economic power struggles are not part of this marriage. Jeff earns the money, although Claudia sometimes works as a substitute teacher. Their roles are quite traditional in that sense, but neither of them is concerned about such things. Emotional strengths and weaknesses are far more important to both of them.

As I was leaving their home, Claudia said to me, "When I married, my mother told me that marriage is an eighty–twenty relationship—the woman must give eighty percent and expect back no more than twenty percent. But she was wrong. It's really a ninety-nine to one relationship. And it's not one way. It flip-flops. Sometimes you give the ninety-nine percent and get the one percent; sometimes he does. It's never equal at any one time, and it's not always fair. If you thought about it, you'd probably think, 'Well my turn has come, and now I want to be taken care of.' But you don't think of it that way. I needed him and he needed me at different times, and we just did what we had to do."

In doing what they had to do, the Winters have managed to equalize the power and the support in their family.

CHAPTER FOUR

~

Changing and Fighting
Changing and Fighting
Changing and . . .

A Los Angeles couple, married twenty-three years, could remember every important fight they had ever had. They had devised a unique system for remembering fights in the hope that memory would prevent their repeating the same argument, or at least in the same way. The trick was, they said, to label their battles. So, for example, there was the Fight of the Farmer's Market, a fight that went on all day as the two shopped in the open food stalls of Hollywood's Farmer's Market. It began when the husband announced that he had bought the family a weekend beachhouse in Malibu, a "fabulous bargain" that he simply could not turn down. Said his wife: "He thought he could make a joke of the fact that he had impulsively bought the house without consulting me, and he kept trying to humor me all day. But I wouldn't let him out of it. It was something we had to settle, because it had everything to do with his attitude toward money and decision making. We couldn't go on this way, having one-sided decisions." Then there was the Fight at City Hall. That one was about her allowing their son to go on a camping trip after her husband had forbidden the trip because of the boy's poor schoolwork. "The fight began when we were on our way to meet out-of-town friends at City Hall, which is one of our landmarks," the husband recalled, "and it continued inside. My wife kept saying, 'Shush, everyone can hear you,' but I kept going anyway. I was furious because she had undercut my authority and let our son play us off against each other. We had to establish some rules for ourselves about that."

A couple in Toledo, Ohio, had a different system for dealing with fights. On one weekend vacation, when they had engaged in a brawl to end all brawls and then made up, they kept the key to their hotel room to use as a symbol of reconciliation in the future. The key, the wife said, "reminds us that we need to keep opening doors between ourselves, because they don't stay open once and for all. Problems are recurring, and we need to find ways, continuously, of breaking through them." Although the key cannot prevent all fights, sometimes when they are heading for a blowup, one or the other fetches it as a symbolic battle stopper.

These couples, like many others I met, were not afraid of fighting. Although given their choice, on many occasions they would have preferred not to quarrel, they recognized that tensions gathered and fights burst open at times, and that the fights did not and would not destroy their marriage. I met a few couples who said they never fought—so few that I can remember only four out of more than a hundred interviewed. One of these couples were in their seventies, and I wondered whether they may have forgotten earlier battles of their youthful married years. Another, a man and a woman without children, seemed to serve, constantly, as both parents and children to one another. Any period of distancing was so painful to them that they tried to avoid arguments at all costs. The third took an easygoing attitude toward everything they did. "Nothing's worth fighting over," said the wife. "What should I fight about—a new dress? What for? I can live without it." It is an attitude that makes life peaceful because it allows partners to gloss over differences. On the other hand, it may also cause them to gloss over issues they should be grappling with, resulting in a kind of bond others would find shallow. The fourth couple approached their nonfighting with the most humor. "I have a terrible memory," the husband explained. "I can never remember what I'm angry about. And Isabelle can't stand confrontation. So we never fight . . . but we do sulk."

Whether people sulk or fight or do their best to evade problems, no marriage is free of difficulties, even if they are occasional. Salvador Minuchin, a psychiatrist and well-known therapist, believes that conflict is an integral part of married life. "The TV view of families presents a distorted idea—that people need to be free of conflict," he declared in an interview I had with him. "Actually, every family has conflict—not only families who seek therapy. Marriages are essentially exercises in conflict."

Minuchin wasn't arguing that married people fight all the time (although some do). When he spoke of marriages as exercises in conflict, he meant that couples must always cope with everyday stresses and frustrations along with out-of-the-ordinary crises that arise within family life. "You go from one stage in which you learn the rules and more or less find your way," Minuchin continued, "and just when you think you have licked the troubles of this stage, you change—things happen. You have a child; a parent dies; a youngster leaves for college; you lose your job. There are continual moments of transition in marriages, and moments of transition are moments of crisis. Each time, your world changes."

The conflicts begin in the earliest days of marriage, and those can be the most difficult, and most significant, problems a couple will encounter. They arise for a variety of reasons, among them the unreal expectations people bring to their marriages. They also come because partners enter marriage infused with ideas of doing things the way they had been done in their own families. "You take two individuals who have their particular cultures and traditions and ways of meeting the world," Minuchin explained, "and now you're going to upset them both. They need to begin to resolve conflicts that grow out of the meeting of two cultures." Even if their backgrounds are similar, even if she is the girl next door or he her high school sweetheart, each comes to marriage with mental images of life as it was at home. Each may want to repeat those images, working hard to impose ingrained habits on the other. Or they may want to change the way things were done at home, causing conflict because of their rebellion.

One woman, a physician married about four years, described the early days of her marriage when she was still in medical school. So determined was she not to be supported by her new husband that she took out loans, not only to pay her tuition but to allow her enough money to support herself within the marriage. Her husband, also a physician but with a thriving practice, was distressed by what he perceived to be her lack of trust in him, her inability to view their finances as shared. In spite of his anger, she persisted in taking out loans until she was able to support herself through her own work. "I couldn't help it," she insisted. "Money was the thing I saw my parents fight about most. My father controlled every cent and dished it out to my mother as he saw fit. I was so scared of being supported financially even though I knew Eddie isn't like my father. The best day of my life was when I started making my own money." Ironically, in not wanting to repeat her parents' fights about money, this woman began her marriage by fighting about money. Her reaction against her parents rather than her desire to perpetuate their ways caused tension in her marriage.

Many problems that arise during those early years of marriage stem from each partner's background. Little things: He eats with his knife; she leaves the beds unmade. She reads at the table; he leaves hair in the sink. (An unmarried aunt who lived with my family for a while when I was a teenager told me repeatedly about a woman whose husband divorced her because her hairbrush was always dirty. Her fearful warning—the same thing would happen to me one day if I weren't neater—took hold, and I became scrupulous about keeping my combs, brushes and the sink cleared of any stray hairs, even a fallen eyelash. Without the benefit of Aunt Gertie's dire admonitions, my husband entered marriage with much looser views of hairbrushes and sinks. His carelessness and my compulsiveness led to some of the mightier battles of our early marital days.) And bigger things: She fills the house with family and friends as her parents did; he wants peace and quiet, with a minimal social life. She guards every penny; he is a happy spender.

People in second marriages may use their first marriages, rather than their family backgrounds, as the gauge of marital behavior they may want to repeat or not repeat. One woman complained bitterly about her second husband's indecisiveness. "He's sweet; he's kind; he's considerate in all the ways my first husband wasn't," she said. "The first one was a tyrant; he wanted to dominate me. But at least he could make up his mind about things." She had intentionally chosen someone the exact opposite of her first husband, but—like couples who compare spouses to their own parents—she could not stop herself from comparing him to her first husband and criticizing him when he didn't measure up.

And beneath the surface of the arguments and angers during those early years are deeper motives for the disagreements, deeper reasons for wanting to repeat old patterns. Each partner brings long-held insecurities and needs to the marriage, hoping that this time the "story will turn out right," as it were, and the lacks left by parents will be filled by spouses. As I said earlier, partners often do make up for some of those childhood deficiencies, offering one another support and solace the way a parent might, but they cannot (and should not) turn into parents. Then the unmet needs of husband or wife, their longings and fears, translate into arguments about sex or money, about manners or possessions.

A couple recounted the impassioned fights they had because of the husband's closeness to his younger brother. The time was the 1960s, the brother a full-fledged hippie—long haired, bearded, "into" love rather than work. The wife in this marriage insisted that her husband have nothing to do with this brother unless the younger man changed his ways—cut his hair, got a job, became a more conventional fellow. Her husband refused to tell his brother what to do. "It's his life," he kept insisting. "I can't live it for him." He could not understand his wife's rage at his brother and her resentment of any time the two spent together. Nor, when she wanted to be honest with herself, could she. She sought professional advice. After a few sessions of therapy she came to recognize her own enormous need to be cared for, a need that went back to childhood feelings of being neglected by her parents. She resented her husband's closeness to his brother, as if that closeness took something away from her, and she expressed that resentment through criticism of her brother-in-law's dress and style. This woman told me that the way she came to handle her own neediness was to force herself to go out and find a job, proving to herself as well as her husband that she could stand on her own feet without being babied.

Weaving their way through these fights about manners and needs are the pulls and tugs over power. Those struggles begin early, as couples jockey for dominance within the marriage, not realizing yet that hard-won positions will shift back and forth as time goes on. So in those first years, the fight over how to decorate a new apartment may really be a fight over who makes the decisions about how the couple presents itself to the outside world. The fight over where to take a vacation may be a battle over whose way of playing will become dominant in this marriage. And the fight over her best friend "who is such a bubblehead I can't imagine how you can spend five minutes with her" is really a struggle over the couple's image and future social aspirations.

Therapists tell me that when couples come to them for marital help, the basic complaint of each partner always is, "if only she would change," or "if I could just make him see how wrong he is." Never does one or the other recognize a need for personal change; each sees the salvation of the marriage to lie only in changing the other. When I said earlier that the battles at the beginning of married life are not only difficult but also significant, I meant that they are significant because they are the first steps for both partners in learning about change in themselves and in the other. Through those battles of will and those battles of family habits, each begins to understand how far the other can be pushed to change, and to what extent each is willing to change himself or herself. And through those battles both get a rudimentary insight into those spheres in which one or the other will never change, an insight that evolves into a clearer vision as the marriage goes on.

*   *   *

The early struggles do not continue forever. Many of them get resolved, but even as they do, changes begin to take place within the marriage and within each partner.

It has become fashionable in recent years to organize changes in adult life into clear-cut stages, in much the same way that children's development is described as occurring in an organized sequence. One of the best known of such plottings of adult life cycles was made by social psychologist Daniel Levinson, who described seven stages of adult life, beginning in the late teens and ending with old age. Based on Levinson's scheme, two psychiatrists, Ellen Berman and Harold Lief, mapped out marital life cycles, correlating stages of marriage to stages of individual adult development.

As charted by Berman and Lief, in Stage 1, for example, during the late teens and early twenties, an individual is pulling up roots and going out into the world. Within marriages that take place at these young ages, conflicts arise over tensions between ties to each partner's original family and the need to adjust to the marriage. By Stage 3, between 29 and 31 years, the individual is deciding about commitments to marriage and work, and marital partners are struggling with restlessness and doubts about one another, especially if they are still caught up in parental obligations. Stages 5 and 6, when individuals are in their forties and fifties, represent middle adulthood. This is a time when partners reorder their priorities in life and when marital conflicts may be churned up over attitudes toward success and concerns about the passing of youth. The last stage, Stage 7, spans from 60 years onward. Now the individual must deal with older age, and marital conflicts center around fears of desertion, loneliness and sexual failures.

Other descriptions offer different categorizations of marital life cycles. One scheme divides marriage into three phases: The first, the honeymoon phase, is a kind of "thank-God-we-have-each-other" time, when partners are happy and enthusiastic about each other. The second phase, called the "pseudomutual" phase, is a time when the couple feel strongly dependent on one another, taking a posture of "it's us against the world" without developing yet as individuals. The third phase brings an open acknowledgment of differences with attempts to deal with them. At that point, partners accept themselves as individuals, but are ready to work at living together and sharing a life. Other social scientists suggest a four-phased breakdown, instead of three, beginning with a self-centered view of the marriage (what it can do for *me*), going through two phases of recognizing and then appreciating one another's individuality, and ending with a set of "rules of the relationship" to deal with problems.

Which description is right? Which really outlines the way marriages are—the seven-stage cycle? the three-phase one? the four-phase one? The answer is all of them and none of them. The most important part of these life cycle schemata, it seems to me, is their emphasis on change, on the idea that marriage is not static but is continually taking on new shapes and forms as partners themselves age and change. And yes, it is reassuring to know that new times and new events that occur in marriage affect everyone, not just you and your spouse. You feel better when you recognize that the birth of a child, for example, adds stresses and tensions to many marriages, not only yours, or that in midlife many men, not only your husband, become restless and self-involved.

The failing of all these classification charts, however, is in their implication that change necessarily moves along the same routes in all marriages, that problems are *predictable* because they follow a set path of unfolding, whether it's in seven steps or four steps. Such thinking leads to simplistic views of marriage that mislead people into misinterpreting problems that occur and anticipating others that may never happen. (A headline in a popular magazine reads: "Not only do big-time woes assail every marriage, they tend to come on *schedule*. Learn the timetable for trouble here . . .")

A friend, a Wall Street broker in his midfifties, recently married for the second time. His first marriage had been during the 1950s, and his life should have followed the predictable patterns of the time. Instead, he was divorced, and in an arrangement unusual for that era, he received custody of his two daughters. He devoted the next twenty years to raising his children, shoving his career and personal satisfactions to the background. A dream of a man, he had many love affairs during those years, but whenever he came close to marriage, he bridled. His friends made many interpretations: He lacked something in his development—after all he should have settled down by now and married again; he was still an adolescent, living out adolescent fantasies; he was afraid to take a chance on marriage and intimacy again. All possible truths. Just as possible, and probably more true, his main motive for remaining single during all those years was devotion to his children, who had been badly hurt by the divorce, and a desire to stay as available to them as possible. Now that his daughters are busy with college and careers, he has remarried. His wife, an executive in a public relations firm, is twenty years his junior and was never married before. Within a year of marriage, they had a baby boy, fat and gray-eyed, born to be doted over. Can one predict the life cycle of this marriage? It is already far from typical. Having married in the fullness of life, both have long since settled their problems of separating from parents. Each respects the other's individuality, yet both are mature enough to handle a strong bond between them. Both have had their fill of sexual exploits and novelties and are happy to commit themselves to monogamous lives. The kind of Stage 5 tensions between personal success and marriage outlined by life cycle theorists are unlikely for them. They have financial security and a string of career successes behind them. They will have their own share of transitions and crises, of course. They will face the problem of his aging while she is still relatively young, the problem of the many years that separate him and his new baby, the problem of incorporating the children to whom he devoted decades of his life into this new family unit. But even these problems are not predictable or inevitable. Life holds too many variables, too many stimuli, too many kinds of experiences to rely on standardized generalizations to foretell the future of any marriage.

One thing we can predict, however, is that change will take place in every marriage and will continue to take place through all the years of married life. And oh, the kinds of changes that can shake up a marriage! Aside from the usual crises that may center around children, work or in-laws, dislocations can occur in less expected ways. Moving, for example, or just redoing a home or apartment, can stir up untapped insecurities and feelings of disorientation. As walls go down or ceilings go up, the entire structure of a marriage can become wobbly. I remember with a shudder the six months during which my own apartment was being renovated. It was then that I discovered things about my husband and he about me to which we had barely paid attention in the previous twenty-some-odd years, and that we have tried to forget in the years since. As I told him innumerable times, I suddenly discovered him to be selfish, unbearably chauvinistic and unfeelingly willing to let me carry the entire burden of the ordeal. As he told me innumerable times, he discovered me to be demanding, rigid and so controlling that nobody else dared express an opinion. What saved our marriage, I am convinced, was our mutual hatred for the building contractor, who was responsible for the misplaced electrical outlets, the leaky faucets, etc., etc. Without him as our scapegoat, who knows what would have happened?

Not only difficulties but even good things from the outside can sometimes bring bad things into a marriage. A job promotion, just as much as a loss, can stir up a storm of controversy and pain, depending on how each spouse reacts to it. A man and a woman who had divorced after twenty years of marriage each spoke separately about the effects of the husband's success in his firm. She: "As he went up the corporate ladder, he became more and more their man. I think he sold his soul to his job, and it is sad, because he had a lot of potential. The man he is now is not the man—the boy—I married twenty years ago. He became very conservative; he made his choices and his compromises. I didn't like the person he became." He: "She resented my becoming more successful. She wanted everything to stay the same, but she also wanted to change her life just as I was changing mine. I said, 'Great, do whatever you want. Go to school; get a job. I don't care what you do as long as it will make you happier.' But she wouldn't. She would apply for jobs and then say either that they were beneath her or she needed more training, and she'd make no effort. I just *couldn't* stand still and wait for her."

The wife's reaction in this anecdote raises another issue. While she probably had good reason to be angry at her husband's new "company manners" and altered attitudes, a good part of her anger at him grew out of anger at herself, that is, dissatisfaction with her own life. She didn't like the emptiness of her days, yet for a variety of internal reasons, she wasn't able to change the situation. She blamed his success and the transformation it wrought in him for her personal unhappiness. Although he became happier with his own life, he was not able to make her happy within herself, and the widening chasm between their perceptions of their lives eventually led to divorce.

It's normal to have change in your life, said Dr. Minuchin. And when does a couple or a family become abnormal? "When your world changes, and you don't." A change in one partner requires some change in the other, or at least an accommodation to the change. In the couple described above, the man changed in ways that his wife felt she could not tolerate, and the more so because she wanted to alter her own life and was not able to. That combination proved disastrous to the marriage.

In all marriages, some of the worst periods of conflict come when one partner changes so much that the other either cannot keep up or does not want to. The marriage becomes unbalanced, and then a decision needs to be made. Does the marriage continue? Should each partner make that extra effort to keep it going? Said Minuchin: "In every couple there are divorce periods. Divorce is a characteristic of any marriage. Some people remarry the same person, others do not. They find an alternative. They say, 'O.K. let me look and find an alternative to this marriage.' "

Minuchin was more accepting of divorce as an alternative to marriage in times of conflict than I am. That is not to say that I don't acknowledge the necessity of divorce as a way to end a bad marriage. I do. What I don't accept is the view of divorce as an alternative equal to the choice of staying married. I don't accept the idea that when conflict disrupts a marriage, or when change causes stress, equal weight should be given to trying to solve problems within the marriage and solving the problems by leaving the marriage. In order for a marriage to last, it must be built on an ideology of coping with conflict rather than seeking alternatives to the union.

The people I spoke with had all been through "divorce periods," times of change that led to stress and disruption. Almost all said that at one time or another, divorce, escape from the marriage, had entered their minds. And what made them stay? Reasons such as "When I married, it was for life," and "We said through thick or thin, better or worse; in other words we made a pledge," and—facetiously but also seriously—"Suction, my dear; we're simply stuck together." What it all came down to was an attachment—that ubiquitous word commitment— not only to one another but also to the marriage itself. These couples are committed to staying married. They do whatever they can to keep their marriage going, and they see divorce not as a viable alternative but only as a last resort. As one woman described it: "There are those little turns, points at which someone else might say, 'That's it; I've had it; I can't watch him eat with his elbows on the table one more time.' But me, I'm different. I'll keep going; I'll hang in there; I want to be around for the end of this story."

Couples who stay together in spite of conflicts and changes make constant redecisions to be married. Although those decisions may not be consciously stated, they are being made again and again, after times of anger and times of distancing. But then I don't believe we actually remarry the *same* person, as Minuchin said we do. While we marry one another over and over, the person each of us is changes in response to events outside the marriage and events in the marriage. In that sense, we are married to many different people in the course of a single marriage, and every marriage that lasts is a "serial marriage," a term used often these days to describe the sequence of marriage, divorce and remarriage that has become so commonplace in our society. The difference is that in ongoing marriages, while the partners change in many ways, each remains unchanged in the commitment to the marriage, and while the marriage changes, it remains, at its center, permanent.

If there was one thing that impressed me more than any other about many of the couples I met, it was their flexibility, their ability to adapt to changes in their lives and to changes in one another. Some years ago, the book *Future Shock* by Alvin Toffler caused a stir in both the literary and the popular worlds. One thesis of the book was that technological changes have accelerated so rapidly in our society, and will continue to accelerate so rapidly, that people may no longer be able to adapt or adjust to those changes. Yet I found myself so often in awe and wonder at the adaptability of people that I suspect that we, as a species, will somehow manage to meet the challenges of that future shock of rapid change. The flexibility of marriages, the aptitude people have for stretching and expanding within the context of their union, inspires me to my optimistic view of the future of humankind.

Much of the time, most of us are not especially flexible. All of us, said Minuchin, "operate within a narrower frame than the one we have available to us." By that he meant that we fall into a rut, we keep doing things the same way, although there are many other methods we could use. Similarly, on an everyday basis we respond to people in set ways, although we are capable of many other ways of dealing with one another. "With your husband you respond one way," he said, "with your children you use other responses; with your friends, you use other responses. But with your husband you keep using the same response." In situations of conflict and stress, however, the flexibility of individuals and couples may come to the fore. Then they are able to expand their responses, to behave in ways they never behaved before—in Minuchin's words, to "use muscles they never used before, and in this sense become more complex."

Two vignettes and a longer description illustrate some of the ways couples came to "use muscles they never used before":

A woman married nineteen years talked about the beginnings: "I was thirty-one when I married. I wasn't madly in love and I didn't especially want to marry—I had a good job and liked being on my own. I thought Lawrence was nice, but I wouldn't have married him or anyone if he hadn't persisted. He really talked me into it.

Then, during our first year, we gave a dinner party. I had stopped working and was trying to get pregnant. I asked Lawrence for some money to buy supplies at the super-market. He gave me a ten-dollar bill. 'Are you crazy?' I screamed. 'What can you buy for ten dollars?' He looked at me as if *I* were crazy. 'That's all we can afford,' he said. We had a horrendous fight, and I thought about it after-ward. I decided this wasn't for me. I didn't need this. I could be independent; I didn't want to be trapped in a marriage where I didn't have enough money to spend. I told him I wanted out.

"Lawrence had been married before and was deter-mined not to have a second failure. He really wanted to be married. We spent a year working this thing out—a terrible year, an angry year, a year of soul-searching and confrontation. At the end of it he understood what it felt like for me to have gone from independence to this de-pendency on his generosity to buy the simplest things. And I understood the financial pressures he felt. I learned to handle money and he learned to trust me. Eighteen years later, we're inseparable. We adore each other."

A man married twenty-nine years talked about midlife crisis—his wife's: "I had a very simple view of marriage when we began. I worked as many hours as I wanted to, and when I came home I relaxed by playing golf and tennis. Pamela took care of the children and of all my needs. She told me recently that we had had a power struggle in the early years of our marriage and that I had won. I didn't even know we had a power struggle. I just assumed the way we lived was the way things should be. Nine years ago my world toppled. Pamela had an affair, which I found out about. Everything exploded. She told me she hated the way we had lived, hated me in my selfishness and disinterest in her and the kids. She was ready to leave me. I couldn't believe it. I was so successful in business. This guy she was ready to go off with was a nothing, a poor shnook of a professor; at least that's the way I like to think of him.

"At first I was ready to let her go. 'Who needs her?' I thought. I'm still young enough, handsome enough and certainly rich enough. I can get anyone I want. And the irony. I swear to you, I've never been unfaithful, although

God knows, I've had plenty of opportunities. But the more I thought about it, the more I could see her point of view. I really had been a selfish bastard all those years. She had been a scared kid when I married her, but she had changed. She had opened herself up to so much more than I had. She loves music, and she used to go to concerts alone, without me. She loves the theater, and the only things I would agree to see were lightweight comedies.

"I decided that my marriage and my family were the most important things in the world to me, and I was going to save them in any way I could. I made a very conscious decision to win back my wife by changing myself, no matter what the cost to my pride. I have to tell you, it wasn't easy. I put Pamela first now, and my work and recreation last. I went to concerts and plays with her. We took walks in the country; we even went on an archaeological dig in Egypt because she loves archaeology. I'll be truthful. At first I had to fake my interest and act a role I didn't really feel. At times I hated her. I would think, 'Screw her, what do I need this for?' But I stuck with it because I knew what this marriage meant to me. And after a while I came to internalize her values. I came to enjoy the things we did together and to regret all the wasted years when I had closed myself off to everything except work. Funny thing is, she became more tolerant of my obsessions as I made myself more available to her. It's a painful thing, trying to change your entire character and approach to life, but I'm the richer for having done it. I have my wife and family back and . . . I'll tell you something I've never said to anyone. That period of time was my finest hour; that change, the thing I'm proudest of in my life."

In the case of both these couples, one partner was determined to keep the marriage going (it just happened to be the husband in both), and that determination and commitment to the marriage led to many changes in the nature of the relationship. Had the other partner been equally determined to leave, or so distorted the values upon which the marriage was built in the first place, probably nothing could have kept those marriages intact. Although the husbands cared more, both wives allowed themselves to be flexible enough to accept change in their husbands and eventually to change themselves sufficiently to meet their husbands part way.

In the third illustration, the couple changed together, constantly, consciously—a bit too self-consciously, some readers might feel. It has taken me a while to sort out my own impressions of their many transformations:

The Hillses have been married for seventeen years. Greta Gruens-Hills is one of the three top executives of a Chicago-based publishing company that specializes in reference works. She began working there in the sales department soon after she was graduated from business school, some eighteen years ago. She had met her husband-to-be, Sean Hills, at that business school. While she moved into publishing, he found work in advertising, and is today an account executive at a medium-sized Chicago advertising company. They seem content in their respective careers, and with four children, appear to have worked out a system for sharing household chores quite satisfactorily.

It wasn't always that way. Even though Greta worked, their home life was structured along traditional lines at first. Like many other women who pursued careers during the 1950s and 1960s, Greta identified with her father. A brilliant Dutch historian, he had moved his family to America when Greta was very young to take over the chairmanship of the history department at a prestigious university. His adored only child, Greta became the focus of much of his attention during her growing-up years. But her mother's submissive, housewifely manners were also imbued within her. Pursuing a career, as her father wanted her to, Greta also played the role of good wife, as both her parents expected her to. Her one rebellion after marriage was to keep her family name, hyphenated with her married one, long before that became a common practice for women.

Sean expected his wife to be a "real" wife too. The only child of middle-class Irish parents, he grew up knowing that his mother had quit her lucrative position as a legal secretary after he was born and did not return to work until he had finished college. That example haunted the early years of the Hills marriage. Greta would rush home after work to prepare dinner and serve it to Sean, while he told her about the difficulties of trying to hold on to a job in the competitive advertising field. She rarely spoke about her own work, and especially not about the rapid progress she was making in her company. "The idea was," said Greta, "that what I did from nine to five was fine for me, but I was not to talk about it. It was not to leak over into his time. I went along with it, because there was no point in not going along with it. If he wasn't going to listen and wasn't going to be interested, why bother talking about it anyway?"

The ultimate in Sean's tactic of ignoring Greta came after she was promoted to sales manager of the encyclopedia division of her firm. She returned from a sales meeting, at which she had addressed sales representatives from the entire country, high and excited by the day's events. "She came in," Sean recounted, "full of her glorious accomplishment . . ." "And," said Greta, "he looked at me and said, 'Gee you're late. Put the dinner on.' " Although Greta said nothing while she prepared dinner, inside she raged. "Part of my attitude had to do with my own work," Sean admitted. "I felt very unsure of myself and I was jealous of her. But a large part of it had to do with my expectations of what a wife's role should be."

Those expectations changed, Sean said, for a very specific reason. One day he began reading Virginia Woolf's, *A Room of One's Own,* and could not put it down until he had finished it. "It was extraordinary," he recalled. "Things Greta had never even been able to articulate were in that book. Now I suddenly saw what she had been up against all the time. With this book as my life preserver, I began to do things differently. Not all at once, but gradually I did change. I reread that book many times."

"He's changed completely," Greta added. "Now we have a pretty balanced sharing of chores. He does the marketing; I handle the checkbook. He takes the children to the movies and playground; I play chess with them."

Greta's turn to change was inspired by another book, this one a popular sex manual, *Nice Girls Do* by Irene Kassorla. "Although it was oversimplified," she told me, "there were things in it that I understood. The whole name of the game in sex, according to this book, is trust, and that was a revelation to me. I realized I had a lot of fears about sex, and they were not dispelled even though I had been married for years. I came to recognize that I did trust Sean, so why shouldn't I be freer with my feelings and actions?" Sean learned something from that book also. "What it meant was that although I had been experiencing a great deal, she was actually experiencing less than I was. I guess basically I had been very selfish, and I didn't realize it."

Then, for the two of them, there was Rollo May's book *Creative Fighting*, which taught them better techniques of fighting with one another. Fighting and reconciliation had been a pattern in their lives since their earliest courtship days, but now they tried to be fairer in their battles. "I learned to think before I yell," Greta said. "I used to just blow off, and Sean and the kids would be frightened when I would get that way. I didn't think I could ever do anything to control those tempers—they just came over me. Now I try to recognize warning signals. You know, you can tell two seconds before it happens that it is going to happen. And then you can nip it in the bud or somehow modify it before you blow up."

Still other changes have taken place in the Hills marriage. After much thinking and talking with other parents, they have changed some of the ways they treat their children. "We saw that unconsciously we were setting up a rather competitive atmosphere at home for the children," Sean explained. "We were paying little attention to the efforts the kids were putting into their school work and much more to their grades. We've tried to stop doing that." And they have changed some of the decision-making traumas that used to interfere with things such as vacation plans or theater dates. "After years of allowing Sean to make plans and then criticizing them I've started taking matters into my own hands," said Greta. "I knew I was on the way to licking this problem a few weeks ago when we were going on a trip. Sean had said that we had to get back at eleven-thirty at night. Before I launched into a long complaining session about the late hour, I went to the travel agent myself and was able to change the tickets. Now I no longer let him do things and then tell him how lousy they are."

This is a couple that gobbles up change the way a

guppy gobbles mosquito larvae. This is a couple for whom change is a separate entity, like another child. Why this is so is difficult to say. Greta appears to be the force pressing harder for change than is Sean. Highly intelligent and articulate, she keeps herself alert to the new and different. More easygoing and accepting of things as they are, Sean has picked up some of her energy to add more movement to his life than he would otherwise have had.

But is it possible to transform oneself as quickly and regularly as the Hillses say they do? Probably not. Is it possible for novels and pop psychology books to shape the entire course of a couple's life? I doubt it. What I suspect is that the changes that seemed so instantaneous in the Hills marriage were probably quite superficial when they began. Only with time did they become incorporated into family life, and only with time and effort will they remain part of it. What I find admirable about the Hillses is their willingness to look critically at themselves and point a finger at what is wrong. The pop books they read do not inspire change so much as they reflect an internal process that has already taken place, a readiness to receive the books' messages. "Trendy" may be the way some people would describe the Hills. Another description, the serious side of that term, is vital, interested in staying on top of things and determined to "stretch their muscles" to improve their marriage. "A really happy marriage," said Sean, "is one that has somebody who is willing to say, 'That way of doing things is not good, and we need to try doing them this way.' Otherwise the marriage stagnates."

For most of us change does not come easily, and flexing our muscles leaves us stiff and pained for a while. People spoke to me about the difficulty of accepting changes in their partners even when the change was desired. In one marriage, for example, the wife's perpetual complaint about her husband was his inability to express emotions, his tight, close-mouthed approach to anything smacking of feelings. After a series of traumas in his life—a business failure, the death of his best friend, an infatuation with another woman—the husband went into a severe depression for which he received psychiatric care. When he came out of the depression and away from the psychiatrist, he had changed into a far more open and emotionally expressive person than he had ever been before. Now the wife seemed to pull away, uncomfortable with the questions he asked and the truths he revealed about himself. Although he had turned into the kind of person she always said she wanted him to be, she had felt safer, it seemed, with her anger and her demands for change than with the actual change itself.

Therapist Carl Whitaker says that couples unconsciously set their own "emotional thermostat"—that is, they know how cold or hot they want their relationship to be, how close or distant. If one turns the thermostat up, the other somehow manages to pull it down, to keep a homeostatic balance. Using that image, we can say that if one partner changes—even with the consent or encouragement of the other—the balance is broken and both need to adjust. Either they reverse roles and the one who was hotter becomes cooler (or vice versa) or they reset their thermostat to a different level of emotionality. In any case, every change within one partner brings about some disruption in a relationship, and with it, often, a clash of temperaments, a conflict of interests. And every change from the outside, every passage or period of transition, leads to its own kind of struggle or confrontation.

I spoke earlier of the battles during the beginning years of marriage. As time goes on, new areas of tension arise. They include fights about kids and fights about in-laws, fights about cooking and fights about cleaning. They include worries about aging parents and worries about aging bodies, concerns about business and concerns about cancer. In remarriages the fighting may center around former spouses, around stepchildren or new children. Many times the fights that erupt between a couple are not really between them at all. They burst out from frustration on a job, rage at a child, inner sadness or angers that are displaced onto a partner. Often, they are cries for change, a way of shouting out hurts even though there is little expectation that any change will take place. Or they may be an appeal by one partner for the other to recognize a change that has already occurred and needs to be acknowledged. The fights take their own forms and become incorporated into marriages in different ways.

To the question, "How do you fight?" I received a variety of answers: "I yell and he withdraws, which makes me yell more," or "She sulks and I slam doors," or "We both go at it tooth and nail, shouting our heads off," or my favorite—a quote from my mother—"How can you fight with a man who cries?"

And how do you make up? "One or the other of us apologizes, eventually," or "We just start talking again," or "We become very physical after a fight; there's a certain sweetness in getting back together," or "I make the first overtures," or "We kind of walk around in silence for a while and then one of us gives in," or "I've found lots of different ways to apologize without actually saying the words 'I'm sorry'—more like signals that I give off." The late Abe Franzblau, a psychiatrist whose wife, psychologist Rose Franzblau, wrote a syndicated advice column for many years, once told me that the rule they had about fights was that the person who was right, and knew it, had to apologize first. Under that system, the wrong one could save face. He also said that they faithfully practiced the old adage of never going to bed angry, always patching things up first. A few other couples reported the same practice, but many others, while acknowledging the niceness of the advice, maintained that it didn't work. When you are really angry, it is almost impossible to make love, or even make up, against a set deadline such as bedtime.

While couples differed in their ways of fighting and getting over fights, almost all agreed about one crucial factor in preventing fights, or at least preventing them from getting completely out of hand: a sense of humor. I can't even count how many people said the secret of their marriage was simply being able to laugh together, often about things nobody else found so funny. Laughing at something that might otherwise irritate is a way of taking distance from a problem and seeing it in a new light.

A Wisconsin nurse described her husband's quick temper, so different from her own rather relaxed nature. "When the battery goes dead in the car," she said, "my tendency is to go get another battery. His is to kick the fender before doing another thing. I used to get real

annoyed when he'd act that way, but now I just laugh
and say to myself, 'Well, here we go—first he's going to
kick the fender, then he's going to get out of the car and
calmly go down and get a battery,' which is just what he
does." She went on to explain her changed attitude: "I
started thinking I hated him the first Christmas we were
married. The tree wouldn't stand up right, and he carried
on so much, I was sure he was going to throw it out the
window. Honestly, I would have left if he had. But probably if he had acted the same way the second Christmas, it
wouldn't have bothered me. I had learned to laugh at his
nonsense."

The importance of humor in marriage is supported by
a study by psychologist R. William Betcher, reported in
the journal *Psychiatry*. Using interviews, standardized tests
of marital adjustment and a series of tests relating to
playfulness in marriage, Betcher studied the ways thirty
couples use humor and play in their marriage. He found
that couples tend to repeat certain playful actions again
and again, and to be spontaneous about others. For example, one of the repetitive forms of playful behavior partners use is to talk baby talk to one another or make funny
faces. Some continue funny games they played as children. One husband described sharing a room with his
brother as a child and lying awake at night, the two of
them, making up funny and insulting names for each
other. In marriage he continued his old game with his
wife, each teasing the other with silly, semi-insulting names.
It was a way for them to rid themselves of hostility and
ambivalence without hurting or really insulting each other.
Another couple devised a game after the wife accused the
husband of constantly saying mean things about other
people. They drew up a sheet on which they would list
the mean remarks each made about others. Their daughter established a "Hostile Remark Fund," fining each of
them ten cents per remark. The game helped channel
their aggression toward others and prevent them from
angrily criticizing one another. Other couples drew closer
in just the opposite way—joking about other people, especially other marriages. This was, in effect, a way of
reaffirming their own values, of saying, "We wouldn't act
like that." Humor and playfulness, Betcher concluded,

help forge strong bonds between partners. They are another aspect of the private secrets couples have, their personal language that is hidden from the outside.

As one person wrote on Betcher's questionnaire, "It is the one clear sign of our feeling of closeness and trust in each other that we feel free to be silly together. It reaffirms a closeness and sensibility to one another that would be hard to express in any other way—it makes me aware of how relaxed I feel with him and he with me."

Unfortunately, humor does not do away with all problems, and arguments and angers do burst out. In the early years of marriage battles tend to be all-out onslaughts in which each accuses the other of being the source of every difficulty, and each attempts to win "once and for all" by spelling out just what is and always has been wrong with the partner: "Your mother spoiled you rotten, and you expect me to continue her handiwork." "I could tell from the minute I met your father that you're as stubborn and pigheaded as he is." "Every time you handle money, you screw up. You've never been good at anything practical." These kinds of global and historical accusations, which characterize early (and many later) marital battles, rarely solve problems, and more often escalate them. Statements that "summarize" for the other's "benefit" everything that is and ever was wrong with the person and the marriage succeed mostly in increasing antagonisms.

The one prime rule of fighting that professionals give, and that many couples have discovered for themselves over time, is "never go back past now." That is, confine the fight to the present, to the specific issue at hand and try to deal with that. Such confinement could lead to a resolution, or at the least to a needed release of emotions, while dredging up the past and turning every issue into a fight to end all fights can lead only to frustration and more fighting. The technique one couple used of labeling their battles, described earlier, is one of the best methods of containing fights. By giving each fight a name and a place, this couple boxed off the fight as an entity in itself to be remembered for what it dealt with. In that way, every argument and struggle did not become a continuation of the one before it or a prelude to the one after it.

Techniques and rules of fighting (about which many
books have been written) are easier created than practiced. When you're enraged, it's hard to fight by the rules,
and at the height of wrath you wonder what there was
about the other person that you ever thought you could
love. The past comes swirling up to engulf the present,
and it seems impossible to separate today's anger from all
the angers that came before. Yet couples do make that
separation. It is almost physical, a kind of switch that
clicks inside when you are about to scoop up the most
painful parts of the past and hurl them. Then you stop,
although the temptations to continue are great.

You stop, also, at least many couples do, from going
for broke in every fight, from escalating to the final threat:
"I'm leaving; I'm not taking another minute of this." You
recognize after a while that threats are meaningless unless
they're real, and if they're real, you have moved beyond
the point of fighting. As a matter of fact, one of the
reasons fights can take place within solid, long-term marriages is the underlying knowledge that the marriage will
last in spite of quarrels. It's safe to fight in a marriage,
safer than it is during courtship or living together times,
because marriage carries an assumption of permanence.
(A statement about marriage that I have heard time and
again is the truism that spouses treat strangers, friends or
business associates better than they treat one another. "I
treat my wife like a stranger," stated from a positive
viewpoint, is supposed to mean that a man is as polite to
his wife as he would be to a stranger. That's all right as far
as it goes. Politeness is definitely a virtue in marriage as
elsewhere. But marriage allows for fights and impolite-
ness because it is a safe haven from the forms and trappings of the outside world. You can expose your feelings,
and your rage, in marriage on the supposition that they
will not be turned against you to hurt you and that you
will not be abandoned because of them as you might be in
other relationships.) Yet even in marriage there are limits.

A schoolteacher in his sixties, gentle and softspoken,
recalled the early days of his marriage, when he was not
so softspoken. "I was an angry young man, angry at my
parents, angry at the world," he said, "and my wife was
so self-contained, never able to talk about how she felt. I

would yell that I was going to leave her, and then I would shout at her, 'Why can't you ever yell back?' " One day she did yell back, "I'm the one who's leaving!" she said, "I can't stand it." The husband was shocked. For the first time, divorce became a real possibility, "in an age when nobody got divorced." He went on, "We didn't even know how you go about getting a divorce. We sat down and looked at each other.

" 'What would your mother say?' I asked her.

" 'What would your father say?' she asked me."

Faced with the difficulty of handling a divorce and dread at having to tell their families, they decided to rethink the whole business. "Look," the teacher said to his wife, "we married because we loved each other. Let's try to look for what it was that made us get married in the first place." That was forty years ago. There have been many fights since then, but very few, if any, that included threats of divorce.

Couples place other limits on their fights, and these have to do with the inside knowledge each has about the other. The one thing we have learned well in our marriages is how to hurt one another, how to unwrap the fragile robe of self-protection that surrounds each of us and get at the essence, the precise point of vulnerability that will clinch our argument—and in the process shatter the other. Just such knowledge and destruction make up one of the most devastating moments in Ingmar Bergman's film *Scenes from a Marriage*. Marianne and Johan have come together to sign a divorce agreement. They begin to shout at one another, and everything that had been held back comes out now, what the author calls all "the hate, all the mutual boredom and rage that they have been suppressing for years. Bit by bit they are dehumanized . . ." Marianne shouts at Johan, "You can commit suicide for all I care, though I suspect you're too much of a coward." And he responds, "Jesus, how I hate you really. I remember thinking it quite often: Jesus how I hate her . . . I hate her, her body, her movements . . ."

We know what will hurt the other most. Always, at the height of an argument, you have your finger on the weak spots. You can claw at those spots if you wish. Or you can protect them, maneuver around them, the way you scratch around the edges of a mosquito bite to relieve the itching, but carefully avoid the red lump that is the bite itself for fear of tearing at it and infecting it, and with it, your entire body. In lasting marriages, even in moments of sheer hatred, an alarm sounds, and you hold back from saying the very thing the other most dreads hearing.

In the book *Anger*, psychologist Carol Tavris argues that, contrary to popular belief, expressing anger tends not to make you feel better, but to make you angrier. That is, the angry words feed on one another until they become fat and blown out of proportion. She recommends that people not express their anger while they feel it. Better to cool down a bit, and then, when more rational, state your position or demands in the strongest way possible. It is sound advice. There are people who follow that formula and find it works well for them, people who walk away before their tempers soar (although the partners of these level-headed people sometimes get even angrier when a spouse won't slug it out at the moment). Others find it more difficult to stop before letting go, especially people who come from families in which fighting was a way of dealing with all controversies. Most people in lasting marriages would agree with Tavris, however, that it is necessary to try to set limits on the number of things that can trigger an angry response. Couples learn over the years what is important and what is trivial, what might bring about change and is therefore worth fighting over, and what serves only to stir up emotions for no useful purpose.

A hospital administrator explained how she had applied the efficiency she exercised on her job to her home life. "There are two things I've stopped getting angry about," she said. "First, if my husband does something I want him to do, but mutters or complains about it, I don't try to make him act cheerful. I don't have to get into an argument about whether he's happy, as long as he does what I want. Second, I don't blow up the way I used to because he doesn't do something that's important to me if I haven't told him what I'd like. I no longer assume he'll just know how I feel or what I expect. I tell him with words." (Her second principle emerged as an antidote to one of the misleading expectations of marriage—that a spouse is by definition a seer.)

Having just spoken of the limitations on warfare that couples impose during the course of marriage, I must immediately insert a qualification. Everybody has met husbands and wives who fight all the time, about everything, from what time to go to bed, to whether to visit friends, to what to have for dinner. Maggie and Robbie, the young couple interviewed on the threshold of marriage, spoke about fighting as a way of life for them. One questions why, and what will happen when their differences become solidified. When you see older spouses fighting constantly, spitting venom and bitterness, you wonder what keeps them together. What could be worth all the pain? The psychoanalyst A. A. Brill liked to tell about a woman who came to him complaining piteously about her marriage. "My husband and I are always fighting," she cried. "That's all we do, fight, fight, fight." Knowing that the woman had grown children and financial means with which to support herself, the doctor asked, "Why do you stay with your husband if you're so unhappy?" She looked at him with something like amazement. "Who else would I fight with if I left?"

Some couples are so attached to one another and so dependent on one another that they get caught up in the old "you can't live with 'em and you can't live without 'em" two-step. Each needs someone else to tear down and to be torn down by—to tear down in order to feel powerful, to be torn down in order to feel recognized, even if it's just as a hitting board. In a perverse way, this *"Who's Afraid of Virginia Woolf?"* relationship satisfies both parties. For other people, constant fighting keeps things hot and alive. It fills an emptiness that might otherwise overtake the entire relationship. Without the fighting the marriage would have nothing, or it would have cold, sheer misery. With it, there is at least the excitement of combat. Sometimes that excitement is a sexual one, the fighting a way of stirring up emotions, the making up a form of capture or surrender, feeding into sexual fantasies.

And then there are people for whom bickering (not acrimonious, destructive fighting) serves as an expression of emotion, a thrust and parry of feelings. Said a widow about her marriage: "For me, fighting was a sign of caring. You don't fight with someone you don't care about. I came from a family of bickerers, and that's my style. But where did my bickering go since Larry died? I don't bicker with anyone now, not even my kids. I keep thinking that if I got into another relationship with someone I cared about the way I cared about Larry, I'd bicker again." Although a state of bickering is not, to my mind, an ideal way to live, there is truth in the concept that you don't get angry at someone you don't care about. Fighting can be a form of connecting with another person.

Some conflicts that arise at various points in a marriage have to be resolved in order for the marriage to continue. Fights flare up around these issues and the fights either lead to some resolution of the problem or become the launching pad for negotiations that allow partners to stay together without, in the end, great loss on the part of either one. An example of that kind of conflict was told to me by a couple married about twenty-five years. The husband grew up in a home in which he felt smothered by three older sisters, who treated him as their pet, delightedly showing him off to friends and relatives who came visiting. The wife was an only child, who had sought out relatives to substitute for the siblings she never had. In the early days of their marriage, she continued her pattern, accepting dozens of invitations from family members for visits, cookouts, bridal showers and so on. Her husband hated the incessant socialization and would often bolt at the last minute from some social engagement she had accepted, leaving her embarrassed and distraught. Their newly established household was torn by strife for more than a year as the battle of the family relations waxed stronger and stronger. As he became more withdrawn, she increased her demands for socialization. In order to stay married, which they wanted to do, they both had to back down, which they finally did. The compromise position, and one that still governs their social life today, was that he would join her in attending those family functions, such as weddings or christenings, that she honestly felt were necessary, and that she would attend alone any others she felt obliged to or wanted to attend, and neither would pressure the other to do otherwise.

Other conflicts never get resolved, and the genius of many marriages lies in their ability to expand enough to encompass those conflicts within them, yet not snap in the process. It's a paradox of marriage that the strongest ones are those in which partners are simultaneously able to change to accommodate one another in some areas, and able to live with unchangeability in others. There may be some characteristics each partner has that will not change, so deep-seated are they, so ingrained in the person's character, or rooted in family background. Or there may be some issues of controversy built into the marriage from its very start that defy resolution. Nevertheless, the marriage goes on and the couple derives happiness from the many aspects that are not controversial. Put another way, problems in marriage cannot always be solved or worked out. The best solution to some problems is to acknowledge that there is no solution, that partners have to live with the conflict as it exists and that the marriage can be strong and good in spite of it.

Living with conflict does not mean that partners are content with the unchangeable; it means that in some areas they accept one another as they are and do not keep fighting again and again for a change that will never happen. The truce might be an uneasy one, and irritations and frustrations might bubble to the surface occasionally, but on the whole each spouse has made a separate peace with the imperfect other.

Henry and Kathy Peters are one of the few couples I met for whom religion was an ongoing source of conflict in marriage. Although there were others who differed in religious beliefs, for most the differences did not seem a primary cause of hostilities. But they were for Henry and Kathy.

Henry is a Presbyterian, Kathy a Catholic. Twenty-six years ago they married in the Catholic church, where he agreed to raise their children as Catholics. But he didn't agree to like doing so. In the small Kansas town in which

Henry was born, Catholics were in the majority, and their bias against Protestants made the Peters family wary of any association with them. Henry's parents were somewhat stunned when their son brought home a Catholic girl as his intended. They were perfectly gracious, said Kathy, but "every once in a while Henry's mother let something slip. I knew they wished I were anything but Catholic."

In marrying Kathy, Henry broke from the proud Presbyterian heritage of his family, a family that boasted judges and presidential advisors among its immediate ancestors. In marrying Henry, Kathy repeated a pattern her parents had set. Her father, a prominent political leader, was Catholic; her mother, whose ancestry stemmed back to the *Mayflower*, was a Congregationalist. Mixed marriages were a rarity back in 1928 when that couple married, and their family and friends had been shocked. Kathy's mother agreed to raise her children as Catholics. "She taught us our catechism and packed us off to mass," said Kathy, "but she herself did not convert." Henry did not convert, either, after he had made the same agreement with the church.

The subject of religion was the first thing that cropped up when I met with the Peterses in their Kansas City home.

"Two contracting parties, me and the Catholic church," is the way Henry described his wedding ceremony. "Separate but equal parties . . ." And his voice carried a slight crackle.

"You've never considered converting?" I asked.

"Good God, no!"

"It's nothing that anybody should do unless they feel it themselves," Kathy said hurriedly. "And Henry is wonderful. He's wonderful without any religion—just goodness for goodness's sake. It doesn't matter to me what he practices."

Silence. Then, "I would say that Henry is impatient with the Catholic church, which he should well be."

Silence again. Then, "I think Henry feels my faith sometimes is blind or a crutch . . ."

"Both," Henry cut neatly into the sentence.

"And he may be right. I disagree, however. But that's all right, we can live with that."

"I've kept my hands off when it comes to religion." Henry leaned back, drew slowly on a cigarette. I gathered now that he was referring not only to Kathy, but also to his children. The Peterses have five, and each, in turn, has separated from the church. "That was the deal I made, and I've kept to it."

"I do worry about the children," Kathy said. Their souls was a subject very much on her mind. "Henry is grown up and he knows what he's about. They're still at a time in their lives when they don't understand their mortality. They don't really know that some sort of faith is going to be important to them, and that it takes effort and time. They're kind of throwing the baby out with the bath."

"I disagree." Henry was stonyfaced.

"When you said you kept your hands off," I asked, "does that mean you haven't spoken to them about how you feel? No snide remarks?"

"I don't believe so."

Henry turned away from me. Kathy stared at Henry, her face slightly flushed. She knew the answer to that question, and it was not the answer Henry had given. "I believe they sensed my own individuality," Henry went on, "and recognized that the faith I was following is not a bad one."

Henry was gloating in his victory. He had sold his soul to the church for the price of a wife, but he was getting the better of the bargain after all. One by one, the children he had agreed to raise as Catholics were lining up on his side. The religious balance, weighted toward Kathy's beliefs when the marriage began, was shifting toward him. And he loved it.

Religion is obviously the sore point in the Peters marriage, and the religious differences fester just below the surface, erupting occasionally, not in angry battles but in sarcasm, in the digs Henry finds opportunities to slip into conversations. It would be a better marriage without that underlying tension, and maybe one day it will be. Maybe when the children have all left home, Kathy will practice her religion privately, without involving herself in saving their souls, and maybe then Henry will not feel compelled to counter her control with his more insidious, and therefore more persuasive, influence. Or maybe not. All we can know at present is that the conflict exists and remains unsolved.

"We can live with that," Kathy said, and they do, because there are many other areas in this marriage that provide warmth and greater protection for the two. They love the family they have created and whom they nurture together. Kathy admires Henry's ability to play with the kids, the endless patience he showed as they were growing up. Henry respects Kathy's skill at "keeping the children in tow," yet managing to remain close to each one, available for any problem that might arise. And for all that, they relish the moments they have alone, when all the children are away at school or on vacations. They spend evenings reading to one another, or at the piano, where Kathy plays and Henry sings. The conflict between them does not destroy the many other things they have.

As time passes, in many marriages the burning conflicts of early days dissipate and fewer issues arouse angry passions. Experts speak about the "disengagement" of couples, their loss of interest in one another and even in the differences that divided them. That description probably applies to a number of couples. For many others a different dynamic takes place. With time, partners in marriages that offer rewards and satisfactions in spite of conflicts begin to internalize one another's outlooks and ideas. They fight less because they become closer in thought.

I asked Dr. Minuchin whether the cliché that women "turn into" their mothers as they age is based on fact. "It's not true," he said. "It's something people think—that they become more like their parents with the years, but it's not so. What happens," he went on, "is that marriage partners become more like each other, even in appearance. They take on one another's mannerisms and gestures so that they almost look alike. More important, they incorporate one another's thinking, becoming more alike as they learn from each other."

Over time, couples arrive at new understandings, creating a fuller, richer entity that is their marriage. Claudia Winters, whose husband finds her "the most supportive woman in the world," put it this way: "Eventually there's a third person who emerges in a marriage. That third person is the compromise person, the combination of the two people and what they give to and take from one another.''

CHAPTER FIVE

~

"Sex Isn't Everything,
but It's a Lot"

*During the evening I spent with the Christens and the Lowes,
described at the beginning of Chapter 3, conversation shifted
from discussions of changing roles and power struggles in each
family to discussions about marital sex. There was a natural
connection—sexual relationships involve issues of power and
dependency; power struggles and problems with intimacy are
often worked out within a sexual context.*

*The discussion took off from a question I asked about the
importance of sex in marriage. Jason Christen, wealthy plastic
surgeon and art collector, spoke with characteristic bravado tempered by a sweet sincerity. His wife, Lila, learning to be assertive
as she carves out her own economic niche, was straightforward
in her views. Stanley and Audrey Lowe argued about attitudes
toward extramarital sex, just as they had argued about attitudes
toward work, with a mixture of heat and humor.*

JASON: In this marriage, Dr. Christen thinks sex is a very
important ingredient. Part of the great relationship Lila
and I have has to do with what goes on in the bedroom.

LILA (*interrupting*): Yeah, it's one of our strongest points.
We get high marks in that area.

JASON: Well, Lila makes me feel like a real lover. I'll be honest. Believe me, as you get older, sometimes you get impotent, and sometimes it's a matter of concentration—you've brought a million things home from the office and you just can't function. Then you begin to question your own abilities. You need a woman who is compassionate about that. God knows the number of times you knocked at her door and she wasn't interested, but you said, "Hey, that's women." Who ever thought it would happen to a man? But by God, it does happen, and you need an understanding woman to put it in perspective. You need a woman who is able to say, "Don't worry, that was today. There's always tomorrow."

LILA: Well, I enjoy sex. I know there are couples, even young ones, who go for years without having sex. For me it's very important.

JASON: That's what I mean. I love a woman who feels good about herself and is very sexual. Sex isn't everything in marriage, but it's a lot.

STANLEY (*coughing slightly, eyes down*): Truthfully, when we were younger, sex was very important in our lives. (*Quickly now*) We still have a lot of sex, don't get me wrong. We both enjoy it very much, but it's not that important to us anymore.

AUDREY (*even more embarrassed*): Oh yes, we both love it; but, as Stanley says, it's not important the way it used to be.

STANLEY (*laughing*): I read someplace that the more sex you have, the more sex you have, meaning, you know, use it or lose it. So I'm very interested in keeping up the frequency, but it doesn't assume the same significance to me.

LILA: Well, I agree with that, and I think most people probably do lose some interest after a while. For us, it has stayed significant, and I certainly hope it continues, into our eighties.

JASON: I think what has happened to us sexually has mirrored the progress of each of us as people. I don't want to get too graphic or clinical, but the way our roles are played sexually has a lot to do with the way she's grown as a woman and I've grown as a man. It was easier when we were younger because the kids would go to bed at eight o'clock and we wouldn't have to wait until eleven-thirty the way we do now. But if it weren't for that element, I think we'd have sex at least as much now as we did when we were younger. The quality is much different now and more fulfilling. In the old days you never thought about the woman wanting satisfaction. Now, of course, it's a major element in our love life. And then, you go through your own aggression and your own passivity, and her passivity and her aggression, and all different things you never thought about before. For me, it keeps getting more exciting.

Have you ever thought seriously about extramarital sex?

JASON: Thought about it? Sure. Who isn't tempted? There are thousands of opportunities if you look for them. But fidelity—that sounds old-fashioned, but I can't think of another word—was part of our original contract.

LILA: Hold on. Here's how it became a spoken contract for us. I said, "If you are unfaithful, I will feel that gives me license to be unfaithful also." He went berserk. He said, "What has one thing got to do with the other?" Don't forget this was back in the fifties. But I said, "Oh yes, I enjoy sex and I could have relations with other men. Don't think you're the only one who has drives; I have them as well." It just made him crazy. And I said, "I could not tolerate it if you ever have anything to do with anyone." And that was the end of it right then and there.

JASON: That was it. We have this contract, this agreement that says that neither will be unfaithful, and if either is, that's an unforgivable transgression, which provides total license for the other to be as libertine and revengeful as possible. Neither of us has ever broken that agreement.

STANLEY: For us, I'd say, the agreement was implicit rather than explicit. We both assumed the other would be faithful. I live up to that commitment we made to each other, but truthfully, I think the fidelity thing has got to be low on the scale of what really keeps people together or really separates people.

AUDREY: You know I don't agree with that.

STANLEY: I know you don't and that's why I wouldn't violate your feelings. But you know, a guy could have a fling with some gal and it doesn't mean a thing to him. Like take today, for example. I was filming this documentary about women on the campuses of formerly all-male schools. And I see this gorgeous girl, this freshman, and she's wearing a tee shirt and no bra and she has tits out to here, each of them as big as a grapefruit. Let me tell you, I really love big "boobs," so for a moment I think to myself, "Wow!" Then I think, "She wouldn't be interested in me," so I'm out of danger. But suppose I had a fling with her? So what? I'd still love and adore you, and you'd still be my wife and this is our marriage and these are our children.

AUDREY: And wouldn't you fantasize about her later?

STANLEY: So what if I did? I know a dozen guys who have had one-night flings and their marriages haven't been destroyed because of it.

AUDREY: I have to put myself in your place. If I had a one-night fling, I would feel terribly guilty. And it would be destructive to my marriage because I can't imagine just going to bed with someone if I didn't have true feelings toward that person.

STANLEY: But that's the difference between us. I think women get more involved. Men can just do those things and they don't mean anything.

AUDREY (*angrily*): How can you say it doesn't mean anything? Just knowing how I feel about such things is enough to make it destructive to our relationship. Wouldn't my feelings about it make a difference to you?

STANLEY: Of course, and I would never act on what I'm saying because of the way you feel. But I don't agree with you. I don't think it would have anything to do with our relationship.

JASON: I guess any one of us could be attracted to someone else. Hell, I can see being sexually attracted to five million women—their body parts are great, they're beautiful, so you make love to them. But trust and caring and compassion and humor and the million different things that make up why you love one person—well, I wouldn't take a chance on losing those things.

STANLEY: Jason, you say it so well, and I do agree with you. But I can dream, can't I?

Does Stanley do anything more than dream about girls with "big bosooms"? Is Jason as faithful as he so eloquently insists? My guess is the answer to the first question is no and to the second yes, but who knows? For all the sexual revolution we have undergone in the past few decades, for all the explicit sex portrayed by movies, books and television, for all the prevalence of pornography on corner newsstands, sexual relations remain a very private matter to most people. Most people, especially married people, do not speak openly to others about the details of their sex lives, and what they do say may or may not be the entire truth. That reticence does not come only from inhibitions or rigid codes of conduct; it comes from the fact that sex, in marriage, is still a profound form of intimacy, still a most personal expression of love and trust, still an arena in which insecurities and vulnerabilities are most glaringly exposed. These are not things that most married people feel comfortable speaking about to others, nor need they.

That is not to say that I didn't ask questions about sexual relationships in my interviews. I did. I asked them of husbands and wives, of single people living with others, of the divorced and the remarried. But I didn't ask clinical questions—how many times a week, what positions, orgasmic or not. Answers to those questions are always available in surveys of sexual behavior, and new surveys constantly appear on the market. Whether these surveys are truly indicative of the population as a whole is unknown. Respondents to sex surveys are a self-selected group of people who are both interested in sex and, for one reason or another, interested in revealing this area of their lives, albeit anonymously. It's hard to evaluate their truthfulness, even when they are anonymous.

In any case, I was after something different. I wanted to learn what I could about the relationship between sexual intimacy and the quality of a marriage. I wanted to hear how people spoke about the sexual aspects of marriage, not when bombarded by an array of questions but in the course of a broader discussion of their life together. Was sex a prime ingredient in making their marriages last? How had their sexual lives changed over the years? How did they feel about extramarital sex? Often I raised the issues in general, abstract terms: "Do you think a good sex life is crucial to marital happiness?" or "Are there circumstances under which it would be acceptable for a partner to have sex outside of marriage?" When an individual or a couple seemed comfortable or eager to talk about sex, the queries were more direct and personal. "How has the so-called sexual revolution affected your marriage?" or (asked of one partner alone) "Have you ever had an affair or a fling outside of marriage?"

As might be expected, attitudes and approaches to sex varied from couple to couple, just as they varied between the Christens and the Lowes. Some, like the Christens, spoke of sex as a vital and vibrant part of their marriage and expected it to continue that way for years to come. "When I married," a woman in her thirty-third year of marriage told me, "someone jokingly said, 'Now that you're getting married, you'll never sleep together.' Well it hasn't been that way for us at all. Of course we're still young—I'm fifty-three and he's fifty-eight—but I imagine we'll go on having sex together forever. We really love it." For other couples, like the Lowes, waves of sexual longings are becalmed with time, and other intimacies become more important. "I love to pick Audrey up after work and go out with her for dinner, just spontaneously, just the two of us," Stanley said at one point. That quiet time together, a time of closeness for both, was as important to them as the closeness of physical love. Many other marriages fall into different niches along the broad spectrum of sexual interests and activities.

One of the difficulties of talking about marital sex with couples is that the enormous emphasis our society has come to place on sexual performance has made people doubt themselves and their own performance. If a wife dares to admit that she doesn't always reach orgasm during sex—or worse still, often doesn't—she assumes she will be immediately typed as "dysfunctional," even if she finds many other joys in the sexual closeness of her marriage. After all, she knows, from much-publicized writings of sex therapists, that women are capable of multiple orgasms during the course of lovemaking. Her inabilities point only to her inadequacy as a sexual partner. (Or her husband's. I know of two divorces triggered by wives who blamed their husbands for their own inability to achieve orgasm. Other issues were certainly involved, but in both cases orgasms, or the lack thereof, were a central factor in the women's wishes for divorce.) If a husband confesses that he doesn't thoroughly enjoy oral sex, the other "Big O," although he gets pleasure from different aspects of sex, he is sure his confession will label him as a poor lover, sexually wanting. After all, haven't sex surveys shown oral sex to be an increasingly favored form of sexual activity among the married as well as the single? And fantasies—so much has been made of a new permissiveness toward fantasizing during sex that people who don't find fantasy a stimulant wonder whether they are dullards, lacking in creative imagination.

The attitudes of a librarian married in 1969 typify the kind of confusion and intimidation left in the wake of the sex bombardment we, as a society, have experienced. "We're very conventional," she said apologetically. "We get undressed in the dark and we use the missionary position when making love. I guess it's pretty old-fashioned, but that's what we do." She looked at me almost pleadingly. "We still have fun, really. Isn't it all right, if you still have a lot of love and warmth?"

Yet marital experts say that anything is all right, from conventional to kinky sex, if there is love and warmth. "It's not that sex is so vital to life," explained psychoanalyst Aaron Stein, "but that sex relieves tensions, and provides in marriage the pleasure of closeness, the satisfaction and fulfillment of the love the couple has for one another. The need to make love is not only a sexual one, it's a need to enjoy one another, to make contact in a concrete way." And in spite of all the talk and all the writing, nobody, except the couple themselves, can set norms for fulfilling those needs. For one couple, that norm may mean having intercourse three or four times a week; for another it may mean playful affection culminating in intercourse less than once a week. Nor can anyone say that the pair with more frequent intercourse has a better sex life. Their lovemaking may be mechanical and distant, a physical function with little emotional involvement, while the second pair may get much deeper and fuller satisfaction from less frequent intercourse.

But sexual behavior does not vary only from couple to couple. Like other forms of intimacy, sexual intimacy varies for any one couple over time, in peaks and valleys of desire and excitement. The birth of a child, for example, may usher in a period of relatively low sexual activity. For women especially, sexual desires flatten out after childbirth until hormones come back into balance. And even then, the excitement and fatigue of caring for a new baby drain sexual energies, and the intense involvement with a child may lessen the involvement with one's spouse.

Surveys of married couples have indicated that men generally feel much more disturbed by the decrease in sex after the birth of children than do women. Mothers tend to regard the interruption caused by children as temporary, even if their husbands complain about it. On the other hand, as women mature physiologically their sexual capacities increase, and many women become more easily aroused and eager for sex during the years when their children are grown and away from home than they had been earlier. In the lives of many men, however, these are the very years when sexual capacities, and often desires, are lower than ever before. Men in their forties and fifties take longer to achieve an erection than they did when they were younger and have a more difficult time sustaining it. When Jason Christen spoke elliptically of Lila's understanding, and of adjusting to his own passivity and her aggressiveness as the years have moved on, he was talking about just such a shift in sexual interests and abilities. Like other men his age, he has had to learn to adjust to his wife's increased expectations, as she adjusted to his more pressing demands in earlier days.

Many other life events influence sex in marriage. Vacations away from children become times of intense sexuality for many parents, times of romantic recapture of earlier, more relaxed days before diapers, homework or adolescents with automobiles invaded their lives. Vacations are so important as a time of sexual renewal for married couples that Aaron Stein argued that a spouse who balks at taking vacations, or insists on spending most of a vacation working, is really trying to avoid sex and the intimacy that goes with it. I would not go so far as to state that as a categorical conclusion—I know too many workaholics who become sick with guilt if they do not envelop themselves in the security blanket of work wherever they go—but given the centrality sex assumes for many couples during vacations, there is surely truth for some people in Stein's assessment.

Not only parents' vacations, but children's times away from home may bring a heightening of sexual longings in their parents. ("Tell your readers," said a writer friend on a warm July afternoon, "that marital sex is very nice, but it's especially nice when the kids are away at camp. Camp does wonders for my sex life.") A new job or promotion can have the opposite effect, stifling sexual vitality while energy is poured into work. Family therapist Carl Whitaker speaks of a man's "affair" with work as comparable to a woman's "affair" with a new baby (or vice versa). A newly promoted executive who had boasted of her husband's sexual prowess well into his fifties described her own changes this way: "I'm working so hard that I just don't have much time for sex. To tell the truth, I don't even miss it, even though I'm used to a high degree. I feel a little guilty about not missing it, but right now I'm loving my work too much to feel very guilty. I'm not worried; we'll get back on track soon." Periods of illness or grief may also become inhibitors of sexual interests, although for some people the death of a parent or a loved relative may quicken the need for sexual closeness, for feeling wanted and cared for.

The ups and downs of sexual vitality go on throughout the years of marriage, and they are a natural and normal part of it. During the earlier years, couples may become anxious about lulls in their sex life. With time, they recognize that there is an ebb and flow, and that lush periods can follow again after dry spells, sometimes creating a bond tighter than before.

But does sexual intimacy continue throughout married life? The stereotypical answer is that it doesn't, that sex grows stale as the body grows frail, and for some couples that stereotype is true. In a memorable scene in an otherwise unmemorable movie called *Best Friends*, an older-than-middle-aged mother is talking to her newly married daughter (Goldie Hawn, married in this movie to Burt Reynolds). "What's wrong is not marriage," the mother says, speaking about changes in her relationship with her husband. "It's age. It beats the shit out of us." A few minutes later, she refers to sex in her marriage with the funny-sad words, "One day we just stopped, and we didn't even notice it."

As age takes its toll, there are couples who do stop having sex, sometimes because one or the other loses interest, sometimes by mutual, unspoken agreement. Some in this arrangement are deeply unhappy about it, making it the cause of arguments or of hard, cold anger. Others feel content to share a close companionship instead of a sexual union. For many other couples, like the Lowes, the frequency of sex declines, and while it does not end, warm feelings and affection often come to substitute for active sexual practices.

There is, however, a cheerier side to the story of sex in long marriages.

Once, in a lecture I was giving, I quoted a sixty-eight-year-old man talking about his remarriage after the death of his wife. The reason he married the woman he had been living with, he said, was to have a firm commitment between them, rather than just "passion on the pillow." I joked, somewhat condescendingly, about his capabilities for passion, only to be greeted at the end of my lecture by four irate couples who approached me, individually, to berate me on my insensitivity and lack of knowledge about sex over sixty. "We have been married for forty-seven years," one woman said sharply, "and what makes you think the passion has left our pillow?"

I have heard her words confirmed many times since then. In spite of illness, aging, medications or lowered physical stamina, plenty of couples enjoy active sex lives well into old age. Actually, this fact has become public knowledge only in the past few years, so strong has been the stereotype of sexless old age. Among recent revelations on the subject is a survey of sexual activities of people over fifty conducted by the Consumers Union in the late 1970s. More than four thousand men and women filled out questionnaires distributed through *Consumer Reports*, the publication of Consumers Union, among whom three-quarters of the women and two-thirds of the men had been married for thirty years or more. As in all such surveys, the fact that the respondents were self-selected—in this case the selection confined to readers of *Consumer Reports*—limits its validity as does the question of the truthfulness of the answers and their emphasis on feats of performance (the winner in the performance category, as far as I could see, was the couple married fifty years, of whom the seventy-six-year-old husband had heart disease and an inability to maintain an erection, and the seventy-four-year-old wife suffered from a spastic paralysis that prevented her from spreading her legs. Still, they reported, they deeply enjoyed sex together, often in the morning, several times a month, usually culminating in orgasms for both). Nevertheless, it is impressive to see the numbers of respondents and the care they took to describe their pleasure in sex so that, as one woman wrote, "Young people should know that sex is not only for the young."

How do couples sustain their interest in sex after years of marriage? "We just do," said some whom I interviewed. Others spoke about giving conscious, and conscientious, thought to keeping the glow. A woman with teenage children, "who stay up to all hours" described the "dates" she and her husband make, sometimes in the evenings, when they know the children will be out, and sometimes in the afternoon, when they can have their home to themselves. A man spoke of the importance of letting his wife know how much he loved her, in words and actions. He hugs and kisses her warmly when they meet after work, compliments her often and is never ashamed to tell her how much he admires her. A couple, a bit embarrassed, told of teasing and exciting one another by sharing sexual fantasies. "We try to live out fantasies for each other as much as we can," said the wife, "and I have to tell you, it keeps things from getting dull."

Older people, in their seventies and eighties, fantasize about the past, and that adds zest to the present. A widower reminisced about his recently deceased wife, to whom he had been married for fifty-five years: "Until the end, we enjoyed each other sexually. Now, I still make love to Susie every night. Don't look away; I'm not senile. I dream about her and in my dreams we're young, and we're making love. I believe it in my dream, and it comforts me and refreshes me." In similar terms, Nate Murray, the gardener, spoke about sex in his marriage now, after forty years. "We cuddle and touch each other a lot. But I'll tell you the truth. You young people speak about fantasies. I'd say I have dreams; let's put it that way. When I'm sleeping I dream of having sex with her, and when I get up I'm all tired out because we had such a good time together."

Sex wasn't always so much fun for the Murrays or for many other couples. The one consistency I can report among all the many variations that I heard on the theme of sex in marriage is the conviction that in spite of problems that may arise, sexual enjoyment often improves over the years. Couple after couple elaborated on the broader satisfactions of sex as their marriage progressed, even if the frequency decreased. They emphasized greater depth of pleasure, greater sensitivity of one for the other, greater ability to trust and therefore to speak to each other more openly about their desires. "If I had to choose between sex when I was young and sex now," said a sixty-year-old woman, "I would choose now. It's slower, easier now.

Such a sense of freedom and knowing the other person, such a freedom in being able to say what you want and what you like."

And almost everybody, old and young, had something to tell about difficult beginnings. Sally Murray, Nate's wife, said that it took her a long time to enjoy sex at all with her husband. "Well, it seemed to me he was always wanting it. In my day, you kind of thought there was something dirty about sex—you just let your husband do it; you weren't supposed to enjoy it much. And I didn't for years and years. It wasn't until our third child was born that I began to relax, and it got a lot better."

Tom Flaherty, a man in his sixties, related with great confidence the stories of younger people he had helped to understand and adjust to marriage. "There are three things that can cause trouble in marriage, I tell the kids who ask me," he said. "One is money, the other is in-laws, and the third is sex. You have to know how to handle all three of them."

"And you?" I asked him. "Was sex ever a problem in your marriage?"

The voice became less assured, a bit hushed, very serious. "Well, you know, Francine, a lot of women, my wife included, think that men are experts when they marry. I was five years in the Marines. I was in the South Pacific for four years, and God knows what she thought. Believe me I was no expert when I was discharged, and it was hard in the beginning, because she didn't know anything either. She was very reluctant, maybe because she expected more of me. I had to learn what turns her on. I had to learn her little signals."

"What kind of signals?"

"She's very modest, but she sends out signals. Like walking up and putting her arms around your waist, or saying, 'Are you going to watch 'til the end of the show?' Or 'Would you want to come in and open the window?' —which, to tell you the truth, has a little latch a two-year-old could open."

"You didn't understand those signals at first?"

"Well, I understood the signals, but I wanted more. I didn't understand that for her there was a time and place for sex in marriage. She needed everything to be just right—the dishes done, the kids in bed. I was impatient. I guess I had to learn to take my time in many ways."

A dancer in her midthirties admitted: "I was never much good at sex. It's taken me about thirteen years to be good at it. And my husband, he just kept working at it with me. A lot of guys would have given up."

And a social worker, married ten years, told me, "I was much more sexual when we dated. It was forbidden; it was exciting. Oddly enough, after we got married, my permission to be a sexual woman, as it were, diminished. You know, the idea that now I'm a married woman and women do it for their men—grin and bear it. I used to have these visions after we got married. We'd be having sex and I'd be loving it, and really excited, and then I'd see—you know that painting *American Gothic* with the farmer standing with his pitchfork and his wife next to him?—I'd see them standing and looking at me. It was like a parental figure saying, 'Do it because it's acceptable, but it's not acceptable to enjoy it.' It was awful for a long time, and I really had to work at getting the enjoyment back again."

The number of honeymoon horror stories I heard reinforced these descriptions of early marital difficulties. Popular wisdom has it that the honeymoon is a portent of things to come, and this may be true in some cases. But quite a few couples in long, happy marriages had unmistakably unhappy honeymoon anecdotes to relate. Typical was the couple from San Antonio, Texas, married now seventeen years, who spent their honeymoon at—where else but—the Tickle Pink Motor Inn in California. They had dated since high school, this couple, and during their college years lived together on weekends. Marriage was to hold no surprises for them. But the moment they arrived in the big, plush, pink rooms of their hotel, the husband turned white. "We had ordered room service," he said. "I sat at the table, and got so dizzy I couldn't keep my head up. I went to the bathroom and threw up. Carrie couldn't believe what was happening. I was sick for the next three days. Of course we couldn't have any sex, and she kept saying, 'What kind of honeymoon is this?' She acted as if I wanted to be sick, and she may have been right. Looking back, I was really terrified of being married. We had started going together when we were so young, and I suddenly felt trapped. Anyway, we checked out of the hotel and went to the airport, and I began to feel better. The airport was mobbed with people, so we rented a car and drove down the coast highway. My spirits woke up and I really felt good. The rest is history."

Social reasons account for the early sexual difficulties of some marriages. The old Victorian morality code framed the unions of most couples married in the forties, fifties and sixties. Even though some recent research has shown that more Victorian women than any of us knew about loved erotic experiences—some of them kept detailed records of the numbers of orgasms they experienced in a year—the official Victorian code had women act and believe themselves to be sexless, docile and fearful of indulging in any sensual longings. That code was passed on from mother to daughter into our own times, impressing on women that to be good was to be modest and shy, and if by chance a wife should have sexual desires, she might indicate them to her husband, as Mrs. Flaherty does, with a little question, a light arm around the waist.

Things weren't much better for men. They were freer, of course. They could fool around before marriage with "fast" girls and "loose" girls, but the girls they married were the "good" ones. And while a wife's responsibility was to accept the sexual acts her husband foisted on her, his role was to teach her, to lead her. Both assignments placed weighty constraints on marriage: the woman often so inhibited, she could get little pleasure from the sexual advances of her husband; the man, like Tom Flaherty, having to prove himself to the "little woman," yet often as scared as she about the realm of the erotic, in which he felt himself no expert.

I spoke earlier about the negative effects of the explosion of sexual information in our society and the great emphasis placed on sexual performance. There is another side, the positive side, the reasons that set off the explosion in the first place—that is, the surge of freedom introduced into relationships between the sexes in the past fifteen years or so. The openness and publicity given sexual techniques made it possible for many couples who began marriage burdened by Victorian moral restrictions to experiment, to try out new ways of loving and let go of old restraints. Women who might have been horrified early in their marriage at erotic thoughts that popped into their minds at unexpected times discovered that such thoughts were a natural spur to increased sexuality. Men who may have wanted to experiment with oral sex or anal sex found out from popular books and magazines that they were not "perverted" for doing so, but normally inventive. And when Jason Christen referred to times of impotence, he felt relatively comfortable, because he had read and heard, as has everyone in this era of sexual revelations, that every man experiences such moments and that they are nothing to be ashamed of.

All this has been to the good. The surge of fresh air that blew away the worst sexual repressions of earlier times has helped marriages in many ways. It is the extremes to which sexual openness has gone and continues to go that have been dangerous.

I believe younger couples, married in the late 1960s, the 1970s and the 1980s, who were supposedly the most sexually liberated, have been as hurt by those extremes as older couples. For many of them, the performance mystique has been even more of a burden than it has been for longer-married people. Because most of these couples had premarital sexual experiences, usually with more than one partner, most know a great deal about "good sex" before they marry. On the one hand, that knowledge is a far better beginning to a satisfying sex life than were rigid Victorian rules; on the other hand, the expectation that marital sex can always live up to the excitements of single life and the variety of multiple partners places a heavy burden on marriage at a time when a couple must make all sorts of other adjustments. Besides, the great emphasis given in recent years to recreational sex—sex for the fun of it—doesn't have much to do with the true intimacy, the gentler emotions of caring and loving that, along with fun, are at the heart of good marital sex.

Beyond social issues, other factors make for sexual strains in the early years of marriage. For all couples, even those who have lived together first, marriage brings strange and new emotions that reverberate in sexual arenas.

Most obvious, to begin with, both partners need to be

able to view one another as sexual beings, a view very different from the one held of the parents and siblings with whom a lifetime has been spent. Freudian concepts along these lines are well known: a boy falls in love with his mother during the early years of childhood, and one of his tasks at adolescence is to work through that love so that by young adulthood forbidden sexual longings for Mother are transferred to an acceptable woman, one he can both love and enjoy sexually; a girl goes through a similar process with her father, and faces the same task in seeking a mate whom she can love and make love with. Making this transition is not as easy as it sounds, and a not uncommon problem in the beginnings of marriages, especially first marriages, is learning to express sexual love. The problem rarely arises when couples live together because, even in our open society, premarital sex still has an aura of illicitness and naughtiness, and a partner is less readily associated with one's parent. After marriage, the partner becomes identified with the good parent, the virtuous father or mother toward whom one learned long ago to squelch sexual feelings (mixed with this identification is the childish belief we still harbor deep within us, although we laugh at it, that our parents never indulged in sexual acts, except, that is, when necessary, in order to create us or our siblings).

So for some people the ability to love a spouse sexually comes slowly, not instantly in a rush of exhilaration after marriage. Sometimes it falls off again and must be renewed when a spouse becomes a parent, and is identified with our mental image of our own parents. Although the remarried may have worked through these matters in earlier marriages, other transitions of marriage may affect them. The issues of competition and power plays, for example, often move right into the marital bed, especially the bed shared by two aggressive people pushing their way up career ladders. A woman's successful career may make a man feel sexually inadequate, unable to assert his manliness through sex. Or it may not affect him at all, but may inhibit her from what she perceives as a need to submit to a man sexually when she is asserting herself professionally. Or one or the other, or both, may be so caught up in struggling to build careers that they lack the ability to concentrate on being affectionate and caring toward one another.

Fears, anxieties and a sense of shame about sex, carried over from childhood, also come to cast a pall on many a marital union, including those whose members thought they were far removed from such nonsense. And then there are the most basic adjustments of any sexual encounters, of adapting to one another's rhythms, of knowing how to touch and when to stroke and where to press in order to delight in one another.

Sexual problems are not confined to the early years of marriage, nor, obviously, does every couple suffer them. The point being made here is that, contrary to publicized images of sex in marriage, marital sex doesn't necessarily begin on a high of thrills and excitement and then peter out. What marriage does for sex is deepen and enrich it. And if time takes the edge off the novelty of discovery, it enhances the discoveries themselves, the exclusive, mysterious, quiet understanding each partner acquires of the other's body—and soul.

Over the years of marriage, couples learn to feel sexually safe with one another, and from safety grows mutual pleasure. Psychoanalyst Erik Erikson described the "utopia of genitality" as one that includes "mutuality of orgasm," although he recognized that not every couple achieves that utopia, and certainly not all the time. Mutuality in sex doesn't need to be that specific, linked only to orgasm and performance. It can come simply from truly shared satisfactions, from knowing, and acting on the knowledge, that there is as much pleasure in giving pleasure to one's partner as in being pleasured.

Over the years, also, couples become more comfortable about being playful, kidding each other without fear of offending. Where laughter may have been mistaken for mockery at the beginning, laughter itself can be erotic to lovers who trust one another enough not to take themselves too seriously. One husband told me shyly about a special squeeze he and his wife exchanged in bed just before making love. It was a squeeze that always made them laugh, and the laughter was a way for each to say, wordlessly, to the other, "I know, after fifteen years of marriage, we're still happy—aren't we lucky?"

Finally, with time, couples build up enough attachments to one another, enough history and love, support and security that if sex isn't always as perfect as they might want it to be, they are able to live with the imperfections, just as they are able to live with unresolved conflicts in other areas of their marriage. The marriage itself means more than its parts.

The couples I met all considered sex a natural and major part of marriage, but no matter how high they ranked it, nobody regarded it as the core of a marriage, the reason for being. Similar findings were reported in a study published in the *New England Journal of Medicine* in 1978. The study, by three social scientists, Ellen Frank, Carol Anderson, and Debra Rubenstein, was based on a questionnaire distributed to a group of 100 middle-class couples who considered their marriages to be working ones and had not sought treatment for sexual problems. The years the couples had been married ranged from one to more than twenty. The questionnaire concentrated on sexual relations, with specific questions about sexual dysfunctions—such as erectile problems in husbands and orgasmic ones in wives—and sexual difficulties, including "inability to relax" or "too little foreplay." In general, the women admitted to both more dysfunctions and difficulties than the men, which may indicate more problems on their part or a greater willingness to admit to problems, or both. Altogether, 50% of the men and 77% of the women reported some sexual difficulties, and 40% of the men and 63% of the women reported some sexual dysfunctions at times, although the study did not indicate how often these problems occurred. In spite of sexual drawbacks, 80% of the couples reported both their sexual relationships and their marriages to be happy and satisfying, and more than 50% reported having intercourse once a week or more, 31% of these two to three times a week. In other words, while these couples would have preferred to have no sexual difficulties at all, for both spouses, the overall happiness of the marriage made these difficulties tolerable, and the difficulties did not substantially detract from marriages that each spouse considered good and fulfilling.

The sex life of any couple is influenced by what else is going on in the marriage. During periods of anger and conflict, the frequency of sex usually declines, and these are periods when sexual problems are most likely to arise (although there are some partners who hate one another in everyday life but seem to have an excellent sex life in spite of their fights—or maybe because of them and the excitement they arouse). Sexual dissatisfactions, in turn, add to the general dissatisfaction in the marriage. But difficulties in sexual performance or activity per se do not usually destroy a marriage even if they do add stress to it. "Sex isn't everything in marraige, but it's a lot," said Jason Christen. And that it is. A lot, but still part of everything else that makes up a full marriage.

For some people a full marriage includes three partners—two spouses and the lover of one (whom the other may or may not know about)—or four partners, including the lovers of each spouse (whom one or the other may or may not know about). Judging from sex surveys, in many households extramarital sex is so tightly woven into the fabric of marital sex that no matter how an outsider may try to unravel all the threads, there will remain deep at the center a crazy knot whose turns and twists cannot be undone.

Kinsey was the first to conduct a wide-scale survey of sexual behavior back in the late 1940s and 1950s, and his findings shocked everyone. By the age of forty, he said, more than 50% of husbands and 25% of wives had engaged in extramarital sex at some point in their marriage. Later, in 1970, a survey conducted by Morton Hunt for the Playboy Foundation found an increase in extramarital sex among couples under age twenty-five, and a 1975 survey of its readers by *Redbook* magazine revealed an increase in infidelity among young wives, with one-third of the hundred thousand surveyed acknowledging extramarital sex. Twelve years later *Playboy* magazine's survey of its readers confirmed that increase, with 38% of women and 48% of men admitting infidelity at least once in their marriage, and among couples under thirty, more women than men reporting extramarital affairs. A survey published in the book *American Couples*, on the other hand, presented lower figures for sex outside marriage than even Kinsey had offered: Of the people surveyed, 30% of men and 22% of women married ten years or more had engaged in it.

What to make of these surveys? As usual, we face the question of who responds to a sex survey, and how representative the responses are of the general population. And the question of timing arises. Were more women in the 1970s and early 1980s, the height of sexual liberation movements, actually engaged in extramarital affairs? Or were more women willing to admit to them because such affairs had become more acceptable by then? Or were the women who were involved in affairs eager to answer surveys in order to bolster the growing acceptability of sex outside of marriage? And to what extent does each survey's mode of reporting reflect social attitudes? For example, in a 1980 survey of its readers the *Ladies' Home Journal* reported in headlines that "One woman out of five has been unfaithful to her husband," interpreting that figure as one among other indications that women have become egalitarian on the subject of extramarital sex by refusing to indulge their men in a double standard of behavior. Three years later, in another survey of readers, the *Journal* presented almost the same statistic about infidelity but reversed the emphasis, announcing that "only 21% of readers report that they have ever had an extramarital affair." Comparing that figure with Kinsey's 26% figure of unfaithful wives, the editors speculated that their figure, so much lower than *Redbook*'s of the 1970s, either brought into question the *Redbook* findings, or reflected "a conservative trend in the 80s." The emphasis on "only 21%" in 1983 as opposed to "one out of five" in 1980 itself reflects a conservative trend toward the mid-1980s, just as *Redbook*'s higher figure may have reflected the more rebellious atmosphere of its time.

We would have to conclude from all the surveys that we cannot reliably say exactly how many married women and men "play around" during the course of their marriages. But that numbers of them do is unquestionable.

Why? Every survey ever taken of attitudes toward fidelity in marriage, from the 1950s through the 1980s, has indicated that monogamy is the ideal of the vast majority of married people, even those who regularly violate that ideal. Unlike marriages in some European and Latin American countries, American marriages are not built on the premise of a split between home life and love life, not predicated on the idea that the purpose of marriage is to rear children and create a stable home while the husband derives his sexual pleasures elsewhere, from a mistress, and the wife—less often, but not infrequently—from a lover. The American way of marriage views the wife and the husband as complete people, capable of providing one another with love and nurturing as well as sex, and capable of sustaining that loving and sexual relationship throughout married life. Couples enter marriage expecting they will be faithful to one another; otherwise, "What's the point of getting married?" as Maggie and Robbie chorused on the eve of their wedding. But circumstances arise and ideals get buried under realities, like a coin that over time becomes hidden under layers of sand.

The reasons vary. Like the Christens and the Lowes, most couples I met denied ever being involved in extra-marital activities of any sort. I believed many of these people; several I didn't believe. Those who spoke frankly of sexual forays beyond the marital chamber usually revealed the stories of their infidelities privately to me, even when they told me their spouses knew the truth; an occasional few spoke together about sexual adventures. Each had an explanation for what made his or her affair, or their affairs, different, yet certain patterns emerged from all of them. Only one of the couples took me by surprise with their revelations and their reasoning, and that was not because of what they had done, but because I would not have expected it of them.

They live in a high-income, monochromatic suburb of Connecticut, the kind that in earlier days, before laws forbade such things, openly restricted Jews, blacks and other minorities from owning homes there. One still doesn't see many minority types among the men and occasional women who board the commuter trains into New York every morning, bound for their executive offices in the heart of midtown Manhattan. The Haldens fit the precut mold of the community in which they had chosen to live the way a tool fits its designated spot in the tool chest,

rounded edge hugged by rounded corner, straight edge
protected by straight side. It was the minister of the local
Episcopal church who had recommended them to me as
an ideal couple, "one of the best marriages" he knew of.
And so, in fact, they appeared.

Clarke Halden, broad, athletic-looking, with intelligent, if somewhat cool, blue eyes spoke admiringly of
having a wife who "does everything right," a wife who
regards raising their two children as a "very serious job,
not just something she does in between everything else."
He liked that about her, as he liked the fact that now,
with the children in school, she had entered graduate
school to study guidance counseling. "When she's happy,
I'm happy," he said, and anyway, going to school, "makes
her more interesting." Caroline Halden had as much to
admire about her husband as he about her, she told me.
She respected his strong, determined approach to anything he undertook, including his career with an international banking firm. "He's a type A personality," she said,
"you know the type that pushes themselves hard—the
candidates for heart attacks, which, of course, always
worries me." But what she especially liked was that mixed
with his drive for success was a more adventurous side, a
side that "wasn't afraid to experimeent with new situations in life, to go out in the world and try new things."

Caroline caters to both sides of Clarke, as he caters to
her wishes ("he's very cooperative in terms of housework
and children," she said several times). Aware that he
requires ample rest for the energy he puts into his workday, she retires early with him so that they can enjoy a
full sex life. Then, after he falls asleep, she often slips out
of bed to take care of personal chores—wash her hair, do
her nails or, these days, prepare schoolwork. As for the
experimental side of Clarke, well, she has forced herself to
try out new things, although she is more timid than he,
because she likes him to know that they can do things
together, that he doesn't have to leave her behind.

"What kind of new things?"

"Oh, skiing, new foods and, well, things with sex."

"Such as?"

"You promise our minister won't read this book?
Well, you remember when sex parlors for swingers first

opened and got a lot of publicity? Clarke brought up the idea of trying one out. He said he was curious, that he was a normal, red-blooded American boy who would like to do it with everybody who walks down the street. He said it would be fun to go because you get sexual variety that way and there's no emotion involved; it's just a physical thing."

"What did you say?"

"I said, 'Oh no, no, no. If you ever did that, I'd feel terrible.' But he didn't mean to do it alone. He wanted us both to go. Then I got to thinking. I wouldn't want to stifle him; I want him to be as happy as possible, and as long as we share an experience like that, it wouldn't threaten our marriage."

"Did you go?"

"We did, actually. At first I just went along and I said, 'Okay, go and have a good time because I really don't think I can handle this.' You have to know what my own background is like. I was a real early sixties person who wanted to be good and save it all for marriage and that kind of thing. My mother never even discussed sex with me. I can remember coming home from the orthodontist, and she was smoking about twenty packs of cigarettes, so I knew she was nervous about something but I didn't know about what. Finally she got up the courage and she said, 'Do you know how babies are made?' And I said, 'Oh sure.' And that was the end of the discussion. Now here I was at a sex parlor, with all these bodies. So I figured I'd just watch and not do anything."

"Is that how it remained? You watched and he acted?"

"Oh no. It took me many many times before I was able to try it. But then, I didn't feel it was anything so bad because we were both in the same room. It was just that we were both having sex with different people in that room."

"What do you think you got out of it?"

"I don't know. It was a thrill, I think. In some ways it was like doing something naughty, like a kid stealing a pack of gum from a store. The first time I thought, 'If my mother saw me here, God would she smoke!' Clarke and I used to talk about what would we do if we saw someone we knew. Then we decided, 'Well, if they're here, it really doesn't matter if they see us.' "

"How did it affect your own relationship?"

"As a matter of fact, I think it made it better. It was something that we shared. No one knows about it—except you. And then, it was very stimulating to us for a while. It was like living out a fantasy."

Clarke had never mentioned a thing about sex parlors and swinging or fantasies come to life. Curious about his reactions and about the state of the marriage, I found an occasion to speak to him by phone about a year after the initial interviews. After a few polite questions, I decided that the best approach was a direct one.

"Caroline told me you two had been going out swinging. Are you still?"

A little stiffly: "No, the shine wore off and it wasn't any great shakes. The thought and the anticipation of each visit were much better than the reality. I think Caroline went only to accommodate me—my curiosity, my lust."

"What was it that appealed to you?"

"The excitement, the variety, the experience."

"And what do you do for that now?" (I had decided to push beyond the stiffness. After all, I was in on their secret.)

A bit more comfortably: "We haven't felt that kind of need recently. We manage to keep things going, and don't forget, we've been married fifteen years."

"How do you manage? Monotony is not an unusual complaint about monogamy."

"Caroline really tries hard. She buys lovely negligees, and she plans special times together. A short while ago she told me we were going out, and she refused to tell me where. It turned out she had made a reservation for a room in a local motel, a really sleazy kind of place, and it was great fun. Then, last week, on one of those really hot nights, we went for a swim at night in our swimming pool. The kids were asleep, and we kept the lights off. We also kept our bathing suits off, and we ended up having sex outside, which was pretty exciting. Those are the kinds of things we do."

"Sounds good. Have you ever considered having an affair?"

"I'd say there are two kinds of affairs. There are those that are very casual, without anything other than sex. No emotional involvement, sort of like a sex parlor. And there are those that have an emotional involvement, and that's detrimental to a marriage. There is only so much emotion you can have, and if you're dividing it among two or more people, you're going to hurt your marriage."

I made a mental note of the fact that he didn't answer my question. It didn't matter. I learned other things from the Haldens, and the themes they returned to—sex without emotion, curiosity, the quest for variety—were themes raised repeatedly in conversations with couples about sex. A bit bored with their perfect marriage and its perfect children being raised in the perfect community, the Haldens had sought a little titillation, a break from Connecticut conformity. Psychiatrists might call their solution an example of "acting out," of the ultimate adolescent wish to live out fantasies that in real life are forbidden ("Hey, Mom, look at me!"). What they found for themselves was a safe break from the everyday, one that posed no threat to the marriage or to the image they had created for the outside world. Sex without emotion, without commitment, with no strings attached. It was the kind of sex Stanley Lowe had spoken about when he imagined himself in bed with a young woman with "big bosooms." The difference was that Stanley did not act on his fantasy because his wife so strongly opposed it. With the Haldens, both partners were jointly involved; neither was cheating on the other, or put another way, both were cheating on each other.

Still, the Haldens' perfect solution quickly palled. The reality, as Clarke said, didn't live up to the anticipation, and now they are thrown back on the normal ingenuity of any married couple seeking to add variety and excitement to their sex life. Their secret intimacies and sex games are fine ways of sustaining that excitement. The doubts I have are these: When they run out of new ideas, will they need to look beyond the marriage again for novelty and stimulation? And if so, will they do it together this time, or will they find new partners separately, and will they tell each other? And then, while Clarke is convinced that he can make a clear-cut separation between having an emotionally involved affair and enjoying casual sex, Caroline seems more dubious. She went along with his "lust," as he put it, at the sex parlor only partly out of curiosity. One suspects the other part was that not going would mean being left out, a first step, perhaps, to being replaced. As freeing as the sex junkets may have seemed to Caroline, she is, in the end, filling the part of traditional wife, the wife who climbs out of bed at night to keep herself well-groomed and attractive for her husband, the wife who buys beautiful negligees and arranges funny surprise evenings in motels so that he stays interested in her.

"I'm a female and he's a male," Caroline said at one point, "and there are double standards." For all the sexual liberation in that marriage, the Haldens still live under the shadow of that double standard, a shadow that could chill the marriage if Caroline doesn't accommodate herself to her man.

But there is more involved here than the Haldens' attitudes and standards. The possibility of emotion-free sex is still an open question, whether practiced sex-parlor style or, more commonly, in one-night flings that supposedly will not interfere with a marriage. In my own research and in broader surveys, attitudes toward recreational sex split decisively along gender lines. Men (although not all) seem to feel that sex can be strictly a physical thing, a release, with no emotions. Women (although not all) believe that sex needs to involve emotions, at least some feelings, at least for them, and they have difficulty understanding or accepting a man's unfeeling flights into infidelity. I heard similar reactions everywhere:

From Audrey Lowe, in response to Stanley: "I can't imagine going to bed with someone if I didn't have true feelings toward that person."

From a research physicist in answer to her husband's argument that an "occasional dalliance doesn't hurt anybody": "There's no such thing as an occasional dalliance. How could you get back in bed with your husband after that? You've given up a part of yourself, no matter how briefly."

From a police officer about a quick affair he had that

his wife found out about: "She took it very hard. She doesn't seem to be able to separate sex from love, and I can. There was no love involved, but she could not understand that, and that's what kind of broke her heart, I think."

Why more women than men can't or don't want to separate sex from love is a moot question. One can use the old argument that their insistence on connecting the two stems from deep-rooted dependencies, their long-conditioned need for care and approval in order to give themselves to a man. Or one can say that women have been conditioned to see sex as acceptable only if they are in love, and then only in the context of marriage, as opposed to men who have always been freer to have sex before marriage without connecting it with love and marriage.

I am inclined to think there is also another reason, and that women's refusal to split sex off from love comes from their roles as integrators (whether this role is socially or biologically determined is not the point). Women pull things together rather than break them apart: They don't set off their careers from their families; they try to mold both into a whole, to stretch themselves to encompass both without detracting from either. They don't make clear-cut divisions between caring for their children and caring for their spouse; rather, they extend their nurturing to both, pulling both within encircling arms to form a rounded family unit. They don't—or they don't as frequently as men—box themselves off from close friendships; they allow work friendships to spill over into personal friendships, park-bench friendships when their children are young to become lifelong friendships that continue after their children have left home. Women are integrators. They tend not to compartmentalize, but to unify, so they—rightly, I believe—see sex separated from emotions, a fling outside of a marriage, as demeaning to the marriage, as something that diminishes the whole.

Many of the men I spoke with, like Stanley Lowe, and including male therapists, made light of the one-night stand, the meaningless lay, the quickie during lunchtime, whether or not they had experienced one. None of the women did, not even those who had had a few flings of their own. While they may not have regarded a short dalliance as a major occurrence in their marriage, most believed that the fact of their infidelity, insignificant as it might have been, reflected on the marriage and on them.

When we look at longer, more intense affairs, fewer distinctions can be made between men's approaches and women's. The differences become more individual now, regardless of sex, the explanations and rationalizations based more on the circumstances of each marriage. By far the reason most often offered for an affair, or several affairs, within marriage is a wish for excitement, for variety. A woman married twenty years told me she was actively seeking affairs "although I have a happy marriage—I've never seen a happier one." The only thing missing in her marriage, she said, is the same thing missing in all long marriages, the excitement of discovery. This is how she put it: "I once heard someone define love as a combination of mutual respect, magical excitement and sex. In my marriage I'd say we have love in terms of mutual respect and sex. But magical excitement—that's the killer." And how does she define magical excitement? "It's seeing someone's face light up as you enter a room. It's being anxious; when you know someone loves you, you're not anxious, and part of the magical excitement is anxiety, wondering what will happen next. And then getting to know someone—that's the most exciting part of all. When you know someone well, the emotional adventure is gone."

She is not wrong. The excitement of discovery as she defined it, not only of discovering but of being discovered, does evaporate with time. The special excitement of secret meetings and the tingling anxiety of wondering whether you are loved—no, you don't get those in long-term marriages. What many happily married couples extol instead is the security of being loved, and the emotional adventure of getting to know someone well, as layer upon layer gets peeled away and knowledge becomes more concentrated and more focused on the inner core of the other.

The temptations to have an affair always exist, for anyone in a marriage. Jason Christen's recognition that he could be sexually attracted to five million women may be hyperbole, but the range is wide, and the fantasies they inspire are extensive. Why some people succumb to those attractions and those fantasies while others do not is a question that has a thousand answers and no answers. My own view is that an affair says more about what is happening within a marriage or within one partner than about the superiority of the extramarital adventure over the marital one.

Most family therapists I have spoken with agree. It's not necessarily true that people who have affairs are deeply unhappy with their marriage or with sex within the marriage. Although some are, others claim contentment. What is true is that an affair signifies some unresolved issue, some problem that has not been dealt with. "Granted that times have changed and we have come to recognize that some people have stronger sexual drives than others and might find ways to have flings from time to time," said Henry Spitz. "When someone gets involved in an affair that goes on for some time, usually the affair and the involvement are statements about the marriage." Often the statements go beyond the sexual component and have more to do with an inability or unwillingness on the part of one or both partners to sustain closeness, to be loving and intimate.

"The affair," maintains Spitz, "is a vehicle for getting someone else into the system. If a partner has difficulty with a two-person relationship, which poses the threat of intimacy or closeness, the easiest way to avoid that closeness is to become involved with a third person."

Theoretician and therapist Murray Bowen originated the idea of "triangulation," the formation of triangles in marriage and family life. During periods of stress, said Bowen, couples—often unconsciously—involve a third person in their relationship, forming a triangle, and shifting some of the pressure and tension from their own relationship onto that third person. Often the third point in a family triangle is a child, through whom the couple channel aggression and anger, or block intimacy with one another. What Spitz was saying was that an affair may offer that same kind of triangulation, a stretching of the band that holds the couple together toward a third pole, one that deflects the emotion and the pressures from the other two. "You detour through a third person, a lover," he explained, "which is no different than detouring through a child or a thing, like alcohol. The affair prevents you from being close to one another."

Even though affairs are usually secret, sometimes a covert agreement exists on the part of the "betrayed" partner, a kind of unacknowledged and unspoken acceptance of the affair because that partner is relieved, too, to have a barrier to closeness in the marriage. Married people who speak about secret affairs that go on for years are usually in just that kind of situation, half marriages as it were, in which a third party takes the pressure for closeness or conversation, sex or stimulation off both parties.

The couple I met who carried triangulation as far as it could stretch, and then some, made no secret of the third party in their life. I have hesitated to include them in this book because the openness of their acceptance of that third party makes them atypical. Yet I have come to think that by being extremes of a type, by serving as an italicized version, they convey more clearly many of the dynamics involved in less unusual situations.

Stanford and Jennifer Chittworth come from Canada: he from an old, upper-crust British family that had moved to Toronto for business purposes shortly before World War I, she from a "mixed marriage" of an English Canadian father and a French Canadian mother who divorced when she was in her teens. The Chittworths live in the United States now, but the third member of their triangle, Jennifer's lover Charles, has a beautiful seaside home in Vancouver.

The Chittworths met some thirty years ago, not in their hometown of Toronto but at a midwestern university, where both were students. At the end of their senior year Stanford proposed marriage to Jennifer. She hesitated. "I wasn't passionately in love with him," she confessed early in my interview with her. "In fact, even after I accepted, I tried to get out of the engagement, time after time. Yet I instinctively felt it was the right thing to do. I had had love affairs and they weren't necessarily a great success. I've often thought that to be passionately in love may not be the best qualification for marriage. Anyway, I knew both my parents would approve of Stanford, and that was important to me."

Unlike his wife, Stanford was a virgin when he married at age twenty-five, a condition he believes was not unusual for a man in the 1950s. When we spoke, he remembered Jennifer's hesitancy about marriage as clearly as she did: "I guess I wasn't enough for her, even back then. I was never everything she wanted, but I said I would take care of her everyday needs, the down-to-earth part of her life, and so I have."

Indeed he has, caring as well for the children they began to produce almost immediately—eight in all, over a period of twelve years. Stanford built a career as a diplomat in the Canadian foreign service, and the couple and their growing family traveled from post to post around the world. Jennifer with her mewing babes and Stanford, busy moving up the career ladder, had little time to focus on matters between them. Besides, Stanford's cool manner, his proper British aloofness (Canada hadn't taken that away from the family), suited Jennifer's less than passionate attachment to her husband.

Fourteen years into their marriage, Jennifer's father died, and suddenly, in spite of the children, her life felt empty. "He had given me the love and emotional support I never got from Stanford," she recalled. "Even when we traveled, his love shone through his letters." Jennifer replaced that fatherly love with a love affair, the first in her marriage, and then a quick string of others. Stanford knew nothing of these affairs, or if he knew, he said nothing. The affair that could not be ignored, however, began back in Canada, where Stanford returned for more training. It has continued to this day.

Charles Knotts was Stanford's boss in the diplomatic corps, a warm, emotional man, not afraid to show his feelings or ask for love. His affair with Jennifer caused a scandal when it began. His wife told everyone, threatened to commit suicide, cursed at Jennifer in public. None of that stopped Charles or Jennifer. As for Stanford, he chose to handle the situation by ignoring it. He went off on a trip for a while, hoping the whole nasty business would go away. When it didn't, he simply decided to live with it. "As far as I'm concerned," he told me calmly, "marriage is forever. I could not conceive of not staying married, and if Jennifer feels our marriage is not complete, I just have to go along with that."

He has gone along with it for thirteen years now. Jennifer spends part of every year in Vancouver, with Charles, whose wife refuses to give him a divorce although they live apart, and part with Stanford, now stationed in the United States. Their children, grown and scattered in various locations themselves, visit their mother in both places.

"But why have you remained married?" I asked Stanford.

"Because we have so much shared history. We had children together; we went through many things together. I don't want to give that up."

"Would you give it up if you fell in love with someone else?" I pressed.

"That couldn't really happen. I have had a fling or two of my own, but nothing serious. By the way, I'm grateful to Jennifer for enriching my life by adding variety to it. It wouldn't have occurred to me to start knowing other women if she hadn't started going with other men. But as for getting deeply involved, I make it very clear I'm not available. I have a wife."

Four years ago that wife informed him that she no longer wanted to have sex with him. "I don't know why," he shrugged. "I suppose she wants to keep herself pure for Charles." He accepted that ruling, as he has accepted all Jennifer's conditions because "there are things that happen to you in life and you just have to accept them. Like disease or death or having failures. There's nothing much you can do so you just accept them." For her part, Jennifer thinks Stanford has been terribly clever. "He wanted to keep me," she pointed out, "and the best way to do it was to give me my freedom. There were times when I certainly would have gone off with Charles had Stanford made a big fuss, but whether that would have been a good idea, to break a marriage because of that sort of passionate thing, well, God only knows."

God may, but neither Jennifer nor Stanford knows what the future will hold. Charles is retiring soon, and has asked Jennifer to leave Stanford for good. She is hesitating. Charles lacks Stanford's intelligence and sophistication just as Stanford lacks Charles's warmth and expressiveness. Together they form almost a complete mate for Jennifer (not quite, but almost); without one or the other there is less than half. Stanford is sure Jennifer will not leave him, not after all these years. "I handled everything correctly," he told me. "If I had broken with her because of her affairs, I wouldn't have her now. I still have her in spite of everything."

Very mature, very sophisticated, very foreign. A different kind of marriage, an alternative. Except for two things: the pain in Stanford's eyes, the listlessness in Jennifer's. A marriage can last long not only because it is successful but also because it is unsuccessful, Jennifer had said to me when we first met. It was a summary statement of her marriage. It is a marriage that isn't a marriage, a marriage that lacks closeness and intimacy, sex, sacrifice and commitment. It is held together by strained fibers of shared history and grown children and fear—Stanford's fear of having to establish an intimate relationship with anyone else, Jennifer's fear of having to give of herself wholeheartedly to Charles. They are psychological twins, each holding back from the one thing that makes any relationship possible, true commitment to one person.

As I said, the Chittworths are an extreme, a blowup of a type, but their oversized version of a marital triangle is simply an exaggeration of other marriages in which affairs serve as a protection against the essence of the marriage—closeness and connection of one to the other.

Many other motives underlie affairs and the timing of them: Anger, hostility and a desire for revenge against real or imagined abuses in a marriage may turn one partner away from home to the great world beyond fidelity (a woman I know is not only becoming deeply enmeshed in an affair, but is setting up her liaison in such a way that her husband is bound to find out about it—that is her revenge on him for his neglect of her as he pursues his career with single-minded determination). Depression, a new job, a new baby, moments of stress when a husband or a wife feels lonely or unappreciated—all are times of vulnerability to that special excitement affairs offer. People who married very young and get caught up in extra-

marital sex may do so because they feel they have missed
something, lost out on the variety they might have experienced had they waited a few years; people who married
when they were older and get caught up in extramarital
sex may do so because they want to feel young again, to
turn back the clock to earlier days of freedom. The motives of any married person involved in an affair can be a
complicated combination of many of these factors, too
complicated for even that person to sort out.

Kent Lawrence, an anthropologist in his late fifties,
told me he had left his wife ten years earlier after twenty
years of marriage for no other reason than the fact that the
sex was no good in their marriage. Never had been any
good, but he didn't realize how bad it was until he became enmeshed in an affair with a beautiful woman, fifteen years his junior. "I hadn't understood how much sex
one needed to be satisfied," he said, "until I began sleeping with Lisa." She was the total opposite of his shy,
modest, bookish wife: uneducated, somewhat coarse and
exhibitionistic, promiscuous, but wildly exciting in bed. "I
doubt if she ever read a book," he said, "but I planned to
marry her; that's how sexually fulfilling she was."

He didn't marry her. He married a woman not unlike
his first wife, a linguistics scholar about ten years older
than Lisa. He is happy in his second marriage, he told
me, and he has never seen Lisa again. But he thinks about
her all the time. He doesn't know what he would do if he
did see her—"she might just turn me on again"—so he
hopes he never does. Meanwhile, he has been faithful to
his second wife. Well, almost. Just a few little escapades
here and there, once with one of his students, more recently with his young secretary. They're meaningless flings,
but he isn't planning to tell his wife about them—she
might not understand how powerful his sex drive is—and
he doesn't want to hurt her because he truly loves her.

One therapist to whom I mentioned Kent commented
quickly, "He's a typical Don Juan personality. He must
have sex problems he can't resolve, so he flits from one
woman to the next." I'm not sure. I wonder whether his
flitting has more to do with the fleeing of his youth, his
need to prove himself one more time, and one more time
after that. He lived with his first wife for twenty years,

had four daughters and was close to fifty when he discovered that their sex life had never been any good. Perhaps what he really discovered was that very soon he would never again be able to think of himself as young; living out sexual dreams, more than anything, is a way of proclaiming one's youth. The fear of aging can be a powerful tempter, a slithery snake luring the middle-aged to forget what they learned from the tree of knowledge but to cling fiercely to the tree of life.

The loss of youth is one among many losses that can precipitate new sexual encounters and new bonding. A child's adolescence and subsequent departure from home may trigger in the parents a painful sense of loss and a longing for change. This is a time when men may become sexually attracted to young women, as young as their daughters; and women, more than at any time in the past, to young men, like their sons.

Illness, a different kind of loss, can lead to extramarital love. There are women who begin affairs shortly after mastectomies, probably as a way to reaffirm life and reassure themselves. The death of a loved one may set off a search for a replacement to fill the space left behind. A man told me, with a great sense of shame, about a wild, mad love affair he had with his married sister-in-law after his wife's death. The woman, his wife's sister, became a substitute for the wife he dearly loved, and for her the man who had been closest to her beloved sister was the only person who could understand her grief and provide the comfort she needed. They clung to one another, and for a brief period, in their state of heightened emotion, they became ecstatic lovers.

Jennifer Chittworth began her history of affairs after the death of her father. So did the woman, quoted earlier, who spoke so warmly about the "magical excitement" of extramarital love, although she's never seen a "happier marriage" than her own. That woman, Nina Payson, had had a profound attachment to her father and he to her. She had married a man who was her father's opposite, almost as a way of keeping her marriage from interfering with her closeness to her father. Now, after his death, Nina finds herself overwhelmingly attracted to men who were like him, in appearance, in personality and in intellect, and is seeking liaisons with such men. It is as though, with death, the sexual taboos between father and daughter have been lifted, and she is trying to recreate and love, again and again, the father she had in every way except sexually.

Like Kent Lawrence, Nina speaks often about her powerful sexual needs as opposed to her husband's weaker ones ("I could do it in a broom closet, under any conditions; he's distracted if a butterfly crosses the room"). And that is not to be discounted. As Spitz said, we have come to recognize and appreciate that people can have different degrees of sexuality and, unless accommodated, those differences can cause great pain in a marriage. But often when sexual issues lead to an affair, they do so because they are overlaid with other issues, as they are in Nina's case.

Does an affair ever help a marriage? If we look to the social scientists for answers, the axiom that works for surveys applies here as well: it depends on whom you read. Back in 1965, when sexual openness was new, social scientists John F. Cuber and Peggy Harroff conducted interviews on the subject for their book *The Significant Americans*. They outlined three types of extramarital activities: those that fill in for serious defects in a marriage; those that take place in marriages in which partners are separated for long periods of time, such as military personnel; and those in which partners do not accept monogamy as a prerequisite for marriage. They concluded that in all three types, marital happiness sometimes improved, sometimes deteriorated, and sometimes remained the same, leading them to suggest that in some situations extramarital relationships can be more fulfilling than enduring marriages.

A few years later another social scientist, Stephen Beltz, conducted intensive interviews with five couples, married for more than ten years, all of whom had begun to allow affairs in their marriages, either openly or by ignoring their existence. Over a five-year period, Beltz found that in four of the marriages, the outside sex became highly destructive, leading eventually to divorce. The fifth marriage survived and grew stronger after all extramarital activities had ceased and the couple had focused on difficulties between them.

And so it has gone, differing findings by different experts, often depending on the values the experts hold and the social values of the time. In recent years, as sexual freedoms have ballooned, we have heard more about the views that support extramarital sex than about those that oppose it. The argument often made is that a marriage that might otherwise fall apart is kept going by an affair that supplies missing ingredients to the legal union. The unanswered question is, What happens to the closeness and love upon which a marriage is based if one party hides a major area of his or her life from the other? In fact, many marriages that are supposedly being saved by extramarital relationships eventually break up because of them. In 1975 when journalist Linda Wolfe was doing research for her book *Playing Around*, she interviewed twenty-one married women whose affairs, they maintained, were preserving their marriages. When she checked on those women again in 1980, only three of them were still married. Said Spitz: "When a marriage continues because an affair relieves the pressures, it tells you only that when you're away from a stressful situation, you feel less stress. The affair has nothing to do with coping with the real issues in the marriage, the real problems."

An affair benefits a marriage, it seems to me, only when it serves as a catalyst, a crisis that forces one or both partners to turn back to the marriage and take a hard look at it. It is not necessary for the "erring" partner to present detailed, soul-searing revelations about every aspect of an affair, unless doing so is the only way to precipitate change. Some people cannot tolerate hearing blunt truths, and some people offer up those truths more to relieve their own guilt, to punish themselves or their partner, than to deal with the realities that caused them. But looking inward—that is important, for the person who has had the affair and for the partner whose life has been touched by it.

A woman on her husband's affair with his secretary: "Withholding, that was the key word in our marriage, for both of us. For him it was withholding praise, withholding approval, withholding support, and for me, withholding sex. He gave me no warmth, no recognition, so I closed myself off from him, physically and emotionally. But from the beginning, from the first year of our marriage, I began accusing him of having an affair with his secretary. It wasn't even true, but I devised the scenario out of my own fearfulness and insecurity, and finally it came true years later.

"I found out about it because I had convinced him to visit a marital therapist with me. This guy was real tough, and suddenly he just pulled it out of Bill. Yes, he was having an affair with his new secretary, this twenty-five-year-old child from London. I was destroyed, I mean devastated to find out that the thing I had suspected all those years when it wasn't happening was happening now. We saw the therapist for six sessions after that, and then continued on our own. We began to look at what had happened to us. We both came from undemonstrative families that had given little love, and we were continuing those family patterns. My father was a tyrant, and I had carried a load of anger around with me, especially at men. Bill needed someone to love him and praise him, and he found that in his secretary. When I began to feel better about myself, I was able to give more to him. As I became more giving, so did he. He had always been afraid to express any feeling for me because he was afraid of being rejected. Now I recognize that his love is very deep, very important.

"Soon after I found out about his affair that day, Bill promised me that he would stop seeing his secretary and give us a chance to work things out. If things went 'all right' with us, he would stop permanently. At first I continued to ask about her, to bring up the subject whenever I could. I wanted to know if he had fired her; I wanted to know where she was living. But one day I decided to drop it. I decided things were good enough between us now that I could live without knowing every detail of her life or all his thoughts about her. I think I finally learned to trust him and he learned to trust me."

Trust. It was a term used over and over by couples when I asked about extramarital sex and long marriages. If 50% or 30% or 20% of married people have affairs, depending on which survey you believe, then the remaining percentages do not. And the reason most of them give for not doing so is trust. "I can't imagine having an affair now," said a woman in the twelfth year of her second marriage. "I did that the first time around. That marriage was never any good, but I still regret my affairs. It's why I know I'll never do it again. Once you have an affair you take part of yourself away from your husband. You begin to lie; you make up excuses not to go to bed with him; you lie about where you've been. How can you think of yourself as a moral person once you've lied to your husband? And then, there's a whole area of your life you can't talk about with him. You want to have an honest marriage? You don't fool around."

And discipline. Next to trust came discipline as a key element in the monogamy these people felt was the basis for a stable marriage. A Los Angeles actor, not famous but successful enough, explained: "It's hard. When I first meet the actress I'm playing opposite, I have to spend time with her, let her know that I want to feel safe with her and want her to feel safe with me. We've both got to feel the love and power of the scene. I would like to go to bed with her. I would really like to, but I've made the decision not to, not with any of them. I don't think the temptations for me are greater than for anyone else. I've got friends who are not in the theater who sleep around like crazy. But it's not for me. I know how much it would mean to my wife. You don't do it when it means that much to the person you care about."

And, again, commitment. A nurse, married seventeen years: "I haven't had an affair because I'm not open to it. I closed that portion of myself off when I married. Sure, I'm greedy like anyone else. I want to live in the country; I want to live in the city. I want to have a lover; I want to have a marriage. But I want the marriage more than anything. Ultimately you give up something when you have only one other person that you share intimacy with, meaning your sex and your guts and yourself. But you gain more; you gain everything."

CHAPTER SIX

~

Ghosts at the Door

"The marital relationship," said Nathan Ackerman, one of the first and most influential family therapists, "neither exists nor evolves in isolation. It has family in back of it; it has family in front of it." To a greater or lesser extent, every marriage is influenced by the family backgrounds its partners bring to it. How these influences affect a marriage depends largely on how aware the partners are and how adept at using their awareness to shape their marriage as they want it to be.

Of all the couples I met, the Gilberts—Lynn and George—were most intent on investigating the family in back of them in order to understand the family they had become. Their story was unique, and indeed haunted by the ghosts of their parents and the shades of themselves as children in their parents' homes. Yet it was not atypical of descriptions others gave of how the families they came from—what experts call the family of origin—have remained a part of their marriages even when original family members are no longer alive.

In the Gilbert marriage, George's family was by far the more interesting. Lynn began speaking about them almost immediately after we met at the Gilbert home in a suburb of Detroit. "I fell in love with George's family as much as I did with George," she said in a voice that seemed to underline key words as she went along. Lynn has the kind of personality people usually describe as chirpy. She smiles when she speaks about even the most painful subjects, and it's only when you look closely that you notice the smile bears little relation to the hurt in her eyes.

"I was seduced by George's family," she went on. "They were charming; they were rich; they had this big farm with cows and chickens and things. Mind you, my family were kind of poor. My mother was a depressed neurotic, and my father a very methodical mathematician. All you ever got at home was 'Pass the peas,' and here was this family with all these dogs and cats running out of the barn. It was very exciting."

The excitement, as it turned out, was only an outer covering, concealing the darkness and turmoil that made up the inner core of the elder Gilberts' family life.

George picked up on Lynn's narrative. His slower, drawling voice contrasted with the bounce of hers; his smile, less determinedly positive, was more a twisted half-grin that acknowledged the many strains of his existence. "My father went through most of the family fortunes pretty quickly—my mother's inheritance and his own—and nobody ever stopped him. The odd thing about that was that he made a fetish of never helping any of his children, insisting that we stand on our own and make our way, yet everything he had came from my mother or his father." Philip Gilbert supplemented the family income by publishing and editing a fairly successful Baptist newspaper in Memphis, Tennessee, where George grew up. Whether he was making money or losing it, his wife, Isabelle, believed that her husband was "the greatest thing since canned corn." Her philosophy, ingrained in her by her own Norwegian parents, was, "Papa is all." He could do no wrong, or at least she would publicly acknowledge no wrong, even though it was common knowledge that along with his accepting wife he kept a mistress.

One of the rites of passage for the five Gilbert children—George's three older sisters, his younger brother and himself—was to discover for themselves at some point during adolescence that their mother was not the only woman in their father's life. With that discovery came the realization that their mother knew of her rival's existence and tolerated it, never confronting her husband or criticizing him because of it. "I had a lot of ambivalent feelings about women because of my mother," George said at one point in our interviews. "She seemed so passive and weak. There wasn't much I could respect there. I thought, 'If Dad feels that way about *her*, what should I think of women in general?' "

Of all the children, George was the only one who tried to speak to his father about the phantom woman in their lives, to say the things he believed his mother should have said. That is, he tried once to be open about the situation.

Late one Thursday afternoon, when George was about eighteen, he went to meet his father after work. Philip Gilbert had a work-home arrangement convenient for his affair. The family farm lay about a hundred miles away from his newspaper office in Memphis, making it necessary for Philip to spend the week living in town and returning to his wife and children after work on Thursdays for the weekend. George doesn't remember exactly what he said, but he knows that with every ounce of courage he could muster he somehow indicated that he didn't like the fact that his father was seeing another woman. The reaction was immediate and decisive.

"What are you talking about?" Philip Gilbert thundered with the anger of a wounded innocent. George kept his eyes fixed on the road ahead. "I don't know where you heard that. It's absolutely untrue, and I'm extremely distressed that you should say such a thing to me!"

George's determination collapsed, along with his self-confidence. "I just said to myself, 'Oh my God, what have I done?' " he recalled. "Immediately, I felt that I had not only erred, but that I had committed some sort of sin. And I felt that if at that moment I could have had a second chance, I would not have confronted him." It would take George another thirty years to have the courage to be able to speak to his father the way he wanted to. And then the words he could say were only in his mind; his father had died years earlier. "Today," he explained,

"I certainly would have said, 'Now just a moment, Phil
. . .' Today, I'm mentally and physically equipped to de-
bate him. But I never was then."

Nor was George able, back then, to speak up about
his father's drinking, which grew increasingly worse over
the years. At first Philip used to "pop nips on Sunday
afternoons because the minister was going to call and he
was nervous about that. Then he'd eat some mints because he didn't want the bourbon and soda to smell."
Eventually the nips turned to long bouts with the bottle,
not infrequently shared by George's mother.

Beneath the surface of a warm, happy family of children and animals roaming peacefully around a farm lay
chaos in the Gilbert home, and that chaos was to stalk
George's own life and almost destroy his marriage before
it could be contained. But first, early on, George tried to
combat the chaos by seeking order. As a teenager, he
decided to become a minister and do missionary work. "It
was a way," he recognized now, "of balancing the inconsistency and the lack of morality that tortured me about
my father. I didn't want to be churned up all the time. I
felt that I'd like to organize my life into some neat package. When I got older and realized that even as a minister
I couldn't create the neatest package in the world, I changed
my mind."

Before changing his mind, he met Lynn. She, too,
was looking for neatness; she, too, was planning to become a missionary. Her plans were not a reaction against
her family, as George's were, but a continuation of the
tightness and propriety of her parents.

Lynn laughed as she called up the one image that to
her symbolized her childhood and parental teachings. "My
family were very strict Presbyterians, and they laid the
guilt on me pretty heavily," she explained. "If I had any
talent at all, they considered that a gift from God; if I
made mistakes, those were my own errors. I couldn't win.
I felt as if I always had to be grateful, as if I had done
something wrong simply by *being*, and for that I had to
make atonement. What brought the message home to me
more than anything was a little framed poem that hung at
the top of the stairs in our house. The last line of that
poem is, 'I wept because I had no shoes until I met a man

who had no feet!' Oh God, the guilt, the guilt, because I had feet *and* shoes.''

The poem was so branded on Lynn's consciousness that it came back to her years later, maybe twenty years into her marriage, when she was working at an alcohol center of a local hospital. Her mother happened to visit one day, and suddenly in was wheeled a man with no feet. '' 'Quick, quick,' I think,'' said Lynn, '' 'amputate me!' I mean, my mother's visiting, and I finally meet the man with no feet. I don't think I can handle this.'' Because the old guilt was churning in her guts, Lynn decided to find out how the poor man had lost his feet. What she learned was that he had passed out on a drunken binge and his feet had frozen. So much for her own crippling sense of having done something wrong by being whole and healthy.

Lynn and George were both eighteen when they met as counselors in a Christian summer camp, each having gone there in preparation for religious careers. ''There was an immediate click,'' Lynn said. ''We found ourselves with the same kind of energy and humor.'' By the end of the summer they knew their feelings toward one another were serious; they also knew that neither any longer wanted to do missionary work. According to Lynn, ''We realized that we liked people to listen to us more than we liked to listen to them or care for them.'' George discovered a few other things he liked: smoking, playing poker and drinking beer, mugs at a time—not especially ministerial material.

They married four years after they had met. By that time they had both finished college, and George went off to fight in the Korean War. Lynn stayed with George's parents while he was away. In his mother, the mother he disparaged, she found both a friend and a mother of a kind she had never had. ''I had had to mother my own mother,'' Lynn told me. ''My sisters (one older, one younger than Lynn) and I had to tiptoe around her because she was always so depressed. Sometimes she just walked out on us; she said she couldn't cope. And she never gave us any support. I can remember coming home from school and being upset about something that happened and Mother would say, 'Well, what did you do wrong?' or 'I can't handle this.' So I got no comfort from her. George's mother gave me warmth and comfort."

Lynn soon would need all the warmth and comfort anyone could give. Back from the Army and working as a junior sales manager in a Memphis department store, George had a mental breakdown, the first in what would be repeated illnesses in the years to come. Many years later, after recurring episodes, George's "breakdown" was diagnosed as manic-depressive illness, a form of mental disease in which the afflicted person swings between extreme moods of wild excitement and inconsolable depression. The highs, the manic episodes, George explained, were a lot harder on people around than on the sick person himself—"If I could bottle my highs and sell them on Broadway, I'd make a fortune. There's just nothing like that feeling of being all powerful. Here I was too cowed to talk to my father, yet when this cowering, quivering kid goes manic he feels he can say or do anything."

Today this illness is treated and managed with doses of lithium, but when George first became sick nobody knew much about the illness or the treatment. Five times in the course of twelve years, he was hospitalized during the manic cycle. Three times, during the depressive stage, he became seriously suicidal.

The first time the illness struck, Lynn looked to George's parents for a continuation of the closeness she had felt while George was in the service. Ironically, her parents, not George's, came through with emotional support and money. Lynn remembers with some bitterness that "this family that I loved, this marvelous family that I had adopted, was uncaring to me during their son's illness. George's mother called me and said, 'Well, dear, I think you had better get a job so you can take care of those two little children.' When I was most needy, they didn't give me anything."

Looking back, George is able to see their behavior during that crisis as part of a pattern that had started much earlier. Philip Gilbert would buy his family Christmas presents, but spend Christmas day away from home. He would send his youngest daughter dozens of roses after her first ballet recital, but miss the recital itself because he was too busy drinking or playing the horses.

"Nobody was able to reach out in that family," George said. "What was given was always a payoff for not really giving." To this day, George has to force himself to buy Christmas gifts for his family or send flowers to his wife because he still associates these gestures with payoffs, substitutes for the real thing, the way his parents substituted tokens for real caring.

Lynn soon learned to rely on herself; even her parents could only do so much to help her. At one point, during one of George's manic episodes when he was especially wild and abusive, Lynn moved out of their house with their three sons, into a motel. Listening to the radio to keep from crying, she heard the producer Josh Logan speaking about his own manic-depressive illness and the help he had received from lithium. She phoned George, urged him to find out about the medication, and moved back home with the children.

The lithium worked for George, as it does for most people with this illness, but it did not work completely. He had several attacks even after he began treatment, and the reason was that his heavy drinking interfered with the effects of the lithium. George had become an alcoholic, like his father. "My father," he reflected, cynically, "was my role model. What a role model!"

To Philip Gilbert's credit, he also became something of a role model for ending his son's drinking. During the years when George was in the Army, his father joined Alcoholics Anonymous and stopped drinking. He changed so much as a result that George didn't quite know what to make of him. "I went away and became a man in the Army," George recalled, "and was going to come back and have twenty-seven scotches and tell him what I thought of him. And I came back and here was this guy, who had never listened to me before, listening to me. I couldn't handle it." The early impact of an alcoholic, self-centered father had left too strong a mark for George to seize very quickly on the new model offered him.

George's drinking cost him job after job. The family moved several times, finally ending up in Detroit, where George now works as a midlevel executive in an automobile company. Wherever he went, George managed to become involved with almost every woman he came into contact with. It was not hard for him. Blond, with attractive features, he has an innocent little boy charm that many women would find appealing. "Like me; tell me I'm strong; tell me I'm competent; tell me I'm sexy" is how he described his own need for women, one after the other. Having the women, however, was not enough for George; he also needed to bring them home, to his own house, his own bedroom.

"My attitude," he said, recalling those days, "was, I have to be honest with you about this. It was really my father's attitude to his wife and his mistress all over again. That is, let the women fight it out over me themselves. But I know now that there was also something else, something much deeper. I had a marriage destruct going on. I did everything I possibly could to make Lynn leave me, to give up and walk out on me, and yet the bottom line was that I was terrified that that would happen. More than anything, I wanted to keep her. I needed in this crazy way to assure myself that she did love me, that she would never leave me no matter what I did. I needed the unconditional love my mother had given my father, but nobody before Lynn had given me."

Lynn stayed with George through it all. When she thinks about it now, she cannot say exactly why she did. "I feel sorry now for that person who didn't say, 'Get out of my house; I'm a human being and I'm outraged that you would treat me this way,'" Lynn said sadly. "But back then I was just functioning because I was taught to endure. I didn't think I was entitled to anything more."

Besides, Lynn had her own madness, her own problems. Years earlier she had become hooked on Dexedrine, a dependency she had compounded by taking up drinking as well. She had started using Dexedrine to lose weight back in the 1960s. It was easy to get a prescription then, and Lynn found a way to have the prescription renewed in three pharmacies at the same time. Because the Dexedrine kept her keyed up, she began to drink heavily in order to fall asleep at night. Often she and George would go to a party together, where George would get bombed and Lynn would need help hauling him into their car. She would drive him home, get him to bed and then sit up alone in the kitchen, the ice clinking in her glass as she downed as many bourbons as she needed to numb her to the life she led. Eventually, Lynn got off the Dexedrine, but the drinking continued for years afterward. Nobody outside the family knew Lynn was an alcoholic because she drank alone, at night, but she knew and George knew, and their children knew.

One day the haze of alcohol and drugs, manic-depression and self-pity that blanketed the world of the Gilberts lifted, leaving them exposed to a pain that was like none they had ever experienced. Their youngest son, Barry, was killed by a car as he was riding his bicycle down a neighborhood hill. The rest of the family immediately blamed themselves and each other. "I had passed him in my car just a half hour before," Lynn said. "I still think, 'If only I had told him to get into the car, he'd still be with us.'" "And I," George added, "I was on the couch having a six-pack of beer watching the Alabama game. And I've thought to myself many times since then, if only I had stopped drinking, Barry would be alive. I would have invited him to sit with me on the couch, and he wouldn't have been on his bike."

A year after Barry's death, the Gilberts joined Alcoholics Anonymous. During that year of grief and recrimination, George had one more manic attack, and both increased their drinking, night after night. They were pretending to themselves that they were drinking moderately when they got into a vicious drunken fight, which their eldest son broke up. The next day George called Lynn to apologize and she said simply, "I've had it. I'm going to AA tonight." He asked if he could come along because, he decided, "I was sick and tired of being sick and tired, and I just said, 'I surrender to this thing called alcoholism.'"

When I met the Gilberts, they had been married for twenty-six years, in AA for seven years, and off drinking. Without alcohol, the lithium George was taking kept his illness under control, and he had had no attacks in years. Both had become involved in trying to sort out what had happened to them in their lives, and why. About a year earlier they had undertaken marital therapy for six months to help them understand some of the causes for their behavior together. Since then they had worked hard at gaining more understanding on their own.

The therapy was triggered by Lynn's rage, at George, at her parents and at herself. Without the dulling narcotic of alcohol, the rage burst out. Why had she allowed George to treat her the way he had? Why couldn't she ever tell him how she felt, why couldn't she scream out her own anguish at his insanity and his drunkenness instead of becoming a drug addict and alcoholic herself? She has traced many of the answers to those questions back to her mother and her life at home. "Being angry was outlawed for me at the age of nine," Lynn maintained. "You know the kind of thing—don't be emotional; we're lucky to be here; you ought to be grateful; we have a family in Hungary that is starving. I felt too guilty to be angry, and I was afraid, because I was sure if I ever showed any anger, my mother would leave me. I learned to be a reactor rather than an actor. I could react to George's sickness, to his drinking and his women, but I couldn't act, I couldn't make any moves of my own."

Actually, Lynn did make some moves, which she downplays now. She did, as she related, take her children and move to a motel for a brief time before she and George learned about lithium. Then, later, during the height of George's infidelities, she found a man, or men, who offered her some comfort, and sex. She alluded to that time only in passing during our discussions, but refused to elaborate because, she said, "I don't think this is helpful to us now." She perceives those acts of rebellion as unimportant in the face of the more dominant theme of her acceptance of everything that George threw her way. Still, I believe they have more significance and show more inner strength than she acknowledges.

In any case, Lynn sees herself as a deprived child, and she *was* deprived at an early age of the love and support all children crave. So strong was her need for warmth and security that she was willing to put up with anything, as long as she was not abandoned again. At the same time, Lynn mimicked her mother's role of martyr, the oppressed one, the one who copes in spite of the burdens placed upon her. ("I always felt I had to cope," she said. "I mean I would be the one who, God damn it, would *cope*.") She allowed herself to be a victim of George's craziness because she had been trained to survive at all costs, and she clung to George, even in his madness, because as bad as that situation was, to be deserted by George would have been unbearable.

For George, the patterns that became dominant had been set far more by his father than by his mother. George idolized his father, but he also feared and despised him. He grew up enraged and indignant at that father who betrayed his mother, yet he felt helpless to change the situation or even to confront his father about it. Instead of confronting him, then, he became like his father, a drunkard, a philanderer. Experts might call George's emulation of his father, "identifying with the aggressor." He took on the very characteristics he condemned, because even in his condemnation he wanted more than anything to be as powerful as his father. Acting like Philip would somehow give him strength and make him feel like a "real man" too.

But the relationship was more complicated still. In the process of behaving like his father, he had to stop himself from becoming too much like him; he had to keep himself from being too strong because once he felt truly powerful he might have to challenge the older man, might have to give vent to the anger that ate away at his insides. So George managed to have his worst drinking binges always at the moments when things were beginning to go well, when he was on the verge of a job promotion or the marriage was moving smoothly. "If I thought I was going to have some responsibility," he said, "then I would drink," and fall back again, the helpless, weak little boy who wanted to be a man like his father, didn't quite make it, and could blame his father for his failure—all at the same time.

And with everything else, George, like Lynn, wanted desperately to be loved. He pushed Lynn as far as he could to the thing he feared most—that she would leave him. She didn't leave him during the worst of times, and today, during the best of their married years, they are together still, trying to unravel the many strands of family history and background that have crossed and recrossed, and twisted themselves around the Gilberts and their marriage.

Like George and Lynn, every person who marries carries across the threshold his or her bag of family influences. And for everybody, as for the Gilberts, those influences go back a long way, back to childhood, when parents' attitudes and ideas, even voices and gestures, become incorporated within us.

Child development experts maintain that young children carry inside them an image of their mothers or fathers or both, and it is this image that guides a child even when parents are gone or when the child is away at school or camp. In time that powerful inner image of the parent dims somewhat as children separate from the closeness that bound them to parents and make friends outside their home. Now many of the characteristics of parents become blended into the overall personality and character of the child, so that the child does not end up a carbon copy of the parent but a unique being, a person in his or her own right. And yet there remains, always, deep within every child, a voice of Mother or Father, reminders of what is "right" and what "wrong," of how to behave and how not to behave.

The more mature a person—the clearer the person is of his or her own identity—the less influenced is that person by the voice within. Such a person feels free to make independent decisions without constant concern about what Mom or Dad thinks, on the one hand, and without anger and rebellion at parents on the other. The less separate, the more connected the person is to parents, the more domineering that inner directive voice. The ideal, which not too many of us achieve, is to be able to be independent of parents, yet remain in a close and loving relationship with them.

It is not necessarily true, as some professionals hold, that people who fall in love and marry invariably and unconsciously choose others who are at the same level of maturity, or separation from their parents. Some do. Lynn and George do seem to have been at about the same point in emotional development when they met and "clicked" and later married. Both were still deeply enmeshed in their families' lives, and looked to one another to complete themselves and help detach them from their parents. Many other couples, however, meet at different moments in life when they are not equally separated or unseparated. Partners who have a large age gap between them, for example, are usually at different stages of maturity and independence from parents when they marry. So are those couples in which one partner has been married before and one has not.

Nor is it universally true, as popular belief would have it, that people always marry partners who are really their parents in disguise, more specifically the parent of the opposite sex who so affected them in early childhood. Again, while we all know people of whom we can say, "He married his mother," or "Her husband is a clone of her father," we would be hard put to say this about every couple we know. Falling in love is a more complicated business. For all the theories, nobody understands just why we choose one person to love and not another. But the partner chosen is as likely to be a combination of both parents, or a variation on brother, sister, grandparent, friend, teacher, movie star or anyone else along the way who excited the imagination as a camouflaged version of a parent of the opposite sex.

Whomever one marries and whatever the degree of maturity of each partner, however, one thing *is* true: people carry influences from the past into their marriages, and the influences spread into the corners of their lives, much the way an ant carries pieces of food deep into its colony, there to be chewed, regurgitated and spread among family members. From our families, for example, come our ideas about how men and women should act in marriage, gleaned from years of observing our parents and the roles they filled for each other.

And from our families come attitudes and approaches toward others that become part of our own way of relating to one another and to the outside world. Jennifer Chittworth, the Canadian woman with a husband and lover whom the husband knows about, told me an anecdote about her mother-in-law, Stanford's mother, that shed light on her husband. Years ago the Chittworths' third son died suddenly of crib death at the age of two months.

Stanford was away from home on government business, and Jennifer had to cope alone with the shock of the death and the loss of her baby while caring for her two older children, still toddlers themselves. A few days after the baby's death, Stanford's mother came for a visit that had been planned much earlier. She stayed with Jennifer for four days without once mentioning the agonizing loss. "She was very proper," Jennifer said. "She considered it bad taste to show any emotion. Her husband had been the same way—very British, you know. In fact after he died, she had worried that she might cry at his funeral and embarrass herself that way. But she didn't; she remained the perfect lady." It isn't hard to trace much of Stanford's inability to show feelings and his fear of closeness in marriage back to parents who closed themselves off from him and from themselves.

Most significant among the many pieces of baggage we carry with us from our original families is the heaviest case of all, the one that holds our image of ourselves, an image that has been shaped to a large extent by our parents. What parents think of themselves and of their children becomes the backdrop against which the children form their self-opinions. Parents who are insecure about themselves usually manage to instill a similar sense of insecurity in their offspring, because in seeing themselves as inadequate, they perceive their children as equally inadequate and transmit that view to them. Parents who constantly criticize and disapprove make their children feel unworthy and unentitled to love. And the opposite—a parent's love and approval are messages telegraphed to a child that he or she is good and lovable. (To complicate matters, however, even loved children can get distorted pictures of themselves if with the love comes total control by the parent, or if the love allows for total indulgence of the child. The former can make for a weak and dependent view of the self, the latter for a child whose sense of entitlement leads to confusion and anger at the slightest frustration.)

All these carry-overs from childhood leave their mark on adult life and on marriage. How we see ourselves gets translated into what we want, expect and demand of our partners. Many, many people I interviewed spoke of their spouse as a partner who "makes me feel good about myself," as if marriage helped rescue them from a wavering self-image imprinted in childhood. Marriage should and can do that, provided the image is not too damaged and the needs are not so insatiable that nothing can fill in the void where self-esteem should have existed. Marriage can also become, however, the plain upon which old battles get refought with the hope of winning this time, old wounds get licked with the hope of healing this time, old hurts get hauled out with the hope of revenge this time.

The intense closeness of marriage reawakens feelings, angers or conflicts we experienced with our parents, the only other people in our lives with whom we were as close. Sometimes one partner misreads the other's behavior as a repetition of a parent's—an innocent silence gets interpreted as the cold withdrawal we had been accustomed to at home or an unimportant show of irritation seems to portend the outbursts of fury to which we had been subjected. Other times, things we may not have dared to say to our parents for fear of their rage or abandonment, things about our parents so painful to acknowledge that we may not have risked admitting them to ourselves, may be said and admitted to—oftentimes blamed on—our partners. Let a partner imply criticism, the same criticism with which parents pounded us, and all the pent-up emotions that didn't come out then are let loose now. Let a partner slight us with an old, familiar slight, and the floodgates that contained early feelings become unhinged, swamped by associations.

In the worst marital situations, one partner abuses the other to make up for deep-felt inadequacies—the man we have all met at some dinner party or another who constantly puts his wife down as a way of blowing up his own deflated ego, much the way his parents treated him or one another. But even in the best marriages, some earlier angers or pains get transferred to a partner. Lynn explained it well when she said that she had come to realize that many of the things George had done were not directed against her but against his father, and many of the things he had said were not in reaction to her words but to the words of his father.

*   *   *

One of the most dramatic accounts I heard of the crippling effects of family background on an individual and a marriage was that of Nina Payson, the woman described earlier who actively sought extramarital affairs after the death of her father.

Nina's parents' marriage had not been a happy one. Her father, a minister, had a charismatic personality that drew throngs to his Sunday sermons. Her mother was a shy, dedicated wife, content to glory in her husband's success, yet pained—and shamed—by his open disregard for her. The important woman in her father's life was Nina, whom he passionately adored. "Whatever I did," said Nina, "was wonderful in my father's eyes. If I sang in the shower, he was sure I'd be a great singer. If I watered a plant, I'd be a brilliant horticulturist." He took Nina with him to concerts and operas, to art galleries and lectures, leaving his wife and younger child, a son, at home together. He never cared much for his son, Nina said, and she wondered whether that disinterest came from her father's poor relationship with his own father.

Nina basked in her father's love. "Not that there was ever anything physical between us," she explained, "but there could just as well have been, so intense was the attachment." And when her father confided that it was she, not her mother, that he loved, the revelation became the pivot of her life. Around it she built her fantasies and ambitions: "My goal was to be like my father, but even more important, to be his ideal woman."

However, with her father's urging, Nina married a man completely unlike him, a quiet, solid, colorless schoolteacher, a man much like her mother, who stayed in the background while Nina forged a career for herself as a painter of some renown. It was a perfect marriage from Nina's point of view. Kevin Payson never tried to intervene in the "love affair" between Nina and her father, and he was devoted to her in a way her father had not been to her mother. She loved having two admirers, and found it amusing to play off one against the other, or stated more accurately, to tease her father by being extra-affectionate to her husband in his presence. Her father went along with Nina's little games because he knew, as did she, that he was the only significant person in her life. As she recalled, when she began thinking about having a child, she discussed the matter with her father before her husband. His enthusiasm over the possibility of a grand-child led her to present the idea to her husband with a great sense of urgency.

Nina's father died shortly after her second child was born, and not long after that, Nina had a mental collapse and made a serious suicide attempt. "Nothing worked anymore after he died," she said, "and I had to figure out how to put things together and make them work again." But, she continued, missing him was not the only cause for her breakdown. She also felt "tremendous anger and resentment" at what he had done to her, how dependent on him he had made her, and then guilt at her anger.

Since her illness Nina has tried to reconcile herself to her marriage without her father around to provide the excitement, the electricity she had needed to balance her husband's serious steadiness. Recently she decided that, try as she might, she cannot live without that spark, and has made an active effort to find men like her father in personality and appearance and become sexually involved with them. She has had a few such affairs, but they don't seem to relieve the aching longing within her or the mas-sive bitterness she feels toward the man who should have known the difference between being a father and being a lover to his daughter.

Every influence on marriage that stems from early family life is not negative. We tend to hear more about the horrors than about the happy effects because they are usually more dramatic and more clearly visible. Yet I was moved by many accounts of positive family impacts, by marriages that had been enriched by the psychological legacies transmitted by one or both sets of parents.

One couple emphasized the "sexual energy" they had both sensed in their families as they were growing up, a romantic acceptance of sexual love that had made it easy for them to enjoy the sexuality of their marriage from the beginning.

A man reminisced about his mother's attitude toward life as a blessing. Before she died, he remembered, she said, "I wonder if the children realize what a gift each day is." That attitude, he said, "her true belief that life itself is a great privilege, has become my creed. I have tried—and I think successfully—to instill it into my wife and my children, and it has influenced the way we live with each other and in the world."

A woman described the perpetual fighting that went on in her home as she was growing up, and admitted that when first married, she carried the same pattern into her life. But a few years after her marriage her parents had a reconciliation. "I don't know exactly what brought about the change," she reflected. "For years when they fought, they would say they were only staying together for the kids. But I think when we were all married and out of the house, they said, 'Hey it's a good time to get to know each other once more.' " Whatever the causes, they seemed to fall in love again, and to treat each other better than they ever had before. Her mother died three years later, a sudden death that shattered her father. Sometime before that, she wrote her daughter a letter describing what her marriage now meant to her and how glad she was that she had stayed with it even during the bad years. The letter and the refound happiness of her parents, their "new marriage" as she called it, served as inspiration to this woman. The knowledge of their ability to transcend their difficulties, even relatively late in life, she said, "is always there, and has always meant something very strong for me."

Other couples spoke about modeling their family lives on their parents' devotion to philanthropic causes, or about feeling close connections to other family members because of the warm ties their parents had created—all plusses, the benefits gained from the original families that, for many people, balance out the debits.

One other major and haunting influence from early childhood remains with us in later life: our connections with brothers and sisters. Compared to the numbers of books and papers written about the relationships between parents and children, relatively little has been published about the impacts of early sibling ties on later life, especially married life.

An important work that does deal with the subject is a book by Walter Toman called *Family Constellation*. Toman's thesis, which was popularized through magazines and books some years ago, is that the sibling position a person holds in his or her original family, whether oldest, youngest, middle or only child, profoundly affects later marital relationships. That is, certain character traits become instilled in children largely because of the accident of birth order in their families. For example, a boy with a younger brother may learn how to be a leader, how to take responsibility for another, how to discipline himself to share what he has (including his parents) with his brother. The younger brother develops other traits. Because he is shorter and weaker than his big brother, he finds roundabout ways to get what he wants, either by being cute and manipulative, or so demanding his brother gives in to him to keep peace. Both boys, like all children, compete for their parents' attention. Where there are three men (the two brothers and their father) competing for the attentions of one woman (the mother), the brothers have less contact with a female than, say, a boy with a sister or sisters. In young adulthood the two brothers will feel more comfortable in friendships with other boys than with girls, and in marriage they will need some time to adjust to understanding their wives.

Toman maintains that the more a marital relationship resembles earlier relationships of family life, the better off it will be. So, for example, a marriage that would have good possibilities of lasting successfully would be one between a man who has younger sisters and a woman who has older brothers. He has learned in his family home how to lead, protect and feel responsible for girls. She has learned to be protected and cared for by boys. They will then be able to get along in a noncompetitive way, each taking on different roles that suit them and the marriage. Among the worst prognoses for marriage, in Toman's framework, is the union of two only children, because neither has had any family experience with a peer of the opposite sex, and each is likely to expect the other to serve as a parent figure, yet be unwilling to fill that role himself or herself when called for.

Toman and other researchers who followed him offered many permutations and combinations of marital partnerships that would or would not work well. How many brothers or sisters are in a family, how many years separate siblings in age, even parents' sibling positions, they argued, can influence the personality of children and their later adaptation to marriage.

The variations are fascinating to play with. How accurately they can predict marital adjustment and difficulties in marriage is another matter. Since so many variables do exist, to say that the results of any union can be predicted seems an exaggerated claim, especially since it ignores such real issues as the temperaments of each spouse, how they dealt with their family positions, how their parents treated them and other experiences they had growing up within their families. (A new variable since Toman's book, written during the 1960s and reissued during the 1970s, is the increasing numbers of parents who are attempting to raise their daughters and sons as equals and the increasing numbers of marriages that are attempting to be egalitarian. A wife who has an older brother may be less than eager these days to take directions from her spouse when she has been brought up to think of herself as equal to her brother, if not in age, then in ability and opportunity. If she marries a man who has younger sisters reared to look up to him and who expects a subservient wife comparable to his subservient sisters, the two might engage in a power struggle the likes of which Toman never envisaged.)

Still, the value of Toman's studies and others like them for married couples is that they provide an awareness of the sources for some conflicts that might arise—an ability to recognize that yes, one of the reasons we're both so stubborn is that we were both the oldest in our families, both used to bossing the others around, and maybe with recognition we can temper that bossiness.

As valuable, or more so, is recognizing the psychological effects brothers and sisters have on each other. In *The Sibling Bond*, two psychologists, Stephen P. Bank and Michael D. Kahn, point out that siblings get to penetrate one another's "core self" in a way that parents never can. Closer in age, they are more likely to confide in each other than in their parents and to reveal things about themselves to each other that they reveal to no one else. As a result of that closeness, sibling relationships can have as great an impact on later life as relationships with parents, and sometimes even greater. In families in which parents are distant or cold, or too busy with other children or family members, siblings might form such formidable bonds that it becomes difficult for marital partners later to wedge their way through the tightness. In other families, a kid brother or sister's idealization of an older sib, especially of the opposite sex, can create a tough rival for a spouse, who gets judged by unattainable standards.

A problem commonly seen among opposite sex siblings, psychiatrist Alexander Levay told me, has to do with the push and privileges parents give their sons as opposed to their daughters. Especially in traditional families in which boys are still expected to achieve more than girls, a talented sister may be kept in the background and not be given the support her less talented brother receives. When such women grow up, they often marry men who are their inferiors, yet these women treat their husbands in the same privileged way their brothers had been treated. At the same time they may harbor great anger and resentment against their privileged husband, as they do against their privileged brother.

Even ordinary, everyday sibling competition gets transported into marriage, so that one partner competes and fights with the other as though they were siblings (there are times, still, in the midst of some anger at my husband, that I am startled to hear pouring out of me the words of the little sister I once was, words addressed to my husband but still directed at the big brother I wanted so much to impress, get even with, catch up to). If the competition becomes fierce, if an older sibling is allowed by parents to torment and mock a younger one, the younger's self-image could become as dented as it would be had the parents themselves abused it. If a younger child is indulged and favored at the expense of an older one, the older might become the kind of spouse who must always prove himself or herself, always be right, the kind whose needs for recognition and approval are unending.

The other side of the sibling coin, of course, is that sisters and brothers provide one another with an understanding of how to get along with other people, and each provides the other with first experiences in dealing with peers, not only parents. For many, that understanding and those experiences will enrich their married life.

Now we come to the vital questions. Are the forces of family background so immutable that we are destined to relive in our present lives with our partners the lives lived in another time with our parents and siblings? Does our early life in our parents' home predetermine how our later lives in our own home will be? According to psychoanalytic theories, yes, those early influences are so potent that without analysis, without a tool for uncovering what lies hidden in our unconscious minds, we are fated to be controlled by those forces. According to theories current among an influential group of family therapists, yes, those early influences are so potent that we can control them only by going back to our original families, literally back to our parents, to our grandparents if we can, and retracing through our eyes as adults the many bonds and interactions that connect members.

So, writes Carl Whitaker, one of the most prestigious of the family therapists, "I began doing family therapy in 1945. . . . As time went on, I heard the ghost of grandmother knocking at the door. Each Dad was apparently trying to restructure his own family of origin, using his wife and children as puppets. Each Mom was also pushing to rekindle her at-home security by using the same nuclear family group. . . . I don't believe in the individual or free will at all anymore. . . . I'm tempted to say over the phone before the first visit, 'Bring three generations or don't bother to start.' " (By "three generations," Whitaker means a couple, their children, and both their parents, a group he considers basic for family therapy.)

So, writes Murray Bowen, one of the pioneers and major theorists among family therapists, "From knowledge about the transmission of family patterns over multiple generations, it is possible to project the same process into future generations, and, within limits, do some reasonably accurate predictions about future generations."

Again, then. Are our married lives predetermined by

what happened in the past, in our families, in our parents' families? In spite of the experts' theories, my answer is no.

Undoubtedly, influences of the past are powerful, insidious, magnetic, often pulling us into their orbit without our realization. Undoubtedly, it is hard to get away from those influences, so firmly do they lodge themselves in our hearts and brains.

Still, if Whitaker has lost his belief in free will, the people I met with lasting, satisfying marriages have not. Their marriages are working precisely because they use their will freely to make the marriages work and to change them when they no longer work or satisfy. One of the themes that runs through this book is the concept that marriages change and that couples and individuals change in response to events and circumstances in their lives—in other words, that people make choices. People make choices, and when necessary, they can choose to alter the way they always have been in order to alter the way they will be and the way their marriage will be.

The thoughts that follow on why people choose to change and how they do so have evolved from my meetings and interviews and from extensive conversations with my husband about his psychiatric work and about our life together.

In the early years, those years in which our views of ourselves and of the world are being formed, what we as children seek and need more than anything is the security of being cared for and protected against the frightening outside. We find that security in the world of our parents, imperfect as that world may be. As adults, we hold tight to the pieces of that world that have become part of us because they represent security still, the security of doing what our parents considered good and continuing along familiar paths that were acceptable to them. To a great extent, most of us adhere to patterns of childhood unthinkingly because we feel comfortable and safe doing so.

We follow those patterns even when they cause pain. Why? Because it may be more painful to break away. A woman whose mother dominated and controlled her all her life, until the mother's death, hated that domination even while she subjected herself to it year after year. But to fight back, to speak up to her mother, to insist on being considered a person in her own right was too frightening. Doing those things would mean incurring her mother's wrath, and with it her mother's withdrawal, more likely abandonment. Within this woman, the child who longed for care and security didn't dare take that risk.

I have been told by psychiatrists that schizophrenic patients sometimes consciously burn their hands with cigarettes or matches, giving themselves terrible pain. For them having that pain is somehow more reassuring than the frightening absence of any feeling at all, with which they are often afflicted. So it is with painful pressures from the past. We live with them, as this woman did, because not having them might leave a void, a dreadful emptiness that we might lack the strength to fill ourselves. Even after parents are old or dead, the behavior we witnessed and the models with which we grew up continue to guide us because, consciously and unconsciously, they represent the familiar and the safe.

Some people go through life content to conform to a course outlined in childhood, filling in the images parents sketched for them, repeating in one way or another good things as well as bad things from their family lives. They continue this course into marriage, as we said, and then afterward, because they are comfortable doing so or because, in spite of problems that may arise, any kind of break with their own past is too threatening to them or to the marriage.

When do people change, or begin to try to change? When the pain of not changing becomes greater or more intense than the pain of changing. Inside and outside of marriage, people begin to give up their early modes of behaving when those ways so interfere with their lives or so distress them that they feel they can no longer continue with them.

George and Lynn Gilbert spent their days engulfed by alcohol and drugs. Both suffered great emotional pain, yet for all that pain, it was safer for Lynn to put up with anything George did than to turn against the familiar ways of her childhood, and it was safer for George to wallow in alcoholic self-pity than to confront his father and with him his own past. The death of their son Barry, and the anguish and wracking guilt it brought, turned them both around. George told a moving story of driving another son, Robert, someplace not long after Barry's death. George had been drinking, as usual, and so preoccupied with thoughts about Barry, he barely glanced at Robert. As the boy stepped out of the car, he stood at the door for a moment, looked at his father and said, "Hey, Dad, I'm still alive," then quickly walked away. Shortly after that George and Lynn joined AA. The time had come to cut with the past and concentrate on the present, on pulling their surviving family together—the family they had created, not the one each had dragged along from another time.

How do people change? How do they exorcise hurtful family demons from their midst? They begin by being aware that the demons are hurting them; they are in pain. That is, they stop fooling themselves by denying they have problems. "I was sick and tired of being sick and tired," said George, who only then could "surrender to this thing called alcoholism"and join AA.

Then they look for the sources of their pain. I don't believe the only way people can get at those sources or become aware of destructive influences from the past is by reliving the past through psychoanalysis, family therapy or any other kind of therapy, although for some people expert treatment is necessary.

I believe people can look at themselves and say, "Hey, what's happening? Why am I doing this?" and then find out what's happening and why they are doing what they are doing.

I believe people can recognize, if they want to, the ways in which they repeat early family behaviors.

In his article on humor in marriage, psychologist R. William Betcher describes a couple who made a game of ridding themselves of the influence of the wife's father in their marriage. He was a gruff, domineering man whose behavior the wife disliked, yet found herself repeating in her own marriage. The scheme they worked out was that whenever the husband became conscious of his wife acting bossy or belligerent like her father, he would call her by her father's name. Then the woman would behave like her father in exaggerated form, making a joke of the whole thing, and in the process curbing the father who was within her.

Unfortunately for most of us, awareness does not so easily lead to action. One of the fallacies people believe—people who have had therapy as well as people who have not—is that awareness automatically brings change, that once we can recognize the sources of our difficulties, once we unearth them from deep within ourselves, they will stop affecting our lives. It doesn't work that way. With awareness we need the resolve and the courage to break old patterns that are harmful, and those qualities do not come easily.

I know a man in his midthirties who lives with and supports his hard-drinking, abusive father, lives with a father who never has a positive word to say to his son, never a compliment, never an acknowledgment of the son's accomplishments, which are considerable. The son has been in intensive therapy. He has become aware of the many unconscious motivations for his ties to his father; he is fully aware of the ways in which his father is using him and abusing him. He speaks of wanting to marry and to have a family.

"Why don't you leave him?" I ask. "Pay someone to take care of him. Visit him, but leave and make a life for yourself."

"I can't," he answers. "He needs me to care for him." He looks away. "I know why I really stay," he says. "I want that bastard to give me the recognition I deserve. I want him to notice me and tell me that he's pleased with me." He smiles. "I guess he never will, but I stay anyway."

For this man, the little-boy longing for his father's recognition and approval is still so strong that he remains bound, a prisoner of a father who will never satisfy his wishes. He knows that; he has all the awareness in the world. But making the break, giving up on his fantasy of one day getting what he wants from his father, is more than he can do. So he holds on and stays in the familiar, if tortured, old mold.

Change brings anxiety. It means charting a new course, moving away from safety. Change is the opposite of security; it causes uncertainties. You don't know what the end results will be. You don't even know whether you'll be better off after you change. For anyone, changing long-established ways and past practices may be the most difficult thing in the world to do. But ah, the rewards of becoming your own person. Some examples:

Zach Newman discovered during his adolescence that his father, like George Gilbert's father, had kept a mistress for years (and had had several other affairs to boot). Zach's reaction, unlike George's, was not to replay his father's act. Instead, at great emotional cost, he cut himself off completely from his father for years, and became adamant in his commitment to fidelity in his own marriage. As for his mother, he didn't come to demean her for her silent compliance in her husband's cheating, as George did his mother. He developed a special sensitivity to her hurt, a sensitivity to women he has continued to express in his marriage, giving depth to it.

A wife and a husband watched a man they knew slap his five-year-old son hard on his face several times for a minor infringement of a rule, then walk away without glancing back at the child, who was crying his heart out. "I guess I can understand him," said the wife. "He was an abused child himself, and such children usually repeat that behavior as adults." Her husband looked stunned. "Have you forgotten," he asked, "that I was an abused child? And I never hit our kids. I have made a point of not falling into that trap. I take responsibility for not hurting them the way I was hurt, no matter how many excuses to do so I can legitimately make."

A renowned art historian grew up in a home he remembers as being filled with misery and hatred. His father, a cold, distant, angry man, treated his son with disdain, his wife sadistically. She retaliated by shouting endlessly at her children and withdrawing to the point of not speaking at all to her husband. This man, Blake Darwin, found his only solace from home in school, where he excelled and received warm praise from his teachers. Once Blake went off to college, he never returned home, although he kept in touch with his parents. When he married, Blake made a conscious decision not to repeat in his adult life what he had experienced at home. The woman he chose is different in every respect from either of his parents, a soft-spoken, scholarly woman who has created,

with Blake, a warm, loving home for their children and
for their many colleagues who congregate there regularly.
(It should be pointed out in all honesty that in addition to
Blake's ability not to be trapped by his past, he was also
lucky in some respects. Temperamentally, he was strong
enough to withstand the onslaught of his home life; some
people are more fragile by nature and more easily destroyed. He was intellectually gifted and this gift released
him from the turbulence at home by making school an
escape hatch and his teachers substitutes for parents. Turning one's back on the worst aspects of family background
is easier when other buttresses exist. Still, Blake deserves
credit for using his temperament and his gifts to control
his life and not be overwhelmed by it. Even with luck
some people would be defeated.)

Finally, a woman in the nineteenth year of her second
marriage compared it to her first: "I married the perfect
man the first time, just what my parents wanted: Good-
looking—very rich—college-educated—very rich—relatively
passive—very rich." That he was rich was most important
to her parents because they had suffered badly during the
Depression years, so badly that the family had moved in
with this woman's grandparents, her mother's parents.
Once back with her family, her mother had reverted to
being a child, completely dependent on her parents. This
woman followed the same path in her marriage, depending on her husband, or rather on his money, to keep her
happy, taking on no responsibilities but "playing house,"
as if she, like her mother, were occupying somebody
else's home. After a few years, she realized that she was
living with a man who was "very dull, very limited and
not for me," and that she was not much of a person
herself. She got a divorce, went to work and then married
her present husband, a strong, tough businessman. She
has struggled to maintain her independence in this marriage and has insisted on continuing her career, although
her husband has had mixed feelings about it. "The last
marriage was my mother's; this one is mine," she said.
"The problems are mine and so are the joys."

I should add that other remarried couples gave similar accounts. The folklore that maintains that people repeat the same family patterns, making the same mistakes,

from one marriage to the next is only partially true. Some divorced people do become so lonely and needy they latch on to the first person they can, and then relive the old blunders. But many other people learn a great deal about themselves in first marriages that break up. Although they may not be able to rid themselves of destructive family carry-overs in those marriages, they often can in the next. Psychiatrist Clifford Sager says in *Treating the Remarried Family* that "about 65% of the formerly marrieds show greater maturity and a more healthy marital interaction in second marriages."

Back to the Gilberts. After they stopped drinking, they started making connections between their lives before and after marriage. The connections, as we have seen, were extensive. Yet, as bound as these two were to their family backgrounds, in some ways both had been freer all along than they realized. Lynn, for example, had the strength to call a halt to George's abuse once when she picked up the children and left him. She came back not only because of her dependency, although that was a factor, but also because she believed that lithium would help him and change their lives. Although she did not find the courage to leave again after that, she did manage to keep her family intact in spite of all the chaos, with much more care and warmth than her mother could have shown. George managed to support the family through all the years of drinking and illness, unlike his father, who lived off inherited money and eventually squandered that. Although George lost several jobs because of drinking, he has been at his current one for seventeen years.

The inner resources, the small core of independence the Gilberts had, helped them when they decided to change their life in earnest. That decision, to join Alcoholics Anonymous and take responsibility for their own destinies, was, said Lynn, "a recommitment not only to life, but to our marriage and to our family. It was finally saying that our family really is everything to us." As the Gilberts have gained control over their lives, they have made peace with the memories of their parents. "I can't just throw my mother out of me," Lynn said. "She had my looks, my spontaneity, lots of good things mixed up back there with the bad. I think I'm still like her in some ways, but I think I'm a corrected version. Better."

In lasting marriages, the past never completely disappears from the present, but old family images and patterns that each partner brings to the marriage become changed, "corrected" and incorporated in new ways within it. Although dim ghosts of our early families may continue to hover outside the door, as time goes on more and more of the real action, the real life, takes place inside, within our new families.

CHAPTER SEVEN

~

Fathers, Mothers, Sisters, Brothers—And Others

What separates humans from all other animals, said one wag, is the fact that we have in-laws. Other animals mature, leave their parents and mate, creating new families and discarding the old ones. For us marriage is just the beginning of fresh entanglements, making our family lives far more complex than before. While shadows from our early lives may appear and disappear, the living flesh and blood relatives that we acquire at marriage are more permanently visible, their presence firmly implanted in the context of a new couple's existence.

With marriage usually comes a brand new set of parents, whom one is supposed to call Mom and Dad or Mom and Dad Smith along with, perhaps, a Grandma and Grandpa Smith and a slew of Smithies in the form of brothers, sisters, cousins, aunts and uncles. By the same token, the families of the bride or the bridegroom acquire a new member, whom they are supposed to regard as a son or a daughter, shelter within their bosom, include in family secrets and pretend to love as much as they love their own. It's not easy for either side, and in many families it takes some years before true acceptance occurs between the generations, sometimes not until a third generation has been born (or as the saying goes, one of the great mysteries of life is how the same worthless, empty-headed young man whom your daughter so foolishly chose to marry can turn out to be the father of the most brilliant grandchild in the world).

With an expression of fear and awe, a bride-to-be said to me, "How is it possible for two families to be able to get together, economically, politically, psychologically?" Although we hear more about the difficulties of those intricate joinings, some families are able to make the connections quickly, and to keep them close and deep. When families click in that way, the rewards can be wonderful.

One woman spoke of her love for her husband's ninety-year-old aunt, a love affair that began the day the two met (this is her husband's second marriage) and has continued ever since. One of the by-products of that closeness is the attachment between the aunt and her greatniece, the couple's daughter. Every morning the girl, age eleven, walks across the street to the aunt's house to have breakfast with her. Her parents don't have much time for breakfast because they both work, but Auntie Sarah has all the time in the world to talk and listen to the young girl, and so they have become fast friends.

Another woman and her husband have been having a difficult time with one another recently because of their religious differences. She is Italian Catholic and he is Jewish. The differences meant little to them when they married, but now, with two young daughters, they are pulled apart about which religion, if any, to have the children practice. They live close to the husband's family, and one might have thought that the proximity would add weight to the husband's side of the scale and load the wife's side with resentment. But that has not happened. The in-law attachments are too strong, existing, it seems, separate and apart from what goes on within the couple's life. "If my husband and I ever broke up," she said, "I wouldn't just be losing him; I'd be losing a family. I'd be losing my mother-in-law, my sisters-in-law, the nieces and nephews whom I love and watched grow up. If we ever decided to move away from this family, then I think our marriage would be in a much more vulnerable position. Marriage has to be more than a relationship between two people—there have to be other supports. There are too many things pulling marriage apart, not enough holding it together. Families hold marriages together."

Experts agree. Family therapists tell me that a basic principle that guides them is a belief that the greater the distance between the generations, the greater the stress placed on an individual family. That is, when parents and their married children have little to do with one another, each family becomes, to use their word, "overloaded." In each family, members expect more from one another because there are fewer people among whom to spread the expectations. When parents and married children can share sorrows and happiness, can exchange ideas and help one another, everyone benefits.

That is not to say that the extended family of old is the ideal. As a matter of fact, the idyllic views we have of earlier times, when parents and grandparents lived happily together on "Grandpa's farm" helping one another in the daily chores of living, are probably gross exaggerations of the realities. In the United States and in other industrialized countries, the nuclear family of a husband, a wife, and their children, living separate from either set of parents, has long been the usual mode among couples who could afford to set up their own households. Those who could not, and lived with parents, usually did so only until they were able to strike out on their own. In other countries, in which a young couple did go to live with the older generation—usually the husband's parents—the strain on them was sometimes unbearable. In India, even today, for example, a daughter-in-law's life in the home of her in-laws is a demanding and often degrading one, in which she may be treated like a servant who must respect and obey her mother-in-law. For some Indian women life begins at middle age, when their children marry and they are freed from household chores by the daughters-in-law who are brought home to serve them as they once served their mother-in-law.

The difference between earlier days and today, however, is that families were so much less fragmented forty or fifty years ago than they are now. The great jump in divorces and the increasing mobility of families have separated parents from married children, brothers from sisters, and cousins, aunts, uncles and other family members from one another at rates that exceed any before. When people speak about turning friends into family, they are speaking about filling a need for warmth and emotional sustenance that family members were more able to offer one another when they lived nearby and kept in close contact. And when social scientists speak of the added burden placed on a family by the distance between the generations, they are encouraging families to keep their ties, in spite of problems, because those connections can be lifelines in a world that has become so complex that individuals and couples often feel submerged by loneliness and helplessness.

But if you stop to think about it, the joining of families does seem at first well nigh impossible. So many loose parts have to be hooked together: The partners need to cut free, then reconnect to their own families; each needs to furrow out a fresh tract that opens in some way to the other's family; and the two sets of parents need to form some link. That last requirement is probably the least necessary for strengthening a marriage; in plenty of families, in-laws have nothing to do with one another. But when a bond does occur, when parents on both sides stay in touch and get along well, that can help the partners accept one another's families. (My parents and in-laws became close friends during the course of my marriage, so close that they phoned one another regularly and visited even when we weren't in town. I wasn't crazy about that friendship at first. For one thing, I could never complain to my parents about my in-laws—they simply did not want to hear what I had to say. For another, the alliance between the two sets of parents sometimes pitted them against us—the parents against the "kids." In retrospect, I consider myself blessed. Their alliance strengthened ours; when they opposed us together it was easier for us to oppose them together, and never did they divide us by allowing us to betray one of them to each other or one of us to either of them.)

The tone of a relationship between married children and their parents and in-laws often begins before the marriage takes place, and can reverberate for years afterward. A man in his late seventies, a great-grandfather, sadly related the "mistake" he had made thirty years earlier when his daughter had brought home the man she planned to marry. "He was so different from us," this man said. "He talked too much; he was dressed all wrong. And I made the mistake of telling my daughter how I felt about him. I criticized him terribly. She married him anyway, and neither of them ever forgave me. Even though we're friendly, my daughter has never been the same with me, and there has always been a barrier between her husband and me."

A young woman, married three years, told me about the distance she keeps from her in-laws because of the way they treated her during the three years prior to her marriage, when she was living with their son. "They disapproved of our living together, okay," she protested, "but to ignore me as though I didn't exist? We would go there on Christmas, and everyone in the family would have bought Joe a Christmas present, but nothing for me, not a thing. Do you think I'm going to forget that? Do you think I'm going to go out of my way for them, now, because I'm officially their daughter-in-law?" These seem like picky things, yet on the explosive terrain where in-laws take stock of one another, even a little friction can lead to a big blowup.

On the other side, some people begin marriage with a most positive view of in-laws, so positive, in fact, that, often unknowingly, they choose their spouse because of the family that comes along. Lynn Gilbert, whose marriage to George was fraught with difficulties, spoke of the "seductiveness" of his family. Susan Spitz, a social worker and therapist, who has been doing some research into the phenomenon of people who "marry families," believes it is a far more common practice than we think. Choosing a family, not just a spouse, or deciding on a person because of his or her family, Spitz says, is a way to make up for past lacks, a second chance at having the kind of family you always wanted. A man may have a need for a strong father to replace the weak one he had, and finds that need met in his father-in-law. Or a woman brought up sheltered and isolated likes the idea of a big, noisy family. One woman told me that the thing that pulled her toward her husband before marriage was his family's tradition of warm, homey Sunday brunches. In her home, family members rarely ate together, and when they did, it was at stony, silent dinners.

When marriages live up to those first family impressions, the arrangement can be ideal and can supply exactly the missing pieces from one or the other partner's background. But the family romance and the marriage itself can also sour when high expectations are not met. A woman described her love for her husband's mother and admiration for his father, who not only looked like Cary Grant, but was as suave and sophisticated as that actor in the best of his roles. "You know the old saw," she said. "Look at a person's parents to see whom you're marrying. Boy, was I wrong. My husband didn't turn out to be anything like his parents. He hated his parents; he went out of his way not to be like them." After twenty-five years of a miserable marriage, this couple were divorced, but the wife remains good friends with her in-laws. "I came to realize," she explained, "that I was very much like his mother. That's why she and I got along so well, and my husband and I didn't."

For some couples, then, attitudes toward in-laws are formed before marriage; for many others the sorting out of emotions and judgments gets under way after marriage, and then it takes some time and doing.

First, as mentioned earlier, there is the issue of the husband's and wife's stance toward their own parents, a stance that, especially in first marriages, is not necessarily sturdy. Many women and men in their twenties and early thirties are still not completely separated emotionally from their parents. And even if they have made the break, they have not yet made peace with their parents, the real peace that says I forgive you your mistakes and I'm grateful for the good things you did (that process that sometimes takes a lifetime to complete).

Now, in the midst of their struggle to establish independence, they take on a new relationship to their parents: they become their parents' peers. From leading very different kinds of lives as singles, they begin to lead parallel lives with their parents. Dad and son (even if son's wife makes more money than he does) talk about such things as family support, investments or life insurance.

Mom and daughter (even in our liberated age) have their own discussions about decorating and dishes, about butchers and laundries. There is a pleasant coziness to this new "buddy" relationship, but it is also somewhat perplexing. While trying to separate, the young couple is being pulled back toward parents; and while parents and children are supposedly equal now, parents still expect to maintain their authority as parents.

As one woman described it: "After I was married, my mother used to call all the time to ask what I was cooking for dinner. I resented it at first because I thought she was checking up on me. Then I realized that what she really wanted was to swap recipes and share ideas. She always found it hard to plan meals, and now that we were in the same boat, she thought it was fine to call any time to chat with me about dinner menus. It was kind of cute, but I wasn't sure I liked it. I mean, I wasn't sure I was ready to be my mother's friend in that way. Our interests weren't the same, even though we were both married ladies now."

Then, while partners are becoming pals with their parents, they are becoming children to their in-laws. Those new parents whom we acquire at marriage want nothing better than to have us regard them as our own parents, to be one of the family. For many the symbol of that new family unity is being addressed as their children address them, "Mother and Father," "Mom and Dad," or variations thereof. My mother once told me that she could not bring herself to call her mother-in-law, my grandmother, "Mother," as she was expected to do. It was not a case of lack of affection—my grandmother had had five sons and adored my mother, the first "daughter" to come into the family, and my mother reciprocated those feelings. Yet as deep as the fondness between them ran, my mother could not refer to her mother-in-law as if she were her mother, a matter of pain for the older woman and guilt for the younger. I understand her behavior. I dutifully called my Belgian-born in-laws "Mama" and "Papa," as did my husband. The names were different enough from my own "Mom" and "Dad" to ease the discomfort of duplication, yet when both sets of parents were together and I asked "Mama" something, I felt I betrayed the "Mom" who sat alongside her. I also felt somewhat mother-smothered.

In-laws are not, after all, parents, and most of us don't look to them for the nurturing we received and expected from parents. It would be nice if the differences in those relationships could be acknowledged, without rubbing all sorts of sensitivities. Granted that the man I met who, thirteen years into marriage, still calls his in-laws "Mr." and "Mrs." is something of an extremist, there are many couples who address their in-laws by first names. That practice, it seems to me, hits the right note of familiarity and friendship, without forcing grown-ups into what is now an inappropriate parent-child association.

The ambivalence about names, which is really an ambivalence about status, has other dimensions in the special vocabulary of in-law relations. When women choose to keep their own names after marriage, as many do these days, some parents-in-law feel a bit slighted, adding to other misunderstandings that might exist. A lawyer, Kimberly Bakst, adamant about keeping her name after marriage, explained how she dealt with that situation:

"Soon after we decided to get married, Randy's parents and I were beginning to see where each of us was coming from. They asked if I was going to keep my own name, and I said, 'Yes.' So Randy's mother asked, 'But how will you sign your name?' To her, getting prepared to get married was like learning your new signature. I said, 'I'll sign Kimberly Bakst.' So Randy's father asked, 'But what will people call you?' and I said, 'They will call me Kimberly Bakst.' We got married in November, and in December, my mother-in-law sent us a Christmas card addressed to Mr. and Mrs. Randy Chapin. I was furious.

"I rehearsed with my best friend what I would say on the phone so that I wouldn't just go wild. Then I called her. I thanked her for the card, and said, 'Mom, when Randy and I got engaged, I knew you really wanted me to call you Mom. It was important to you because that meant I was a family member. I wasn't crazy about the idea, but I knew it meant a lot to you and Dad, and I wanted to do it for you. It made me feel good to make you feel good. By the same token, my name is Kimberly Bakst. I know it is odd to you that I care so much about that name, but it is mine, and I would love you to address me as Kimberly Bakst.' My mother-in-law was quiet for a moment. Then she said, 'I don't get it. You mean you want me to write on an envelope, Kimberly Bakst and Randy Chapin?' I said, 'Yes, that's just what I mean.' She said, 'But I've never done that before with anyone.' So I said, 'Try it.' And she has, ever since then. Of course that hasn't stopped my in-laws from expecting me to jump up and do the dishes with the women while the men just sit, but that's another story . . .''

Kimberly's anecdote reveals another aspect of in-law connections. That is, many, if not most, of the misunderstandings that arise between parents and married children stem not from malice on either side, but from the different perspectives with which each views the marriage, the different places each is coming from, as Kimberly put it. The fantasies and hopes, and the self-views, of parents and children diverge greatly after children marry. Young couples are usually still in the throes of finding their own footing, seeking and wanting independence from their parents. While parents may respect that independence, they still regard themselves as being responsible for teaching, directing and guiding their offspring. They may be friends, but they are also their children's mentors. After all, that was the role they had for years and years. They were their children's ultimate resource, the emotional center of their lives. Even when their children are adults, parents want to see themselves as indispensable, and they cannot allow themselves to believe that what they say to their children or how they instruct them after marriage may really no longer be relevant to the children's lives. Parents live with the fantasy of being needed as they have always been needed and loved as they have always been loved, and if marriage vows represent for their children a statement of final separation, some part of their parents doesn't really believe that.

Along with this fantasy of irreplaceability that many parents hold goes the conviction that whatever they do in terms of their children is for the children's benefit, for their own good. As firmly as they can, they repress (so that even they don't recognize it) any notion that in the process of advising or helping their children they may also be trying to exercise control over them as they did in the past. So while Kimberly saw her in-laws' refusal to address her by her premarried name as a form of constraint, a criticism of her unshakable feminist commitment, they regarded their behavior more as exercising their prerogative as parents. From their viewpoint they were helping their son establish his position as head of the household, and helping their daughter-in-law understand that, in spite of her "new-fangled" ideas, the traditional way of doing things was most acceptable to them and to the world as they knew it. They had the good sense to back off after she explained her position. She had the good sense to explain that position by placing it into perspective for them.

Not all parents or children have such good sense, and many a family rift or tensions in a child's marriage grow out of parental blunders that may not be malicious, just blindly foolish. A wife of twenty-eight years recalled the bitterness in her newly married household because of the gifts her father lavished on her. When "Dad" bought his "little girl" a mink jacket for her birthday, her husband lapsed into an angry silence that lasted for days. "He felt," she explained, "that this was something a husband, not a father, should buy, and of course, he couldn't afford any such luxury. He thought my father's gifts made him look less masculine, less a provider, less the important person in my life. We talked about it for a long time. What bothered him most, I think, was the fact that he couldn't afford to buy the things my father could, and by accepting my father's gifts I was still tying myself to him instead of to my husband. It wasn't easy, but I did tell my father that I would prefer for him not to give me expensive gifts in the future."

This kind of parental help that turns out to be a hindrance to a marriage becomes especially acute when parents give married children financial support. Undoubtedly, at times such support is crucial to survival or makes the difference for a married child between getting an education or not. Yet even under the best of circumstances, it is extremely hard for people to establish emotional independence when they are still financially dependent on parents. No matter how careful both parties are, there are always some strings attached, some vested interest on the part of parents in seeing how their money is being spent, some sense of obligation on the part of children to repay parents by pleasing them and following their wishes, even if they conflict with a spouse's wishes. And mixed in with all the goodness and giving often is resentment, by the parents because of the money they are doling out, by the married children because of the dependency they still feel at a time when they want to be free.

Sometimes, again unwittingly, a parent's excessive financial or emotional support may be just the thing that pushes a marriage around the bend. A recently divorced man, still shaken by the event, blamed part of the couple's inability to work out their differences on his mother-in-law's overwhelming desire and ability to prop up her daughter. "Her mother comforted her and praised her, as if she could do no wrong," he said with more sadness than bitterness. "Don't misunderstand, she didn't attack me or anything nasty like that. She just made it clear to my wife that whatever she did was all right, that she would back her up, with money and love, no matter what. We never even got to slug it out because her mother was there to cushion every fall. It breaks my heart for her as well as for me because it was made so easy for her. Will her mother always be there to pick her up, brush her off and send her on her way? You can't find your soul with that kind of support."

His account reminded me of an incident Tom Flaherty had related about the early days of his marriage, more than forty years ago. After an all-out battle, his wife had packed her bag and gone "home to Mother." Only in this case Father intercepted. "You don't belong here," he said to her when she arrived at their house. "Go home and fight it out with your husband." She did, and their marriage survived the fights. Her father was no less caring than the mother of the young woman who split with her husband; he was a bit tougher, perhaps, or at least not so caught up in his old role of protector and defender of his daughter that he lost sight of his new part as a bit player now, with his son-in-law at center stage.

I don't want to create the wrong impression. There is an opposite extreme to those parents who care too much, who are too involved in doing what is good "for the sake of the children," and that is the parents who don't care at all, who are uninvolved and unsupportive of their married children. These are the parents who, in the name of a child's independence, will not come up with a much-needed loan or tide married children over temporary difficulties, the parents who give up both parenting and friendship once their children marry.

A couple in Cleveland described such parents. They belonged to the wife, and made that very clear by being "cold, cold, cold," to the husband—but none too warm to their daughter either. They were mainline Philadelphians, deeply "offended" (the term they used) by their daughter's marriage to a middle-class Italian-American from Detroit. The wedding was held in Detroit because the bride's parents did not want their friends to attend and meet the groom's family. Since then, in the sixteen years of the couple's marriage, these parents have visited only on two or three occasions, and then for some special event, such as a christening or graduation of one of their grandchildren. Once in a while they invite a grandchild (the couple have three children) to visit them in Philadelphia, but never more than one child at a time, even though their home is very large; too much commotion otherwise, they explain. They never invite their daughter and their son-in-law, nor do they send birthday or Christmas gifts, nor do they phone, except in emergencies. "I'm glad there's some geographic distance between us," the wife said, "because I know they'd be just as distant if they lived close by, and then I'd really be angry."

A couple who seem to have found a balance between being emotionally too close or too far from their married children are the Newmans of Florida, Zach and Sylvia, and they achieved that balance only after great pain and great effort on their part and the part of their son and their daughter-in-law. The Newmans are traditionalist Jews, if not Orthodox then fairly observant of Jewish law and ritual. They gave both their sons substantial Jewish educations and looked forward to the day when they would have grandchildren to continue their beliefs and culture. So when their younger son, Michael, brought his fiancée home to meet his parents, the Newmans were shocked. Almost a takeoff on the Katharine Hepburn–Spencer Tracy movie *Guess Who's Coming to Dinner?*, the young woman who came for dinner at the Newman home was black. And a Baptist.

"I cried for a year," said Sylvia. "I told him, 'Michael, you're going to break my heart.' And you know what he answered? 'Mother, what about my heart? I'm going to live a long time after you're gone. This is my chance for happiness.' "

"You see the difference in generations?" Zach broke in. "I would never have spoken that way to my parents. 'I'm going to live for a long time after you're gone.' But he was being honest."

"He wasn't honest at first," Sylvia continued. "He went with her for a year and a half before we ever met her. And all that time he was accepting the blind dates my friends were arranging for him. He's a very attractive man, even if he is my son. A jewel. But that's not the point. He knew how we would react, and he was scared to tell us. Later they told us that they used to sit in the park and cry, the two of them, because they were afraid of what we would do."

What the Newmans did, once it became clear that Michael had made up his mind, was think hard. Between her tears, Sylvia knew in her heart that she "loved Michael so dearly, nothing could take away from that." And Zach reasoned, "I suppose there are much worse things that can happen to your child than have him marry outside your faith, no matter how important that is to you." Cautiously, they decided to give Belinda, Michael's fiancée, a chance, and to try to get to know her. Knowing her, they found her to be, in Zach's words, "a wonderful, wonderful human being."

"Right away," said Sylvia, "she called us 'Ma' and 'Pa.' She showed such respect for our religion, and I think that's because she's religious herself. That was the part that surprised us."

"We were thinking at first that maybe she would convert to Judaism," Zach went on. "We wanted that very much. But then when we realized how religious she was, we said to each other, 'How can we force her to give up her religion? How would we feel if he gave up his?' So we didn't pressure them about it. Now, what's interesting is that he became more Jewishly religious because of her.

To make that possible, she keeps a kosher home. She called up Sylvia and asked her all about the dietary laws. We were thrilled."

"I'll tell you," Sylvia moved in again, "all our friends adore her now. Truthfully, I still get a pang in my heart when I attend a friend's child's wedding, and it's a real Jewish wedding, and Michael was married by a justice of the peace. Then I think about all her good qualities, and how he told me he couldn't live without her, and that has to be enough. You learn a lot when you're a parent, and especially when you've been hurt. You learn what you can insist on and what you should keep quiet about."

"We're keeping quiet about something else now," Zach said. "We're really keeping out of something we both have strong feelings about."

"You mean their not having children?" Sylvia looked at him.

"Yeah."

"They've decided not to have children." She turned to at me. "They feel that in this world it would be too hard for a child of racially and religiously mixed parents, even with all the changes these days. Zach and I think they're making a big mistake; we're longing for a little grandchild from them, and believe me, I never thought I'd feel this way. But they made a life for themselves and they know what's right for them. I don't think it's our place to say anything."

For the Newmans, the journey to that point at which they could accept their own place in relation to their son and his wife had to be a difficult one. I admired them for having made it, and I admired Michael and Belinda for having given them the time and the chance to make it, without pressing on them or each other while they did.

All in-law stories do not have such happy endings. In many families, even the small irritations and minor grievances among in-laws get blown up into open warfare— hence the slew of in-law, especially mother-in-law, jokes that for years were the stock-in-trade of stand-up comedians (we hear fewer mother-in-law jokes these days; perhaps the women's movement has shown up their tasteless- ness or perhaps because families have become so fragmented and isolated, people are less prone to knock a good thing).

In some families, in-law problems become a cover-up for more serious problems that exist between husband and wife, or parent and child. A man may blame his mother-in-law for butting into his life, intruding with her ideas into every corner of his family, when what he is actually angry about is his wife's inability to make a decision of her own and her enormous dependency on her mother. Parents might vent bitter hatred on a daughter-in-law for turning their son away from them, when what is really gnawing at them is their son's coldness and lack of interest in them. It sometimes happens, in fact, that people choose partners who they know will not get along with their parents and then stand back and let the spouse fight their old battles for them, or use their spouse as an excuse not to see their parents (this is not a happy solution to one's differences with parents—aside from other unpleasantnesses, when one spouse fights constantly with the other's parents, the animosity between them can easily spill back over into the marriage itself).

And then there are situations in which one partner quarrels with the other or with in-laws over issues that really concern his or her own ties to parents. I remember criticizing my husband early on because of what I perceived as his inability to stand up to his father. My father-in-law was a man of quiet charm, who in his soft-spoken way still managed to convey his likes and dislikes, especially to his son. His pet peeves in our student days were the casual clothes, and most specifically a certain kind of inexpensive, soft, tan leather shoe, that my husband loved to wear to everything from football games to family weddings. My father-in-law never let an opportunity pass without making some comment about the shoes, and slipping in a word or two about the tweed jackets and open-collar shirts that were his son's standard uniform (a product of a more formal European culture, my father-in-law always wore dark suits and somber ties in those days). Yet it seemed to me my husband let every opportunity to respond to his father pass. He would ignore the comments and digs, and go on wearing his rumpled medical student clothes while I would fuss and fume that he needed to assert himself with his father far more than he did.

"Why don't you ever answer him?" I would argue. "Why don't you tell him that what you wear is your business, not his?"

"Why bother?" my husband would answer. "He's not going to change his ideas, and I'm not going to change mine. I dress the way I want to, and his comments don't mean anything to me, so why fight?"

"But he should know," I would insist, "that you're a grown-up now. He has no control over your clothes anymore."

"That's just the point," would come the response. "He has no control over me, so why should I get angry with him and upset both of us?"

It took me some time, years actually, to recognize that my anger at his unwillingness to confront his father in this area had more to do with my response to his father's remarks than his. He was freer than I of parental ties; I was still fighting battles, trying to set boundaries between myself and my parents. Parental criticism could affect me because I was still looking for parental approval; I cared very much about my parents' and in-laws' likes and dislikes, and about pleasing them. Anger was the only way I could put distance between us. My husband didn't need the anger because he had marked off the distance, set apart his territory from his parents'. They could try to encroach on his, but it didn't distress him. He had a clear understanding of where they ended and he began, even if they sometimes didn't, and with that, he conducted his life.

In-law arguments may stem from far deeper divisions within a marriage that get masked by the arguments themselves. A husband described the tension within his marriage for years because of his wife's attachment to her mother. The two women spoke on the phone several times a day, visited back and forth several times a week and shared, it seemed to him, knowledge about everything that went on in his home life. The only thing that saved the marriage during those years, he believed, was the fact that he worked such long hours that he wasn't around to hear all the conversations between mother and daughter.

Suddenly, this man lost his job. It was a terrible period for him, lolling around the house or going out to look for work every day. Eventually he decided to work from his house, as a consultant. He wondered how he would stand seeing his mother-in-law in his home or suffer the knowledge of how many hours his wife was devoting to her. He discovered, to his surprise, that the more deeply he became involved in family life once he began spending time at home, the less frequently he saw or heard about his mother-in-law. What he came to realize was something his wife knew but had not wanted to face: his preoccupation with his own work had pushed his wife, who was dependent on her mother anyway, into the insufferable closeness he had hated. The "mother-in-law problem" in this man's marriage was in reality a problem caused by his own emotional absence, leaving an emptiness his mother-in-law filled. As he has become more caught up in life at home, his wife has been able to free herself from her mother, at least from the sticky entanglement in which she was trapped.

The worst kinds of family fracases come when parents are excessively controlling and children must fight to fend them off. Although, as I said, many parents want to hold on to their children longer than they should, some parents simply do not want to let go at all. For such parents, a son's or a daughter's marriage is too threatening to the bond they have with that child. They don't want to be displaced, and they refuse to accept or recognize the fact that they have been. In some distorted way they think that by asserting themselves in the marriage they will "show" their children—that they will not give in, that they count, that they can still call the shots.

If such parents succeed, it is often at the expense of their child's marriage. If they fail, it is because their child used extraordinary strength to stand up to them and to declare, either openly or through action: *My spouse now comes first in my life.* It is a declaration of independence nobody can make but the child, and it is one that takes a strong mind and firm commitment to one's freedom and one's marriage.

And even then it takes great effort to hold out against parental pressures. One of the reasons is that the corollary to parents' fantasies that whatever they do in terms of their children is for the children's own good is the children's fantasy that, in fact, parents do have their best interests at heart. Unless our upbringing was horrendous, most of us believe that our parents want what is good for us, that they understand and support our need for independence, that they welcome our marriages and our spouses and families—and to varying degrees this is true about most parents. When parents fall short of these fantasies, it's easier to make excuses for them than to accept the idea that they may not care for us as much as we want them to, or as is often the case, they are placing their own egos ahead of concern for us. It's easier to go along with parents, to give in when we can, than to confront them directly and risk hurting or angering them. And yet the declaration must be made, one way or another, if the marriage is to succeed.

Direct confrontation is not always necessary, if each partner feels confident about where he or she stands in relation to parents and one another. Claudia Winters remembered her parents' disapproval of her marriage to Jeff because he had not finished college and established himself in a profession as his brothers had and as Claudia's father had. "It bothered me terribly," Claudia said, "because they would make snide comments about Jeff to me as if it were all right to speak to me that way about my husband. But I didn't answer them. I just turned away from them, and pretty soon they got the idea that I had no interest in what they had to say and that they could not influence me. My attitude was, 'Oh, they don't know the half of how happy I am with Jeff.' "

Unfortunately, in some situations, the only way to break loose from the ironclad grip of parents who won't let go is to push against it bodily. That is what a St. Louis businessman named Scott Spinner did, but it was ten years into his marriage before he mustered the strength and daring to do so, and then only because he was provoked into action by his wife. Dawn Spinner knew about struggles with parents before she married Scott. For reasons she never fully understood, her parents had made her the focus of all their fights during her growing up years—arguing constantly between themselves and with her about the hours she kept, the boys she dated or the food she ate. She had a vague suspicion that fighting about her had somehow kept their marriage intact, as if that were the only common interest they had. And, in fact, two years after she married, her parents broke up.

After her marriage, Dawn turned to Scott's family for the warmth and comfort she had not received from her own, as Lynn Gilbert had turned to George's family. She was hit with the same disappointment. Outgoing and expressive, Scott's warm parents turned out to be possessive and controlling to a degree she could not have anticipated. Soon after their wedding, Scott's father insisted his son leave his job and join the family in their restaurant supply business, making it clear that not to do so would be an unforgivable transgression against the family.

Although Scott was miserable in his work, he obeyed his parents. He obeyed them also when they insisted that he and Dawn have dinner at their house every Sunday, along with his two sisters and their husbands, and that they spend all holidays with the family. Dawn began to feel trapped, and feeling that way, she encouraged Scott to look for other work so that they could at least get out from under the financial tent they inhabited with the family. The entire Spinner clan took up arms against her then, accusing her of wanting to separate her husband from his family. Scott kept himself aloof from the feud, continuing his role of dutiful son in spite of his parents' increasing coldness and rudeness to his wife. Although he complained bitterly to Dawn about his unhappiness in the business, he made no attempts to extricate himself.

One day, in a freak accident, Scott tripped and broke his ankle as he was crossing a street. He was rushed to a hospital, where he called Dawn. She, in turn, phoned his parents, but refrained from telling them how bad the break was or that Scott needed surgery. They arrived at the hospital just as surgery was ending. As they began questioning Dawn, a nurse appeared and asked for Mrs.

Spinner. Dawn moved toward her, but her father-in-law pushed her aside and, with his wife, headed forward.

"This is Mrs. Spinner," he said, "and I am Mr. Spinner, Scott's parents."

Flustered, the nurse responded, "I was looking for his wife."

Dawn stepped out, and all three silently followed the nurse to the surgeon's office. As the physician described the break, which had been bad, Scott's father became increasingly agitated. "He's like a child," he shouted. "Irresponsible, like a child. Why couldn't he watch where he was walking?" He turned to Dawn. "Irresponsible," he repeated, "you're both irresponsible kids."

With that, the elder Spinners left the hospital. Dawn waited in Scott's room until he was returned from the recovery room. Then she sat near his bed while he slept, and she wept quietly to herself. "We were married ten years," she said. "His father was still calling us irresponsible kids, and both his parents were treating me as if I didn't exist."

Scott was back in his room about four hours, still drugged with Demerol to stop his pain, when his parents arrived again. This time his father's diatribe was aimed directly at him. "Why can't you watch where you're going?" he shouted. "Why are you still such a child?" Distraught at her father-in-law's behavior, Dawn rushed to get a nurse, who quickly bustled Scott's parents out of the room, ordering them not to return until the next day.

Some weeks later, after Scott had returned home, his mother called to complain to him about Dawn's behavior at the hospital.

"She would have gone in to see that surgeon without us," she said. "I could tell from the way she walked ahead when the nurse asked for Mrs. Spinner."

Scott listened to his mother's complaints. Then in a quivering voice he had trouble controlling, he said, "Look Mom, let's get something straight. When I am on an operating table, or anyplace, anyplace at all, and somebody calls for Mrs. Spinner, they want my wife, not my mommy. Is that clear? For me, she is *the* Mrs. Spinner."

Shortly after that, Scott resigned from the family business, and started a small business of his own. Eight years later his family have still not forgiven him. Although he, Dawn and their two children keep in touch with his parents, and visit occasionally, their contact is much less frequent than it had once been. That is the only way, Dawn and Scott have decided, to maintain their independence and their integrity as a family of their own.

"What you really want," said Dawn, "is the image of the Waltons. You want everybody in the family to sit down at the table and love each other. But it doesn't happen that way. It took us ten years to break free. And then we realized that they can't hurt us unless we let them. We realized that to escape, you've got to close your eyes and your ears, and you've got to build a little retaining wall around yourself so that it shelters you. There are the days when they get through, and it hurts like hell. But you learn to protect yourself."

What a sadness it is for a husband and wife to have to barricade themselves behind a "retaining wall" as protection against parents who want to believe that everything they do is in the best interest of their children. At least the Spinners have stayed in touch with his parents, no matter how difficult that has been, and at least their children have continued to see their grandparents, aunts and uncles, to have even a half-taste of what it means to be rooted in a family. I spoke with other couples who had broken off all contact with their families, recognizing that in doing so they were excising a part of themselves, but feeling that that was the only way for them to survive as a couple.

Family therapist Murray Bowen has written at length about the dangers of what he calls "emotional cutoff" from one's parents. Couples who break completely with their parents, Bowen maintains, put their own marriage at risk. Instead of working through their problems or finding a way to live with them, they are running away from them, making it likely that those problems will surface again, this time in their marriage. There is also a greater chance that their children will break away from them as they did from their own parents, having seen this pattern as a way of dealing with family differences. In addition, says Bowen, "the person who runs away from his family of origin is as emotionally dependent as the one who never leaves home. They both need emotional closeness, but they are allergic to it."

There is much truth in all these observations. In many cases, people who are able to separate themselves from their parents in a mature way don't need to shut themselves off. Had Scott Spinner been more sure of his individuality, more able to stand up on his own for himself and his wife, his parents might not have encroached on his life as much as they did. It might not have taken the trauma of the hospital experience for him to set limits for them had he not been too dependent on his parents still, too needy of their love and approval to be able to challenge them—until he could handle no more.

But there is another side. Under some circumstances, it seems to me, the maturity or emotional dependency of a son or a daughter is less the issue than the parents' pressures and demands. When these are excessive to the point of harassing a child or so interfering with the child's marriage that it is endangered, cutting off completely may be the best way, with all its bad consequences. The wife of a well-known actor described her break with her family:

"My parents objected to my marriage from the beginning. For one thing, I'm ten years younger than my husband. For another, he was born in Europe—he's not the kind of red-blooded American my parents would have liked for me. And then, he had been divorced before. So all together, they weren't happy. They began badgering me to break off with him before the wedding. They had already broken up my sister's marriage, because her husband wasn't classy enough for them, and my sister is a mess. To this day, she's a mess. I wasn't going to let that happen to me so I tried to ignore their comments. But they wouldn't let up; every phone conversation brought another jibe, every visit was filled with nasty words and digs.

"A year after my marriage, my father asked me to lunch. In my innocence, I thought it was going to be an anniversary celebration to patch things up. Instead, right after we ordered our meal, my father looked at me with a fearsome look on his face. He said, 'Okay, this has gone far enough. I want you to end this marriage now.' I was shocked. I don't know how I did it, but I stood up, and I said to him, 'You will never speak to me this way again. And you will never do to me what you did to my sister, because I'm walking out of your life now.' It was very dramatic, and I sounded like some tough cookie, but when I walked out of the restaurant my knees were shaking. I could hardly stand. I crossed a street and almost got hit by a car because the tears were pouring out of my eyes and I didn't know where I was going. It was horrible."

After that she did not see her parents again for ten years. In recent years they have made peace with each other, and if her parents don't love her husband (she recently celebrated her seventeenth anniversary), at least they don't malign him in her presence anymore. As I said, this was an extreme situation, and it is only in extremism that such a total cutoff may be preferable to keeping ties between parents and married children, no matter how frayed they may be.

As the years go on in a marriage, in-law issues change. Many people speak about a mellowness that marks their relationship with parents and in-laws as they grow older. Jeff Winters, for example, mentioned casually that his mother lives down the street from him and that the only problem they have is that "we don't see enough of her." Claudia remembered that when they were first married, more than twenty-five years ago, Jeff used to stop in every day to see his mother. After about a year of that, Claudia expressed some dissatisfaction with the arrangement, and Jeff quickly cut down on his visits. Since then, his mother has made a conscious effort not to overinvolve herself in her son's life. So much so, that when she wasn't well recently, and Jeff visited her more frequently than usual, she worried about taking him away from Claudia. "Of course," said Claudia, "his spending time with her didn't faze me in the least—now."

In my own experience, the issues that once grated don't disappear as parents and children age; they simply become less important in the overall scheme of life. You cherish parents more as they become older because you know the time you have together is becoming shorter. You cherish their experience and their memories. In-laws, for example, are the strongest connection one spouse has to the other's childhood. As they get older and look back more often to the past, they tell stories that become the myths and traditions of your family, the history that you transmit to your children, and they to theirs. You learn from parents as the years flip by because you can allow yourself to learn without feeling overwhelmed by their knowledge or their desire to convey it. It's easier to ask their advice when both they and you know you will not necessarily take it. And it's interesting to discover the many facets of their personalities that appear after they retire or take up new work. Just as they once served as models for you in childhood, their ways of handling the concerns of their older age are tucked away someplace within you, not for now, but for that time later that you don't want to think about when these will become your concerns too.

Then, of course, there are the problems. A middle-aged couple with elderly parents may feel themselves under great pressure. To be in the middle years of life, for many, means to be squeezed on both ends, by old, needy parents above and adolescent children pushing for independence below. And there, at the center, is the couple, grappling with their own aging, their own sense of life flying by. Old family issues that have been dormant for years may be stirred up again now as roles become reversed and children become their parents' caretakers. The financial drain on a couple that is supporting one or the other partner's parents may be enormous, while the emotional drain takes its own toll: anger at parents for becoming old and sick and guilt at never being able to do enough, meaning that you're not able to save them from death.

For some people, especially those who did not get along well with parents, a parent's illness or aging brings out earlier dependencies. Everything else becomes unimportant—wife, children, career—in a last-ditch stand to grab the love or approval that was missing in earlier years.

Exactly that need for love made a tough businessman, Evin White, almost crazy during his father's last six months of life. Evin struck me at our first meeting as the kind of man who had steeled himself from sentiment. He had good reason to. As he put it, almost nonchalantly, "My father just never liked me," and he grew up not daring to like or trust many people himself. Evin gave up trying to understand the reason for his father's dislike long ago, attributing it with a shrug to his being the youngest of five sons so that by the time he arrived, his father "was bored with family life and bored with fathering sons." In spite of the dislike, for a while Evin worked in his father's highly successful import-export business in Boston along with his brothers. His father's animosity was so persistent, however, that he left the business and moved to Rhode Island, where he started a real estate brokerage company that has become quite successful.

About two years ago, Evin's father became ill with emphysema. As he became sicker, he began phoning Evin more and more often. Evin's first response was caution; he did not quite trust the sudden turnaround in the relationship. But his heart softened as his father began to speak of regrets he had about his life and to ask Evin's forgiveness for having been treated so badly. With every passing day, his father seemed to become closer to him, pleading with him to hold the family together in the future because he was the stablest of them all. Now Evin's armor was pierced and for the first time he allowed himself to acknowledge the hurt and the hunger he had felt for acceptance. He began to see this period in his father's life as a time to undo what had been done in the past, to put it all behind them, and in the time remaining to create a new, warm relationship.

When his wife Stacey expressed some doubts about his father's newfound affection and suggested that Evin was being used by his father because his brothers were not willing to give up their time to be with him, Evin blew up. "If a man is suffering," he cried, "you help him. You stand at his side and say 'It's all right, I'll be here.' " And so Evin did. During the last six months of his father's life, he flew back and forth between Boston and Rhode Island several times a week, and spent every weekend at his father's bedside. It was as though he had no family of his own, so distant and unimportant did his wife and children become to him in his all-out dedication to the father who finally seemed to love him.

"He didn't deserve Evin's care and love," said Stacey when the Whites were telling their story. "He was a horrible, evil man."

"He was my father," Evin rejoined.

Then he went on with his narrative. "My father died, and I was the only family member with him at the time." His eyes lowered and his voice became hoarse. "And I was not even mentioned in his will. Nothing. The money doesn't mean anything to me. I have as much as I need. But my father didn't care enough about me to mention me in his will. He didn't even care about my children. Maybe Stacey is right. He was really a bad person. And I almost gave up my entire family for him, the way I carried on during those last six months."

Most parents are not like Evin's father, and when they die, they leave a large space in their children's lives that nothing else can quite fill. For many people in long marriages, the death of parents draws the couple closer together as they step up now to take their places on the front lines of mortality unshielded by parental bulwarks.

In some marriages, spaces are filled not by parents but by siblings. People speak of warm, enduring relationships with brothers and sisters that enrich their marriages, and a number of couples expressed surprise and delight at how close they had become to sisters and brothers-in-law, who were like siblings or good friends to them. When siblings create problems in a couple's marriage, the causes are similar to the causes for parental problems—overinvolvement, a need for control, dependencies and the inability or unwillingness of one sibling to make it clear to the other that a spouse comes first.

One man attributed the breakup of his marriage to his sister-in-law's influence. "My wife was so close to her sister," he said, "that I couldn't get between them. All the emotions that went on in our marriage were between the two of them. I was the odd man out." Ironically, after his marriage ended, his sister-in-law called to commiserate with him, although she had encouraged her sister to break up. He interpreted that phone call as her attempt to continue to feel important after her power base within the marriage was gone.

It could be. Sisters or brothers who interfere in a sibling's marriage do so because they want to maintain the power or influence they exerted in earlier years. Such people were usually the oldest or most favored in a family, the one to whom the others looked up in childhood. They carry their lofty positions into adult life so that they become a presence within the marriage (they may not be physically present, but they are there, every time a spouse suggests, "Let's ask my brother Mike what he thinks," or "I don't want to decide about that until I discuss it with my sister Alice"). And because siblings generally do not go through the same struggle to separate themselves emotionally from one another as they do to separate from parents, their influence, when exerted, can be even stronger than the influence of parents.

The sibling relationship that is most likely to make itself felt in a marriage, it would appear, is that between brother and sister. I have no scientific proof for that statement, only the accounts of couples I interviewed, and the evidence of history. Back in ancient times, the historian Herodotus described a cruel scene in which a woman was given a choice by the Persian king Darius of whose life should be saved, her husband's, her children's or her brother's. She chose her brother because all the other lives were replaceable for her; his was not. Her choice was reflected in much more recent times by a woman in the Arab country of Yemen, who explained to the scholar S. D. Goitein, "A husband—I can get; children—I can bear; but a noble brother—from where shall I get him?" In a book about Islamic communities during the Middle Ages, Goitein points out that this "brother-sister syndrome," as he calls it, extended throughout Mediterranean countries and the Near East in early days and continued through modern times. One of the reasons for the extraordinary closeness of brothers and sisters in the past, he says, is that parents died young and brothers became responsible for providing for their sisters and arranging their marriages (at a time when all marriages were arranged by families rather than left to the whims of the two people involved). The sister's responsibility came after marriage. If a married sister held a stronger economic position than her brother, she was expected to help him out. She was also expected to intercede on his behalf with other family members or with government authorities if he fell into trouble.

Those old traditions may be gone, but their spirit lingers on. In many households brothers still act protective of sisters and sisters still mother brothers, and those positions may persist into adult life. Brothers and sisters also play out with each other the sex roles they will have later; they are couples in miniature, and some find it hard as adults to be replaced by another man or woman. For all these reasons sisters and brothers may become entangled in one another's marriages unless each sets a clear limit on how far the other is allowed to go.

For years as I was growing up, my family lived next door to a couple with no children whose marriage was subtly being torn apart by the husband's sister. A beautiful and vivacious woman, this sister had been her parents' favorite, and she grew up strong, self-centered and sure of herself. Widowed at the age of forty, she chose not to remarry, but to spend as much time as she could with her beloved brother, whom she adored. Although he was the older of the two, she was the stronger, the more controlling. She phoned him several times a day to report on her activities and her loneliness, had dinner at his home twice a week and joined the couple for weekend outings or afternoons at the movies.

The wife, gentle and good-natured, without a cunning bone in her body, was no match for her sister-in-law and she knew it. She rarely spoke to anyone about her home life, but everyone saw the strain she was under as she competed for her husband's attention with his sister. Occasionally she would talk to my parents about wanting to go away with her husband but being unable to because he would not hear of leaving his widowed sister home alone. And occasionally the sister, Marguerita, would show us a gift her brother had brought from one of his business travels. She was quick to point out that Maria, his wife, received a gift also, but she made sure we recognized that while Maria's may have been more expensive, it was surely less fashionable. She had seen to it that her brother was aware of the differences in the tastes of his wife and his sister.

From the outside, the couple seemed to have a proper relationship, always polite and considerate. Looking back on them I've wondered whether he knew how stifled his wife felt in the constant presence of his sister. If he did, he never acknowledged it. Sometimes he would mention to my parents or one of the neighbors that Maria was depressed and he could not understand why. I doubt he ever allowed himself to realize that the hurt she carried within her came from never feeling special, from being treated as an equal with his sister, loved, perhaps, but no differently than the other.

Maria died of a rare blood disease, although the front stoop psychiatrists of our building diagnosed her illness as terminal sadness. Marguerita was unable to attend her funeral, for that very morning she sprained her ankle and could not walk. But within days she had moved in with her brother to cook and care for him. And there she lives still. The two of them are quite old now, but Marguerita fusses over the brother she has all to herself, and he is content in her care. If they talk of his marriage to Maria, I suspect it is as of a distant event, an interlude in the lifelong attachment of this brother and sister.

We must speak also about the influence of friends on a marriage. I asked everyone I interviewed about friendships, both as a couple and as individuals. Most couples have groups of friends with whom they socialize as a couple and individual friends, his and hers, whom they may or may not share. Mostly, the individual friends are hers. Men, as many studies have shown, tend to bond together, to work in groups, play team games or team up with their colleagues. But when I asked them if they have a best friend aside from their wives, their answer, with some exceptions, was no.

Why men don't develop deep friendships as so many women do is open to question. It may be that, trained in childhood to hold back their feelings, they never allow themselves to reveal their vulnerabilities to each other, although they may open up to the women in their lives. Or it may be that men learn to compete with one another before they learn to trust one another, and true friendship requires a basis of trust, even when competition exists. I don't know all the reasons. I do know that most of the women in long-term marriages with whom I spoke did have close friends, one or more, with whom they shared intimacies and experiences. They could turn to others for some of the emotional support for which their husbands relied only on them. Claudia Winters, for example, mentioned two women with whom she spent a great deal of time while her son was dying of leukemia, "because of my need to talk about things." Her husband, Jeff, talked about his pain only to her, or not at all. A few women described women friends with whom they prayed regularly and the closeness they felt during those quiet moments.

What does it do to a marriage when one spouse has close friends and the other doesn't? Some husbands admitted to being jealous of their wives' friendships at first, but after a while they came to accept and admire them. What often happens is that a woman's friendship with another woman, or with a man, turns into a family friendship, the women arranging social events for all to share. If the coupling doesn't work, the women may remain friends themselves without involving their spouses. (Newly married young couples often fight about friends, worrying in the midst of their arguments how, if they really love each other, they could have such different tastes in whom they like. Remarried couples and those married some time learn to accept the differences, and go their own ways in choosing friends.)

The dangers of one-sided friendships come when the partner with the friend confides everything that is going on in the marriage to that friend—all the fights, all the sexual difficulties, all the in-law quarrels. Once the doors to a marriage have been opened in that way, they are hard to shut again. The outside has been let in, and the cover of intimacy that surrounds the marriage has been cracked. If a spouse reveals the details of an affair to a friend, it seems to me the betrayal becomes twofold. Not only is there a secret in the marriage from which one spouse is excluded, but now the secret is known outside the marriage, further excluding the spouse, further weakening the bond between partners.

In the best of marriages, friendships are vital and

cherished, but secrets are kept for the couple themselves. In the weakest marriages, friends are used as buffers to prevent an intimacy that neither party wants and both fear. Psychiatrist Henry Spitz told me of seeing a couple for marital therapy several times, when, in the course of conversation at one session, the wife mentioned a man's name he had never heard before. "John said the same thing," she was exclaiming. "John?" asked Spitz. "Who's John?" "Oh," came the answer, "didn't I tell you about John? He lives with us. Roy's so busy with his work, I can just talk to John or go out with him any time I want to."

On occasion, a friend who has been let in on all the secrets of a marriage can help save it at a moment of crisis. Unfortunately, friends have a way of becoming too sympathetic, too willing to take sides and urge partners to actions they may not really want. A designer who was planning to separate from her husband for a short while in order to sort out various issues between them looked at me with tears in her eyes. "My friends think I'm leaving Dan for good, so they say all kinds of terrible things about him," she said. " 'He's a bum, he's this, he's that.' But you know what? He's mine. He's part of me. Whatever our problems, they're our own. I don't want everybody to encourage us to split. We're married seventeen years. I need some help in keeping this thing together." And a man bitterly blamed his brief separation from his wife on her best friend's constant urging. The couple were having their difficulties, but the friend was having her own marital troubles. As if to free herself, she pushed this man's wife into leaving him and looking for another man. The wife left, was miserable without her husband, and returned to him six months later. She has little to do now with her former best friend.

A final issue to be considered is this: Can women and men have platonic relationships outside of marriage, or are all such relationships threatening to each person's marriage? In *The Extramarital Affair*, psychoanalyst Herbert Strean argues that every strong platonic relationship between a man and a woman includes some sexual feeling, and that the emotional commitment in such a relationship may be just as destructive to a marriage as an extramarital sexual relationship would be. I would agree only in part. I have seen friendships between men and women that are so highly charged, so intrusive in their marriages because of the all-consuming interest each person has in the other, that it doesn't much matter whether they engage in sex or not. But to deny the viability of truly platonic friendships based on interest, respect or admiration is to cut out an entire area of comfort and pleasure.

It may be true that platonic relationships between men and women have a sexual component. Not always, but often an attraction exists—that may be what led to the friendship in the first place. Judging from my own male friends and what others have told me, we continue to be attracted again and again throughout life to certain types of people. They are the types we *did not* marry because somehow we knew they would be wrong for us as mates. But we like them and have fun being around them, and if we can have them as friends, we have the best of both worlds. It takes some awareness and caution to keep such friendships from escalating into something more sexual or more serious, but that's all right. A good marriage can sustain these friendships without being threatened.

Of course, if one spouse balks at the other's opposite-sex friendships, that is another story. Then both have to seek out the cause for the jealousy or opposition. Is one spouse using the friendship to tease or torment the other? Is the other spouse too insecure to trust such a friendship? Are there reasons why it should not be trusted? Sometimes friends, both same and opposite sex, become the focal point for all the conflict and frustration in a marriage. As one divorced woman explained, "All our fights were about my best friend, as if without her our marriage would have been just fine. I finally said, 'If you don't like Connie, I'm not going to be your wife.' It was crazy. Without Connie we would have had the same problems; we just would not have had anyone else to blame them on."

Parents, in-laws, siblings, friends—at their worst, they can interfere with a marriage, but at their best they bolster and enhance it. Each marriage, with its partners and its families and its friends, is like a new civilization, similar to what came before it, but different enough to be uniquely its own. Each marriage, and the children it creates, begins the world again.

CHAPTER EIGHT

On Kids and Couples

The drive to the summer camp my daughter attends takes three hours. On visiting day we drove three hours to visit her for three hours, and then we spent three hours on the road driving home. It was the hottest day of the summer, and radio newscasters, speaking with the controlled excitement usually reserved for assassinations and other major upheavals, announced that the temperature had reached a record-breaking 98 degrees. Their announcements were no surprise to us or to any of the parents making the drive to visit their children at camp. It is always hot on parents' visiting day. No matter which year and which Sunday it falls on, that day, everyone knows, is going to be fiercely hot, most likely the hottest day of summer.

It is hot in many ways aside from the weather. You've been apart, you and the children, for several weeks. You're nervous about what you will see, and you're nervous about what they will see. Such a short separation, yet there is a strangeness between you. Some transformations have occurred, inside them, inside you, between you and your spouse. What will you find in them? What will they find in you?

For me, my daughter's departure for camp always

brings the same reaction. I return from seeing her off at
the camp bus, and the apartment seems dead. Silent. I
can feel her presence—the loafer she never got around to
picking up still lies on the dining room floor, her closet
door is still open, the leftover stuffed animals of babyhood
peering out of the dark. But there is a stillness, an absence
of excitement. Silence. I say her name out loud and blush
at my own craziness. She'll be gone only two months.
How can I feel so empty?

"Little survivals" is what psychohistorian Robert Jay
Lifton calls such separations. Children and parents go
through many small but painful separations during the
years of growing up. Kids begin school, their first move
away from home. They leave town to take jobs or go to
college. Parents go to work, leaving their children at home.
They take trips; they become ill; they divorce. Each leave-
taking brings its own kind of sadness and mourning.
Gradually, the children survive and we survive, accommodating to the distance or loss in our own ways.

It takes me a few days to accommodate to the separation from my daughter after she leaves for camp. I suffer a
few days of intense longing, of mother arms that have
nothing to enfold, of remembering the times before she
left when I forgot to tell her she was beautiful or special or
mine. A few aching days of missing her drag by, and then
a kind of numbness sets in. Part of me becomes numb to
wanting her, to wondering where she is when I'm thinking about her and to whom she is speaking when I'm
speaking about her. I suppose it's the parent side that
becomes numb, and to compensate, another side reawakens with vigor, the young side, the bride side, the free
side.

You're set free when the kids leave. That is the only
honest way to describe what happens. An invisible weight
slips off. You can go to sleep at midnight and awaken at
noon. You can watch television all night and make love all
morning. You can go out to dinner at ten o'clock at night
and speak loudly when you return home, never bothering
to say, "Shh, the kids are asleep," never peeking in to
cover a restless sleeper or pat away a nightmare. You're
free, and in the long warm light of summer, you and your

spouse get to see one another and know one another again without interference.

When you drive to camp on the hottest day of summer, you wonder whether the love you have of your newfound freedom shows on your face along with your other love, of them, the children. Will they know that while you miss them, you don't miss them that much anymore? Will they be able to read in your eyes that while you write to them constantly, you don't think about them all the time? Probably not. I remember being a camper and seeing my parents on visiting day. I assumed their smiles came only from their happiness at being with me, for I was sure that back home they had nothing to cheer them, back there, their days were hollow without me. I would have fleeting moments of guilt during their visit because of my sense of being disconnected from them. I belonged in my grass-covered camp with its rough wooden cabins and sapphire skies while they belonged in their grey city world where ridges of heat and dust hung motionless over dirty asphalt pavements and all life stopped while the children were away at camp. It never occurred to me—it would have shocked me to realize—that they were disconnected from me too.

The sun was still beating down with unyielding determination when we left camp on visiting day. It had been a good day. My daughter looked strong and tall, filled with confidence. She talked constantly about this one and that one, about the counselors, the sports, the activities. She never guessed our secret, that Daddy and I were having our own fun without her, and by the time the visit ended, I had forgotten about that also. I felt the pit in my stomach, the emptiness of not having her with me as I shut the car door and waved a last good-bye. She waved, turned around and sprinted away.

"I miss her so much again," I said to my husband as we drove off. "How will I get through the rest of the summer without her?"

"You'll manage," he smiled.

On the way back, we stopped to eat at an Indian restaurant, which served the kind of hot, spicy food that kids hate. Then we took in a late movie. We reached home at one o'clock in the morning, a clean, neat, quiet home, and went to bed satisfied. It had been a good day and there were still weeks of separation to look forward to.

What does having children mean to a marriage? Contradictory things. It means feeling a kind of love different from any that came before it, a love that makes you know without a shade of doubt that you could give up your life for another human being. It means suffering rages and frustrations so intense that they slash through the most protected core of your psyche. Having a child means experiencing a joy that gurgles up from the wellsprings of your own childhood, and it means living with restrictions that can bind so tightly you wonder if you will ever escape. Children can bring a couple closer than they ever thought possible, and they can split a couple farther apart than two chips of wood springing from the blow of an ax on a log. And it all goes on at the same time.

Until a while ago, nobody questioned the connections between children and marriage or thought to separate the two. Love and marriage, kids and carriage were seen as a package deal. One logically followed the other. People assumed that not long after marriage, a couple would begin having children, and if a couple did not have a child, it was because they were not able to, not because they didn't want to. Bertrand Russell, the liberal-minded philosopher who shocked his contemporaries by advocating free love before marriage, spoke of marriage as a vehicle for producing children. He proposed that single men and women enjoy one another sexually but that once they decide to marry, they accept the responsibility of having children. "Children," he wrote in his book *Marriage and Morals*, "rather than sexual intercourse, are the true purpose of marriage, which would not be regarded as consummated until such time as there is a prospect of children." And psychoanalyst Erik Erikson viewed procreation as a crucial stage of adult development, emphasizing that adults need children for their own maturation. "Mature man," he said, "needs to be needed, and maturity needs guidance as well as encouragement from what has been produced and must be taken care of."

Only in recent years, beginning in the 1960s and

building steam in the 1970s and 1980s, have people cast doubt on these assumptions. The emphasis on zero population growth, which became popular during the 1970s, led couples to reconsider having children as an automatic and natural part of marriage. Many women who entered the work force began postponing childbirth or deciding to forgo it altogether as they pressed ahead to advance in their jobs and careers.

Reflecting this changing attitude toward children in marriage, a slew of professional studies and popular books began arguing the case for childless marriages. Typical of the professional works was one by two sociologists, Norval D. Glenn and Sara McLanahan, which surveyed more than two thousand people fifty years and older, some of whom were childless and others whose grown children no longer lived at home. The people were asked to rate themselves on their "global happiness," and the researchers concluded that children had little effect on the global happiness of their parents. Furthermore, these researchers disputed the commonly held idea that "important psychological rewards for having children are derived from the later stages of parenthood." They found that many older people feel neglected by their offspring and establish their strongest and most satisfying relationships with others the same age rather than with children or grandchildren. When reported in the popular magazine, *Psychology Today*, this research was headlined, "Parenthood's Dim Rewards." The same pessimism, but without scientific trappings, appeared in an advice column by Ann Landers in 1975, when readers were asked whether, if they could make the decision over, they would have children. Of the fifty thousand people who responded, 70 percent said no, they would decide not to become parents again.

I question the broad conclusions of these and similar surveys. In the Glenn-McLanahan study, for example, the survey query that measured global happiness was, "Taken all together, how would you say things are these days—would you say that you are very happy, pretty happy, or not too happy?" No questions relating to the special satisfactions or gratifications of parenthood were included. Had they been, they might have elicited other, more specific, responses that would add insight to the "global happiness" generalizations. In the Ann Landers survey, nobody knows who the respondents were—it is possible that the majority of people who went to the trouble to respond were people who were angry or frustrated with their children. In a less well-known survey that asked the same question, reported by Daniel Yankelovich in *New Rules*, 90 percent of the respondents answered that they *would* have children if they "had it to do over again."

But the point is that surveys and studies by popular writers and social scientists gave a stamp of approval to expressing the negative side of having children more openly than ever before. By the mid-1970s, the birth rate had fallen and "nonparent" organizations were sprouting up everywhere to drive home the message that marriages did not have to include children to be valid.

Yet even while these new attitudes toward children began taking hold, statisticians noticed another trend. Although the birth rate of the population as a whole was decreasing, the birth rate among one group of women was rising—women in their thirties and early forties. Many couples, it seemed, had not banned children from their lives; they had simply postponed expanding their families. Now, women who had delayed having babies in order to pursue work and careers began "hungering" for children, as one woman put it, before it would no longer be possible for them. This "baby boomlet," as *Newsweek* magazine labeled it, has led to an abundance of new child-care publications, and much discussion about the pros and cons of having children late or early in a marriage.

Where does all this leave us today? In a fairly good position. The couples I interviewed who had children, as most of them did, had given little thought to whether they wanted children when they married, or how soon they should have a child after they married. "You got married; you had children," one woman said, expressing the outlook of most. "You didn't think about it." None of these couples has regretted having children, but some have wished they could have had more time alone before their first child, or had simply been more aware of what a child would mean in their marriage before becoming parents (some of the negative attitudes toward children in the research cited above might actually have reflected this wish on the part of parents that they had known more about what they were getting into rather than regret that they had gotten into it). The changing attitudes toward children, emphasizing choice rather than social obligations, have added meaning, it seems to me, to having a child. When mates consciously choose to become parents because they want to rather than because society expects them to, they have a greater chance of being wholeheartedly dedicated to their child.

Kimberly Bakst, the lawyer who insisted her in-laws address her by her own surname, spoke of the baby she and her husband Randy Chapin were expecting in about four months.

"Had you always planned on having children?" I asked them.

"No," Kimberly answered. "It was a big crisis in the first months of our marriage. I felt very strongly that a woman couldn't have a career and a child. I am a feminist and a lawyer, and I thought if I have to choose, I would choose a career. Also, I didn't think I wanted to bring a child into this world of woe."

"What made you change your mind?"

"Randy cried," she said. "He had such strong feelings about wanting children. We were having a big discussion, it was maybe our fifth month of marriage, and he just began to cry. It was one of the few times I have seen him cry. The tears really got to me. I thought, 'If this means so much to him, I have to rethink my position.' I did, but he agreed to wait until I felt ready. I found that the happier I got with my life, the more positive I felt about having a child. Now I'm ready."

Being ready, for Kimberly, also means that she feels secure in her career and is planning to take a few months off after the baby is born before returning to work. Randy would like to take a paternity leave, but his firm is not inclined that way. Even if he doesn't get time off, however, he plans on "full participation" in all aspects of childrearing. Neither is sure that their plans will work out, but they are prepared for change, if need be. "I am scared, real scared," Kimberly admitted, "but I'm also optimistic. This child is going to be a reality in my life, and I'll just confront things when I get there because this is so important to us."

Whether things work out just as they wish, they are beginning with a conscious plan and a conscious decision about how they want to structure their lives. That type of awareness adds control to a marriage. It may not make childrearing a snap, but it eases the anxieties, the anger and the sense of being trapped that many parents of earlier generations felt, especially women.

One danger in such control and awareness comes when a couple postpone and postpone having a child until the perfect time, only to find that at that time they are unable to conceive, or they have other problems. A sad note along those lines was struck by journalist Susan Jacoby. Married in her twenties, Jacoby had put off having a child until she was more firmly established in her career. By the time she achieved what she wanted, when she was in her midthirties, her marriage had fallen apart. Now in her late thirties and unmarried, she has reconciled herself, but with pain, to the idea that she will never have a child even if she remarries one day. "No one warned us," she wrote in *Vogue*, that "waiting for the ideal moment to become a mother might cause us to lose the moment altogether." As in all areas of marriage, balance is needed, in this case between choosing the right time and nature's own timetable.

Deciding not to have children at all is another kind of choice some couples make, although even in our time of many options only about 5 or 6 percent of all couples do make that choice. The couples I spoke with who had chosen not to have children fifteen, twenty, twenty-five years ago or so were not sorry about their decisions, but they were apologetic and somewhat defensive. "I guess we were selfish," they all said. Or "We were so involved in our work (or for some, our families) that we wouldn't have been good parents anyway." Today, the more open acceptance of voluntary childlessness has allowed such couples to be more accepting of themselves and less apologetic. (A poll conducted by the firm of Yankelovich, Skelly and White found that 83 percent of Americans now believe it acceptable to be married and not have children. A smaller percentage, but still a majority—59 percent—

rejected the statement that "people who do not have children are selfish.") We are moving in the direction, then, of accepting people's choices about children, and that acceptance makes the choices more real and more appropriate to each couple's life.

The childless marriages I studied seemed to be no worse or better than the marriages with children. Most of the couples without children did not begin marriage determined not to have children. The decision seemed to evolve as the years went on. A Kansas husband and wife, married twenty-two years, and typical of others, had been in college when they met and married. "Of course, when we were in college we didn't want a family," the wife said. "Then we both became busy with our careers [she is a musician, he a graphics designer]. The longer we were married and didn't have children, the less interested we became in having any. We were able to travel and do things we wanted without having to worry about kids. Now I can't even imagine myself with a child. I don't think I would have been a very good parent."

Only one couple had been sure from the start that they did not want children. Becky and Richard Peele had begun marriage, some thirty years ago, with heavy responsibilities. He was supporting a widowed and sickly mother; she was caring for a retarded sister who lived with her elderly mother. "Everybody assumes," Becky said, "that we were unable to have children, which is okay with us. But the truth is, it was a conscious decision. We both felt we wanted to fulfill our responsibilities to our families and that took time and money. We needed something left over for ourselves."

"People probably look at us with disgust," Richard added, reflecting the defensiveness I heard from other childless couples. "But we don't care about that. We've never regretted our decision. The people I know with children have all had problems."

"The most marvelous people," Becky agreed, "don't necessarily have children who are free of problems. And even without the problems—our closest friends have a son whom we were very close to as he was growing up. We went everywhere with that child from the time he was three years old. I loved him, and it was wonderful to be with him, but when the day ended, they went into their place and shut their doors, and we came back home and closed our doors, and we were perfectly satisfied. If it had happened for some reason that we'd had a child, I'm sure we would have done just as well or just as poorly as everyone else. But it didn't, and we're happy as a family with just the two of us."

What I observed in those families of two is a calmness, a kind of serenity that is not possible with children in the picture. Life is more ordered, more organized and more predictable. Whether partners without children are emotionally closer to one another as some of them maintain is debatable. They are free to spend more time together, to do what they wish when they wish, to arrange their lives as they see fit, with little interference from sources outside themselves. But the intimacy in a marriage comes from many factors, not least among them the work—and fun—of rearing kids.

In many marriages without children, the creative energy parents use in rearing and guiding their young is often channeled into other forms of creativity. After years of working for large companies, for example, the graphics designer from Kansas has just put all his money into starting his own business. "It's something I've always dreamed of doing," he said. "If I had kids to send to college now, I couldn't do it. This is my way of shaping something." Other people without children spoke of taking on volunteer work in areas far removed from their everyday occupations, of teaching, and especially of traveling extensively. (Traveling can provide a different kind of creativity. It allows you to explore worlds beyond yourself and to integrate those explorations into your own experience.)

Do couples without children miss out on a vital part of life's experience? Many people with children would say so. They would have to admit, however, that such couples also miss out on the anxieties and disappointments children can inject into a marriage. As one mother of three described such comparisons: "I have a friend who has no children who comes to visit occasionally. She looks at the kids and she thinks they're so cute and she wishes out loud that she had my life. And I look at her with her silver fox coat and beautiful nails and wish that I had her life. But we both know inside us that we wouldn't want to trade places."

Once a couple has a child, everything in life changes. Raising children may be the most rewarding job in the world, but it is also undoubtedly the most difficult—an "impossible profession," Salvador Minuchin called it. Or in the words of one mother, "With kids, you're damned if you do and you're damned if you don't, meaning you never never know what's right." True, there are hundreds of experts out there telling us in books and articles what's right. The problem is that what's right with one is wrong with the next. Fashions in childrearing change and so does expert advice. In the end, as everyone knows, you and your spouse and your child have to figure out how to handle each other.

Having a child is like getting married: you have to experience it to understand it. As prepared as anybody is, nobody is really prepared, at least not for the first child. The way you eat, the way you play, the way you work, the way you think—they all become different with the arrival of a baby. One of my favorite anecdotes was told to me by a professor who described bringing his wife home from the hospital with their beautiful newborn son. They settled the baby in his sparkling bassinette, played with him for a while, then put on their coats and headed out to get some pizza. Partway through the door his wife cried, "Oh, my God, we left the baby alone," and ran back. They had simply forgotten that a new person had joined their lives and that many years would pass before they could casually leave the house together without thinking about him.

For a couple, a child is an interruption—a constant interruption that needs to be fed, cared for, loved. The baby interrupts the flow between parents, the one-on-one intimacy that had existed before. A third being now becomes a focal point in the marriage; he or she also becomes a medium through whom flow the issues and tensions with which partners themselves may be grappling. In her humorous but serious novel *Heartburn*, about the breakup of her marriage, Nora Ephron describes the effects of having a child this way:

"After Sam was born I remember thinking that no one had ever told me how much I would love my child; now, of course, I realized something no one ever tells you: that a child is a grenade. When you have a baby you set off an explosion in your marriage, and when the dust settles, your marriage is different from what it was." And she goes on: "All those idiotically lyrical articles about sharing child-rearing duties never mention that, nor do they allude to something else that happens when a baby is born, which is that all the power struggles of the marriage have a new playing field. The baby wakes up in the middle of the night, and instead of jumping out of bed, you lie there thinking: whose turn is it? If it's your turn, you have to get up; if it's his turn, then why is he still lying there asleep while you're awake wondering whose turn it is?"

Among the people I interviewed, arguments were said to center around children more than around any other issue in the marriage. Neither money nor sex nor in-laws nor work was mentioned as often as children as sources of disagreement in a marriage. For some couples, the tensions begin early on, almost as soon as the baby is born. A wife's deep involvement with a newborn baby can make her husband feel left out, almost like a sibling whose mother has abandoned him for the other child, the younger and cuter one. In turn, the husband's sullenness or jealousy can push the wife ever closer to the baby for comfort and emotional support. Even when a husband involves himself in caring for a baby, as so many do now, it may be hard for him to break through the physical and psychological closeness of a mother to her infant, especially if the mother is breast-feeding.

Added to this issue, a certain amount of sexual distancing often takes place after the birth of a child. For a woman, the disinterest may be due to hormonal changes or to the enormous physical satisfaction she gets from holding and cuddling her baby. For both parents, there is the exhaustion and emotional drain of caring for an infant, an exhaustion that may continue even as a baby gets older and certainly as other children arrive. Children's

demands and needs tire parents out, and the preoccupation with children in a family can shift interests and energies away from sexual desires. (They shift back again, of
course, and many couples help things along by taking
time out for themselves—getting a babysitter or a family
member to stay with the baby during evenings or weekends while they concentrate on each other.)

Children may inhibit sex also simply because they are
there, in the next room or, at the most unexpected times,
in parents' rooms. A topic of perennial interest among
parents is whether to lock their bedroom door so a child
cannot enter when they may be making love, and what to
say to a child who does see them in the act. In either case,
a child's presence in a family may make sex between
partners more self-conscious than ever before.

It may also raise career tensions. Many a couple, like
Kimberly and Randy, who are cool and confident before a
child is born about their ability to handle a child and two
careers, find the actuality more difficult than expected.
The smoothest-running dual-career families are those that
can afford, and find, excellent help to care for home and
children. In most others, partners constantly juggle and
trade off time with each other. Who takes off from work
to take the baby to the pediatrician, later to the dentist?
Who stays home with a child when she's sick? And who
loses a workday to go to a school play (an activity at
which no one can substitute for a parent)? "When you're
a working mother, you give up everything except your
work and your family," said one woman. Working fathers
make their sacrifices too, and the sorting out of who does
what can generate anxieties in the marriage.

Then there are less expected work issues. For some
men, liberation flies out the window when a baby is
carried through the door. No matter how accepting they
may be of a wife's work or career, once they have a child,
they want their wives to be home, if not full time, then
much of the time. They may be willing to "help out," and
they may agree to hiring an outsider to handle some
duties, but they expect, as their fathers expected, the
major responsibility to rest with their wives. In such situations, the baby becomes the catalyst for a deeper struggle
going on between the couple, the power struggle Nora

Ephron describes, but even more, the struggle over roles and work and each spouse's interpretation of the marriage.

"I just think," said one husband to me in front of his wife, "that a baby needs a parent at home. I think one of us needs to be here for him now, and one of us will need to be here later when he gets older and goes off to school and comes home from school."

"Does she have to be the one who's here with the baby? Isn't it possible for you to be here some of the time?" I asked.

"I can't organize my work that way," he answered quickly (he's a dentist), "but Debbie can find part-time work."

Debbie shrugged. "We're negotiating," she said, as if wanting to stop the conversation before it got pushed into a track from which she knew she would have trouble extricating it. "The problem for me is he makes more money than I do, so I'm on weaker grounds. But we'll work this thing out."

I expect they will, but it will take quite a bit of negotiating. The baby has set in motion other conflicts between them that have to do with how they view themselves and each other. Had it not been for the baby, the dispute might have taken other forms or may not even have arisen for many years. It has arisen now, and the baby became the trigger for setting it off.

Children can be explosives in other areas. The parents of four children portrayed their most heated battles as resulting from the kids' sloppiness and their way of strewing belongings in every room of the house. The husband would shout at the children, and when his wife tried to calm him down, they would get into a brawl of their own in which he would accuse her of being too easy on the children. The longer we spoke, however, the clearer it became to me (and to them too, I believe, although we didn't articulate it) that his anger at the children about their sloppiness was also an expression of his anger at his wife's careless housekeeping. "Gail can leave an open can of tomato sauce in the refrigerator for weeks, until it's covered with green mold, and not even notice," he said with a tight smile. Or "I've had friends come to visit and they go into the kitchen to see if the oven is as dirty as I told them it is. And it is." Or "I'm used to seeing cobwebs wherever I look in this house." Instead of shouting directly at his wife about her habits, which may be too threatening to their relationship, he detours his anger through the kids. She responds by defending the children, which is also a way of defending herself, and both avoid an open battle around the things they dislike most about each other.

Children are sometimes used more openly as an excuse to cover up for difficulties between parents. A spouse who wants to avoid sex, for example, may use the excuse that the children will hear, and then will complain that kids interfere with sex in marriage. In more serious situations, children become scapegoats for the angers and disappointments of mates. The parents may blame the child for everything that is wrong between them—"If Tommy weren't doing so badly in school, we would have no problems in this family" —refusing to recognize that Tommy's difficulties may be not the cause but the result of family troubles.

In the most problematic family situations, a child becomes unmanageable or ill in some way as a result of bearing the burden of family problems, thus accelerating the problems themselves. One therapist spoke about a seventeen-year-old girl he was treating who was anorexic. Like others with this disease, she had starved herself into skeletonlike thinness, and her distraught parents had hospitalized her, fearing she would die if she were not treated quickly. The parents seemed totally puzzled about what might be troubling her. After several family meetings, the psychiatrist gained some insight into the pressures that had led the girl to her illness. She had been, from her earliest years, her father's favorite, partly because she was the youngest of three children and partly because she bore a haunting resemblance to his beloved sister who had died in a Nazi concentration camp. The girl flowered in her father's love, but began to shrivel under the hatred and jealousy that spilled out of her mother precisely because of that love. The more attention the father paid to his daughter, the angrier the mother became at both father and daughter. Although she never spoke about her feelings to her husband and seemed outwardly as pleasant to the daughter as to her other children, the mother managed in a thousand little ways to convey her anger. Caught between her parents' rivalries and rages, the girl retreated into herself, rejecting both of them in the most extreme way she could, by not eating and becoming deeply ill.

The issues that arise between most parents because of children are not usually so severe. If most of the arguments couples have center around children, most of the arguments about children center around questions of discipline. How hard, how soft? When do you lay down the law; when do you let matters drift? When parents disagree on these questions, it is usually because each spouse has come to parenthood with preconceived ideas carried over from his or her childhood—some ideas that each wants to repeat, others that need revision. A son still remembers with pain the rigid rules his father insisted on, and determines to give his children as much freedom as possible, while his wife thinks the strict ways of her family would be as right for her children as they had been for her. A woman smarts at memories of being neglected by her parents in favor of her older sister and becomes devoted to her youngest child at the expense of the older one. Or a man favors his oldest because as oldest in his family, he enjoyed a position of special honor and responsibility. The different visions each spouse brings to the marriage lead to battles about how to educate children, whether to help them with their homework, how much of an allowance to give them, what chores to demand of them, or when to let them ride a bike or drive a car.

An actor spoke about the bitterness just those kinds of differences caused between him and his wife: "She's so much tighter and more controlling with the kids than I am. She would tell them, 'You're not allowed to ride a bike here,' or 'You can't do this or that.' I had a lot of freedom when I was a kid. I was raised without a father. I was out there, doing a lot of crazy things. They may not necessarily have been healthy, but they made up my personality. I don't want my kids so tightly controlled that they are afraid to take any risks." His wife had her own complaints about him: "He sets standards for the kids that are academically so high, he scares the living daylights out of them. Sometimes I think he's especially hard on our eldest son because he wants the boy to make up for his personal failures. I tell him this, but it's hard for him to step back."

Making up for personal failures—that is the other side of the discipline differences, the dark side, the side nobody wants to admit to or even talk about. For in spite of all the good advice and the truly good intentions parents have of allowing children to be individuals, of sending them out into the world free to be their own persons, there is a part of all parents that coils itself around their children then steps out into the world along with them and waits, unprotected, as the world gazes on their young. Parents' egos become caught on their children, and when parents fight about discipline and how tight and how loose to be with the kids, they are often fighting about the image of themselves they want their children to bear with them into the world.

Now this is not altogether bad. Although parents have been warned repeatedly by childrearing books and articles that they dare not make their children "extensions of themselves," the fact is that children *are* extensions of their parents in many ways. Into our children we pour our beliefs, our ideals and our values: what we consider good and important and what we want them to value and consider good and important. Children are extensions of us when they carry what we prize most within them, and transmit our ideals to their children.

The problem with "extension" is that we sometimes become confused between what we want our children to value because those values will enhance their lives and their children's lives and what we want them to value because those values will enhance the way the world views us. "Extension" becomes bad when we become so hooked into instilling what we believe into our children that we forget where we end and they begin. We are allowed—I believe parents should be allowed—some ego involvement with our kids. We are allowed to feel proud when they perform well in school, or on the athletic field, or on a job, because that good performance is a reflection of values we taught them. And we are allowed to feel bad when they do not do well, bad for them if they are hurt and bad for us. What we are not allowed to do is lose sight of their own abilities and inclinations and squelch them or forget to cultivate them while we inject our ways of doing things into our offspring. We are not allowed to have kids make up for our personal failures, even while we encourage their success.

When parents grapple with problems of discipline, then, they are often grappling with themselves and each other.

In the strongest marriages I came to know, it seemed to me that the different ways of disciplining that parents brought to their marriage were not necessarily molded into one monolithic whole. The parents did not feel they had to arrive at a consensus all the time or always present a united front to their children. Rather, over time, each came to accept the other's natural inclinations and to work around them. Often one parent was the organized one, the one who saw to it that everything ran smoothly, and the other was the one who played, who amused the kids or humored them out of their troubles. Or one parent was the disciplinarian and the other the "pushover."

A wife and a husband spoke at length of the husband's strictness with the children. "Sometimes I feel as though I'm on an island," he said, "and the rest of them are out on the sea enjoying themselves. I have such a feeling of isolation at times when I see my wife and kids having fun together, and I'm alone worrying about all the dos and don'ts of life." Yet both he and his wife have realized that the very fact of his being the tough guy in the family has allowed her to be the easygoing one. "We fall into our roles," she said. "But if he weren't the policeman, I guess I would have to be."

Although parents' roles are not always as dissimilar as they are in this family, the differences that do exist allow parents to have separate and distinct relationships with their children.

The wisdom we have inherited as parents is that we must be consistent, we must stand together, we must not let the kids play one parent off against the other. Yet what many parents in strong, happy families know is that some inconsistency is good for children and that what family therapist Murray Bowen calls "parental we-ness" can be bad for children. Bowen writes of the detriment it is to a child to be locked into a "two-against-one" situation with parents in which the child feels overwhelmed by the alliance between parents, and can fight back only by somehow causing a rift between them. When parents relate to their child as individuals, as a male and a female with different ideas and different temperaments, the child gets a better understanding of how to get along with males and females and with people of different ideas and temperaments.

That is not to say that parents should disagree on every decision that affects the children, or should not try to arrive at some consensus on major matters. But on a day-to-day basis they do not have to agree on everything nor do they have to hide all their disagreements from their children. It is useful for kids to learn that parents can have different opinions, that they can argue and approach questions in different ways yet continue to respect and love one another. And parents have everything to gain from not trying to force each other into a mold of firm consistency, from not locking horns in a power struggle over whose way with the children is right, but acknowledging that both ways can be right.

Children can add pressures to a marriage and because of these pressures everybody, from great-grandmas to young Ph.D.'s in psychology, advises couples not to have children in order to save a failing marriage. (I know of only one troubled marriage that was saved by the addition of a baby. The troubles there, however, came from in-law interference. The wife's parents hated her husband and didn't hesitate to show their hatred. After the baby was born they were so thrilled to have a grandchild, they became more affectionate even to their son-in-law, and that brought a much-needed calmness to the marriage. But this case was an exception to a wise rule.)

All that has been discussed so far, however, may give the impression that children bring *only* tensions and discipline problems. So let's backtrack. Children change the life of a couple; they can cause conflicts in a marriage. These are truths that all parents know. They also know what one new father said to me, that having children is "everything. It's just everything." They know that children can inspire the greatest happiness, the greatest creativity and the greatest intimacy within marriage, and that the sources for the strains and conflicts are the very sources for the happiness, creativity and intimacy.

What can be more joyous and more creative than nurturing a child? What more breathtaking than striving to reach a balance between the child's abilities and possibilities and your own hopes, dreams and wishes for that child? If tension comes from that striving, so does excitement, so do riches. Raising a child means learning, constantly learning new things, and the learning adds richness and excitement to a marriage.

And what can lead to greater intimacy for a couple than uniting in the experience of shaping another being? Although children can be a buffer in a marriage, a screen that prevents partners from focusing clearly on one another, they can also be a compressor, a means of pushing partners tight up against one another. There are times in the course of a marriage when mates talk about nothing but the children, not as a way of avoiding other intimacies but because of their joint, passionate interest in those children. "You can't know how many hours my husband and I have spent in the bedroom trying to decide what school to send Kasey to," said a city mother, torn, as many others are, between public and private schooling for her child. Those moments of single-minded absorption in the children are also moments of intense attachment between partners.

The intimacy and closeness children bring to a marriage also stem from the second chance partners get to look at themselves and their own childhoods. I spoke earlier about the means people find to break from the past by becoming aware of the harmful or inhibiting effects of their early family lives. Rearing a child is a way of awakening that awareness. In their relationships with their children, parents have an opportunity to retrace their connections to their own parents. Although they cannot undo what was done to them, they can be aware enough not to repeat what they didn't like, and they can become closer by sharing their knowledge of the past and their awareness with one another. Even the arguments over children can bring partners nearer to each other. Because fights about children often push to the fore underlying issues in the marriage—issues of power, control, jealousy—they can help a couple get to those underlying issues and deal with them, if the partners are willing to step back from the immediate battles.

Finally, caring for kids together leads to changes in both partners, and these changes bring them closer. The actor mentioned above continued speaking: "Over the years my wife has loosened up and I've gotten tighter. I used to beat her over the head with her tightness about the kids. I used to say 'tight ass' and really get angry and fight dirty in front of the kids. Now I'm able to see what gets her tight and help her to see it. Now the children are doing many more things that I would like them to do, and that's with their mother's consent. It's a stretch for her, but she's risking it. As for me, I've learned more about helping the kids without making so many demands on them. I used to get so angry at my son when he wasn't doing well, and I would just walk away from him in disgust. Judy is different. She'll be in there with him for however long it takes to get him through and to help him in a very constructive way. It was what she did for me when I was young and just beginning in this acting racket. I've learned a lot from watching her with the children just as she's learned from me. We're both very involved with them, and it's a real bond between us."

The changing, the closeness, the creativity all become stretched—sometimes to the point of breaking—in families in which there is some problem with the children. In such families the strains may become more dominant than the pleasures, and only with effort are parents able to work their way around their children's difficulties to support one another.

Just as spouses begin marriage with great expectations, so parents look at a newborn baby with expectations only of perfection. An infant is so beautiful, so whole, so miraculous, it's easy to envision a future filled only with sunshine and rainbows. To the extent that we, as parents, are able, we try to create that future. And if, with time, we temper our expectations with the more limited realities of our children's abilities and potentials, we still swell with satisfaction at the offspring we have produced. If our kids are happy and successful at whatever they do, their happiness and success reassure us about our marriages, about our joint ideals and our ability as parents. If there are difficulties in the children, if in spite of everything, they have serious problems, parents feel somehow betrayed and diminished. They look at their children and they think of what they had hoped for, what might have been, and the hurt runs deep into their hearts.

I saw that hurt in Henry and Kathy Peters, the Kansas City couple who had strong religious differences. We had spent several hours talking about their life together and especially their religious views. They spoke lovingly of their five children and the close ties among them. At one point, I casually asked about their youngest son, Billy, who was away for the summer. The silence deafened me. Then:

"I'll be very candid," Henry said. "Billy was something I wasn't prepared to cope with."

Billy, sixteen, had been brain-damaged at birth, Henry went on to explain, not severely enough to be considered retarded, but enough to give him serious learning disabilities. The disabilities led to school failures, which led, as they so often do, to behavioral problems, including, most recently, drug abuse. But what hit Henry hardest were his son's academic inabilities, his lack of skills, the cutoff of any potential for the kind of middle-class life Henry and his other children enjoyed.

"No, I wasn't prepared for that in one of my children," he continued. "In terms of intellectual and educational things . . ." He broke off. He started again. "My father was a judge. My grandfather was a very, very bright man who quit school in the fourth grade and as a result was thirsty for knowledge."

"My heart aches for this child," Kathy cut in.

Later, I wrote myself a note: "Kathy's heart aches for Billy; Henry's ego aches." But it wasn't fair of me. "Our society," Henry had said, "is not willing to take people as they are, to say, 'Okay, forget it; you can have a worthwhile life without any schooling.' " In the Peterses' society, schooling and professional achievement mean everything. They are having to learn together to ignore society and concentrate on their son. As he gets older and goes out to seek work, they know they will have to accommodate themselves to his limitations so that he can live with himself.

"Billy looks at Henry and sees his success and ability to do whatever he wants to do," said Kathy, "and he just knows, he knows that he will never be like that."

Kathy is managing better at accommodating than Henry is. "Billy is special to me," she said with some feeling. "It's like anything else. The harder you work at something, the more it means to you." Henry still makes demands on the boy, still sets "tough standards," as if those demands will make Billy be like everyone else in his society. But he knows in his heart that will never happen, and he is coming around. With the help of Kathy, he is pulling back, trying to understand and accept. "It's frightening as hell for Billy," he said. "I feel so sorry for him, being so different." He looked at Kathy, and she smiled at him. They both feel the pain, a double pain, for the boy and for themselves. Together they're searching for a way to live with that double dose.

Another couple, the Percys, struggled with a fact about their children that is condemned far more by society than is a learning disability. The issue was the homosexuality of two of their three sons, and they handled it by becoming highly active and visible in an organization called Parents of Gays.

At first glance, Mark Percy hardly seemed the kind of parent who would be accepting of a homosexual son, let alone involved in an organization supportive of gay people. Tall, white-haired, dignified in a most straight-laced way, he had served as an Army officer for a good part of his life and had gone to work in the State Department upon retirement. His wife, Giselle, a lively, attractive woman, had been born in France. She spoke English rapidly with a charming French accent, a contrast to her husband's slow, measured, midwestern inflection. Both told the same story. They had found out about their eldest son's homosexuality about ten years ago when the young man was nineteen.

"It was Memorial Day weekend," Mark said, "and he was visiting us. He said he wanted to talk to us, but we had company over all day, and we just never got to talk. We had gone to bed, and there was a knock on our door, and he said, 'I *really* want to talk to you.' He looked very serious, and Giselle and I thought he was going to tell us he was engaged, because he had been going out with different girls we knew about. You can imagine our surprise when he said he wanted to tell us he was gay."

"What was your reaction?"

"Shock, I guess. Then my first question was, 'Are you sure? I mean, how do you know? Do you want to talk to somebody to make sure?' And he said, he knew and he didn't need to talk to anybody. And I was satisfied that he knew what he was talking about."

"Then, did you just accept him?"

"Well, we have never *not* accepted him. I mean he was the same boy he had been five minutes before."

Giselle spoke now, less authoritatively. More real.

"I was miserable at first. I thought, 'What did I do wrong?' And the next day I didn't dare go out shopping. I thought people could see it in my face. But then, a few days later, I had lunch with my son. I'll never forget it. It was wonderful. We talked about politics; we talked about books; we talked about museums; we talked about movies. And the fact of his being gay never even came up! I was so happy because I realized, as Mark did, that he's the same person, gay or not. When I got home, I pinched Mark and I said, 'You know, he's the same person!' Then I called my son up and I said, 'You're the same, but I need an education.' "

The Percys educated themselves about homosexuality by reading books and talking to other people. Then they joined the Parents of Gays organization and eventually became officers in it. By the time their second son told them about his homosexuality, they were more able to accept it than he was himself.

"Curtis knew we were backing his older brother, yet he couldn't tell us until he had come to grips with being gay himself," Giselle explained. "He resented his lot in life."

If the Percys resented their lot, they had decided not

to say so. I didn't trust the easy acceptance of their sons' homosexuality that they described. I didn't believe that Mark Percy, with his high Episcopalian manners and background, with his pride in his own father who had been a football hero at Harvard in the early 1900s, could be so comfortably acquiescent about his sons. I didn't believe that Giselle could go through just a few days of misery and then happily embrace her son's style of life.

What I did believe was this: At some point the Percys recognized, each in a separate way, that the sons they had raised would never live out all the dreams and expectations they had for them—the conventional dreams of homes and children and loving spouses that most parents want for their children—that, in fact, their unconventional lives would be disdained by much of society. Whatever anguish those realizations caused them they kept to themselves, speaking of their feelings only to one another and after a while putting those feelings aside. Instead of trying to change what they acknowledged could not be changed, they altered their own orientation, to their children, their marriage and society. They became a team dedicated to helping other parents and reeducating social attitudes. They became politicized. They appeared on the *Phil Donahue* show and on *Good Morning America.* They lectured around the country and gave interviews to magazines and newspapers. Because they could not turn their children's lives around, they turned their own lives around and in the process changed the nature of their marriage. "Our work with other parents and our commitment to our sons drew us together in a new way," said Giselle. "We became more honest with each other than we had ever been before, as a couple and as a family."

As children grow, the concerns of parents change. Couples find ways to bypass sexual interruptions caused by the presence of youngsters. They invent methods of keeping the kids out of their bedroom (many *do* lock their doors; and many let their kids know clearly that "Mommy and I want to be alone now"). They negotiate childrearing responsibilities and forms of discipline. They plan time to be alone, to reestablish the old intimacy, the kind that doesn't include a child. And then: Adolescence arrives to shatter whatever calm may have been established between a wife and a husband.

Children's teenage years, it has been said, mark the time when kids threaten out loud to run away from home, and parents make their own secret plans to do so. For some, those years are dark and dreadful woods in which teenagers have to fight to untangle themselves from their parents in order to find their true selves. As they do, their angers and tensions engulf the entire household. But even those who do not have violent outbursts of rage or days of withdrawn silence often have wild mood swings. One day they're sixteen and the next day they're six; one day they cry piteously to be given the independence they crave and need; the next day they want to be snuggled and kissed goodnight, comforted and reassured. Most disturbing for many couples are the intense rebellions their teenagers may undertake, turning against everything the parents hold and stand for. The professor's son who drops out of school and the conservative police officer's daughter who becomes involved in radical causes are cutting themselves free from parents in ways they hope will leave the deepest gashes. And they do. Parents blame themselves when their children reject them, and sometimes they blame each other.

Adolescents have been known to wreak havoc in a marriage when they align themselves with one parent, goading that parent into turning against the other. They may do this in order to manipulate and get what they want by weakening the bond between spouses; they may do it because they are frightened and insecure and they want to attach themselves to the one parent who seems strongest, safest or most comforting. In either case, parents become confused and hurt. It's one thing to relate independently to children, another to be ripped apart by a hostile and disruptive teenager. Parents may find themselves in vicious fights with each other as one feels left out, like the collapsed side of a triangle. Or the "outside" parent may retaliate by ignoring the child or trying to hurt him or her. (Neither reaction, of course, helps the marriage or the child—what works best is holding on to each other while trying to understand the teenager's needs.)

It sometimes happens in a marriage that has been

shaky all along, and even in some that have been steady, that parents themselves get caught up in teenage behavior. The excitement, the enormous sexuality of adolescents (one can almost see the hormones floating through the air around them), can be seductive and thrilling to parents who may be in the throes of fighting encroaching middle age during these years. The wife who has an affair with a younger man or the husband who begins hanging out at singles bars is acting out fantasies of being young and attractive like the kids, young and sexy and ready to fly from all responsibilities.

All these things may happen when children become adolescents. What may also happen is that a marriage is infused with a new vitality, a new zest because of the teenagers in the house. Not every adolescent becomes ferociously rebellious or bent on destroying parents in order to form a separate identity. Daniel Offer, a Chicago psychiatrist, has written extensively about normal teenagers who establish their independence and make the adolescent passage with a minimum of disruption in the family. What these and other teenagers bring to their homes is life and vigor.

Kids turn their parents on to new things—I know a couple who began hiking, skiing and taking long walks in the country, all inspired by their children, and continued these activities long after the children had moved away from home. Teenagers make adults think hard thoughts about ideas and motives, about convictions that had been comfortably accepted for years. They ask the difficult questions because they are looking for absolutes, for truths: Either you believe in God or you don't. If you do, why don't you observe every rule of your religion? If you don't, why do you observe any? Either you care about poor people or you don't. If you do, how can you live in a capitalistic society where people suffer poverty? If you don't, how can you stand yourself? They probe everything you hold dear, and they force you to probe yourself, to explain yourself to them and in the process to explain yourself to each other. Although few couples emerge with a completely new set of values as their children push through adolescence, many do emerge with a clearer idea of where they stand on a variety of issues. A liberal rabbi, for example, who has been outspoken in his views on providing women religious equality with men, said that he had given little thought to the subject until his teenage daughters had "opened his eyes" to existing inequalities.

The years of their children's adolescence are years when parents can be more open than ever before in revealing themselves—that is, in permitting their children to see them and know them as real people with concerns, insecurities and problems of their own. Kids should not be burdened with their parents' problems, but neither should they be sheltered from all of them. It helps parents to be able to be honest with their children about themselves; it helps children to know that parents have anxieties just as they do, that they have a shared history and life of their own beyond their life with their children. It helps children because it sensitizes them to adult problems, and encourages them to shift their thinking away from themselves onto others.

A mother of four spoke with a shaking voice about the fury and accusations her seventeen-year-old daughter heaped on her and her husband. This couple had inherited great wealth and loved to lavish it on their children. They dressed the youngsters in beautiful imported clothes when they were small and hired the finest nursemaids and governesses for them. Now the daughter has pointed an angry finger at them precisely because of the clothes, nursemaids and governesses. She hated the fancy dresses, she told them, and hated learning French and having to be on her best behavior all the time. And why didn't her parents take care of her themselves, she wanted to know, instead of having all those nurses for their children?

"I told her," said this woman, "that she was right, that her father and I had done many wrong things. But I also told her that she had to understand where we were coming from, that we are both persons with our own history and family and problems. This was a second marriage for both of us. We were trying to find our way with each other and trying not to repeat old mistakes. We wanted to make things perfect for our children. We tried our best even if we failed at some things. I wanted her to know that. I told her that the wrong things we did were not her whole life. We did some things right too. And I wanted her to know that everything didn't happen then. There is also now. We're still a family; we can help each other and go on from where we are now."

In some families the worst period of teenage turmoil is the year before a young person leaves home to strike out alone. It seems as though the only way some kids can separate from parents is for them to make home life so hateful that it is easier to leave and easier for parents to let them go.

Not that it's ever easy to let go, no matter what the commotion. When a child leaves home, even when there are plenty of children left behind, a void exists for everyone in the family. That pit in my stomach as I drop my daughter off at the camp bus every year is just a prelude, I know, to the emptiness I will feel when she leaves in a few years for a college away from home. Parents whose children are grown and gone speak of a sense of bereavement after they leave, a mourning for the laughter and the gladness that only the young can bring to a home.

But they also speak about relaxation and the relief of not having the daily responsibility of caring for children. For years, the "empty nest syndrome" was the most touted psychological theory about women's reactions to their children leaving home. Like mother birds without their young, women were described as being lonely and desolate when their babes flew off. More recently experts and laypeople have recognized that the "empty nest" feeling can hit fathers as hard as mothers, forcing them to face their own aging along with their longing for their children; and that for many women and their husbands, the "honeymoon suite" eventually replaces the "empty nest." These are the couples who find new pleasures in one another once their children are away, taking up old hobbies, traveling, going to movies or plays together. Although they may miss their children terribly, they are able to stack up other satisfactions, applying their freed-up energies now to areas that had lain dormant. A woman who had devoted herself to her children summed it up: "I've given and I've taken. Now it's time for Jerry and me."

The new freedom from child care does, of course, stir up new adjustment issues. Alone for the first time in maybe twenty years, husbands and wives need to face one another head on, almost need to get acquainted again. "It's an entirely new grid now," said the father of a college-bound only son. "It's so strange," said a woman whose second child had joined the first in taking a job out of town. "I became pregnant in my fourth month of marriage. We hardly knew each other then, and once the children were born they became the center of our lives. Even when they weren't home, so much of our time was spent thinking about them and planning for them. Now they're really gone, and we're both feeling almost shy with each other. Who is this other person? What do we know about each other?"

Sometimes the young ones who have flown away feel guilty themselves about having abandoned their parents (a reversal of the pervasive guilt that seems to go with the territory of being a parent). A college student described being "worried sick" that her parents might split when she left for school. "What would they talk about, I kept thinking," she said with a laugh. "I thought the only thing they ever talked about was us kids, and since I'm the youngest and last one to leave, they'd have nothing left in common." As it has turned out, her parents seem to be doing just fine without her, her mother beginning a career as a social worker, her father taking time out to read, play golf and relax in ways he never had a moment for in earlier years.

And other things take place in the postnesting years. Many women who devoted themselves to rearing children now go back to school or launch new careers or return to occupations they had left years earlier. The transition causes some discomfort in most households and greater upheavals in others, and with good reason. At the very point when husbands may be thinking of retiring and spending more time with their wives, the wives are becoming more caught up in outside work and interests. The other side of this coin, however, is that with the changes in their work schedules and interests, husbands and wives get a chance to develop those sides of themselves that had been undeveloped for most of their lives: she, the aggressive, "masculine" side; he, the more sensitive, emotional "feminine" side, and in that development they are able to draw closer in understanding and appreciating each other.

Lest anyone think, however, that when children leave home, they stay away for good, consider this: The number of young adults still living at home with parents increased by 85 percent between 1970 and 1983. Some of these young men and women had never left home; many others have returned. Why? They couldn't find jobs or apartments. They were between marriages or live-in partners. Or simply because it's comfortable and cheap to live at home with the folks.

A group of researchers at the Family Institute of Westchester studying this growing phenomenon of what is called "delayed launching" has found that many parents feel disappointed and irritated when their children move back home and that the return interferes with the quality of their marriage. Said Kenneth Terkelsen, a psychiatrist and director of the project, "People have been looking forward to that period of time when they can be alone and together and get to know one another again. Then the kid shows up." Terkelsen said that although some couples made a point of telling his interviewers how much they liked having their children back again, the great majority of others expressed unhappiness.

Along with the unhappiness or disappointment some parents feel when grown children reappear at their doorstep come a certain amount of confusion about loyalties.

Who comes first, a spouse or a child? This is a question that runs through all family relationships, and in the best of marriages, the answer changes with the years. When children are young and parents need to devote most of their attention to them, a woman may be more a mother than a wife; a man more a father than a husband. With time the alignments shift back and forth, depending on the immediate needs of the children and the parents. Mates who are so locked into each other that their children feel excluded much of the time may believe they have a good marriage, but they do their children a disservice. On the other hand, children always press for the most they can get of each parent, and parents have to be on guard to save part of themselves for each other. As children grow up, the part parents put aside for themselves becomes larger, the part for the children smaller. That is why when grown children return home or bring their problems to their parents, parents may become confused or distressed. Where do they place their allegiances now? How far do they extend themselves for their children and how far for each other?

A Canadian woman, Stephanie Falkner, has been torn by just such questions and by the decision she felt she had to make. Stephanie and her husband, Jack, live in Sarasota, Florida. They moved there from their lifetime home in Canada four years ago after Jack suffered a stroke. Although he recovered well from the illness, it became the impetus for him to make the move to Florida that he had long wanted to do.

"I hated the cold weather in Canada; I hated the accounting business I was in. I felt I was constantly fighting the clock, that one day I would just drop dead from the cold and the overwork," Jack argued, sounding as though he were trying to convince me. Actually, I knew that the target of his argument was Stephanie, who had resisted Jack's urgings to move to Florida for years. She had family and friends and a comfortable life in Canada. She knew all the shopkeepers, worked for volunteer organizations, had neighbors who greeted her whenever she walked out her door.

But the most important thing the Falkners had in Canada were children—three grown children, an eighteen-year-old daughter and twenty-year-old son who lived with them, and a twenty-three-year-old married son who lived a few blocks away. Stephanie didn't want to move to Florida and leave her children behind in Canada, and the children refused to leave Canada.

"I did something that went against my grain," she said, her voice tight with emotion. "I have such a tremendous sense of guilt at leaving my children. I know they were grown up, but they still needed me. We were so close and now I hardly ever see them. I miss them enormously and I miss my old way of life."

"We had to go," Jack said softly.

"Let's be honest," Stephanie's voice was harsh now. "You *wanted* to go. You complained for twenty-five years."

She stopped. "I guess we had to go after Jack had the stroke. He was so young when it happened—not even fifty—that it had to mean something was wrong with the way he was living. And he's been trying so hard to see a light at the end of the tunnel for me. Things are getting better."

No one can say Stephanie has been gracious about her move to Florida, and no one can deny that this marriage has been shaken. Yet it will survive and steady itself because she has made up her mind about her priorities. Alone, she said to me, "This has been a wrenching experience for me, and I know that my unhappiness has made it harder for Jack. The children came first for a long time in my life, and it was difficult to change that way of thinking. In spite of all my bitching, Jack knows that now he's number one. I belong with him. This is where we started and this is where we'll end, together."

If priorities become ambiguous in what the social scientists call "intact" nuclear families, they become almost chaotic in families of stepparents and stepchildren. Studies show that more than 40 percent of remarriages end in divorce within five years and the largest proportion of these are marriages that involve children from a previous marriage. Indications are that remarried couples without children have the highest chance for success, followed by those with grown children and those with children only of their own marriage. Marriages that include children from one spouse's previous marriage rank next, and those with children from both their previous marriages have the least promising outlook. No wonder. The more people involved in a relationship, the more complex it becomes, and the greater the chances of problems. The complications can be myriad. For example:

How does a parent arrange adequate time to be with a new spouse and children so that no one feels cheated?

How does a new spouse exert authority over stepchildren without stepping on the tender toes of biological parents?

Who pays for what and for whose children?

What happens if a stepparent doesn't like her or his partner's children? "My kids are very bright, animated and fun to be with," one newly remarried woman told me. "His kids are limited, mundane people. They're the kind of people that in no way would I have anything to do with, except that they are part of the package." I wondered how well that package would hold up.

And if the children don't like the stepparent? One teenage daughter gave her father a "her or me" ultimatum. The father chose his new wife, but is anguished because he no longer sees his daughter.

How does a remarried couple, both with children from previous marriages, carve out time and space for themselves? One such couple, married now for eighteen years, took the children of both their former marriages on their honeymoon with them. A good time was had by all, and warm family feelings launched the new marriage. But that was a risky undertaking, and for another couple it might have caused disaster.

Is it possible for a couple to have romance and passion in their new marriage when stepchildren are constantly underfoot? Sometimes the romance and sexuality with which a remarriage begins stimulates sexual fantasies and feelings among children, especially teenagers, causing new strains between stepparents and stepchildren.

All the combinations of feelings and frictions, the ambivalences of love and hate that parents and children both experience, the competition, jealousies and resentments that color relationships in first marriages become intensified in remarriages that include children from former marriages. "The worst of it is," said a man recently remarried to a woman who had custody of two sons, "that you have no role models. Most of us came from intact homes. We try to recreate the same kind of home we had, but it's so different with stepchildren. For every one of us, it's like reinventing the wheel."

I spoke at great length about that reinvention to an unusual woman, Allie Vail, who, in addition to having married a man with three young daughters, spends part of her time living thousands of miles away from her husband and his children.

Allie is a fashion designer, known among the young

for unconventional, somewhat flamboyant sports clothes that take their cue from Japanese stylists. Her husband, Russell, is also a designer, and the two run a business together, she from New York, he from San Francisco. The arrangement has worked beautifully from a business standpoint and—at least for the eight years they have been married—from a personal standpoint as well. The two spend ten days together each month in San Francisco, ten days together in New York and ten days apart, when she is in New York and he is in San Francisco. They spend two weekends a month in San Francisco, one weekend in New York and one apart.

A complicated-enough situation, made more complicated by the presence in San Francisco of his three daughters. Allie was married once before, just for a year, just long enough to know she had made a mistake and to end the marriage before having children, and she regards Russell's children almost as her own. Although Russell does not have custody of the girls, who now range in age from eleven to fifteen, he does have visiting rights for weekends, holidays and a month in the summer. His divorce was of the vituperative order. He had walked out on a marriage that outwardly seemed perfect; inwardly, in Russell's words, "it lacked passion, intimacy and communication." His former wife has never forgiven him, and makes no effort to conceal her bitterness from her children.

Although Allie met Russell after his divorce, that has not prevented his former wife from being strongly antagonistic toward her. "I wanted to be her friend," said Allie, remembering the naive dreams of her first year of remarriage. "After all, I'm with her children every weekend. But it hasn't been possible. Even though I'm not responsible for the breakup of her marriage, she blames me, and she lets the girls know how desperately unhappy she is." Still, Allie is pleased that the children have never turned to her and said, "You're not our mother," or "What are you doing here?" or "I hate you." The fact that they haven't she credits to Russell. "He obviously made it very clear to them, one, how much he loves me, two, how terrific he thinks I am, and three, that I wasn't in any way taking him away from them."

Allie is being modest in giving Russell all the credit.

From the day she married him, she made a conscious effort to understand his children and involve herself in their lives. "I didn't rush things," she said. "I don't believe in instant love. I told them, 'You and I don't have to love one another. Your parents have to love you; my parents have to love me. Russell has to love me and I him. But *we* don't have to love one another, so we have to work extra hard at learning to do so.' And we have. At least I have, because I know how much those kids mean to Russell. When he doesn't see them, he misses them. He speaks to them on the phone every night—you know, he needs his fix."

When Allie gets off the plane in San Francisco on a Saturday, Russell and his children meet her at the airport. From there the first stop is the supermarket, where they shop for weekend supplies. "We stock up on kid food," Allie explained, "then we go home, eat and talk. Before we know it, it's Monday and the workweek starts." They don't work an ordinary nine to five day—there are fashion showings, press parties or meetings many evenings, so that weekends become their time together, time to relax. "As much as I love those girls," Allie said, "I look forward to our one precious weekend alone in New York. In San Francisco when the children are around, they're really *around*. Russell and I sit down to talk and there's a child there—'Hi, what are you talking about?' There's never any privacy with a child around."

"In all honesty," I asked, "don't you resent those children?"

"I don't resent the children," she answered, "but sometimes I resent the situation. Our vacation two years ago is an example. We all went away together over Christmas, to a beautiful ski lodge in Utah. Everybody had a terrific time, except me. At first I didn't understand why; I just knew I was having a bad time. Then, afterward, when Russell and I were alone in New York, I said, 'I know why the vacation was awful for me. It's because there wasn't enough of you to go around. As much as I adore your children and they adore me, it's you we really want. We are all desperate to have time with you.' "

Allie thought for a minute. "I am grown up, Francine," she said. "I know that everybody can't come first all the time. I think there are times when the kids really should come first. But I decided on that vacation that I have to come first more. I didn't come first enough of the time and I felt I should say so."

There it is again, the question of who comes first, spouse or children? In a remarriage with children present, it's a question that never disappears, and Allie accepts that. "You go into a situation like that," she said, "and you're mindful of all the things you shouldn't do. You do not ask a father to choose between you and his children. One feels tempted to do just that, but I know nobody wins that way." The way to win, she decided after that vacation, was to speak out when she had to, but also to cut down on their social and business life to free up more of their evenings and provide time alone for the two of them. She has found, also, as have many stepparents, that as the children have grown, "they have become more relaxed. They know Russell loves them, and that he left the marriage and not them. They know I love them and that I'm not trying to take him away from them. They're ready to know now that we have a life and we have a relationship of our own."

The one bumpy area that has not been worked out in this complex, long-distance marriage is an issue that in a traditional nuclear family would be decided between husband and wife, but in stepfamilies is often a group decision: Should Allie and Russell have a baby of their own?

"The discussions are endless, and everybody has something to say." Allie winced. "I'm going on forty, so I have to decide very quickly. Russell would love to have another child. The girls are ambivalent. Sometimes they think it would be wonderful because the baby would be "related" to them through their father, and that would make us all closer as a family. Other times they worry that I might love the baby more than I love them because this one would be mine. The one thing they're sure about is that if we have a baby it has to be a boy. They're not interested in having another girl around."

Ultimately, Allie knows the decision will have to be hers. "If I don't have a child," she reasoned, "I will always in some ways be wistful about having missed out on that. But I don't think I will be devastated. When I think of having a child, I think of having to give up time with Russell, and I don't know that I want to delay having that kind of time with him for another eighteen years. Given the three children I already share with him, I'm not sure I'm willing to give up any more of my time. When we're alone together, it's wonderful, and after all, that's why we got married."

To be together is, after all, why all couples marry. In stepfamilies, that priority can get lost as parents and children jockey for position. When remarriages and stepfamilies turn out well, as Allie's seems to be doing, the priorities eventually sort themselves out, as they do in all happy families.

Like Allie's stepchildren, more than a million kids have their homes disrupted by divorce every year, and about one child in six is part of a stepfamily. Apart from the unhappiness divorce arouses in children, experts wonder how living through a divorce affects a child's own view of marriage. Will the children of divorce want to marry? Will they stay married?

The most extensive studies of the effects of divorce on children have been made by Judith S. Wallerstein, a psychologist at the University of California at Berkeley, who began studying the children in sixty divorced families in 1970, and followed them during the next ten years. Among other things, she found that many children continue to suffer emotionally years after their parents divorce. As they get older, some avoid marrying altogether, and some postpone it, determined not to "rush in," as their parents did. Others express anger at their parents' mistakes, and vow not to fail in their marriages themselves.

Whether the marriages of these children will succeed, Wallerstein and others maintain, depends to a large extent on how the children are made to feel about their parents and themselves after the divorce. Children benefit most, these experts say, when both parents stay in contact with the children and with one another so that they can cooperate in caring for their offspring. They benefit, also, when their parents treat one another respectfully and regard one another as worthwhile human beings in spite of what has happened between them.

For years, common wisdom held that no matter how bad a marriage was, it should be kept together "for the sake of the children." In the past twenty years or so that maxim has been turned on its head to read that children reared in a home in which the parents stayed together only for their sake would be more damaged than if the parents split. Given the high divorce rate today and the number of children living with a single parent, nobody is quite sure anymore which "truth" is the more accurate. What everyone does agree on is that children do best in themselves and in their later marriages when they grow up in a home with a strong, good marriage as their model.

Allie Vail, determined to keep her commuter marriage working and working well, held up her parents' marriage of forty-five years as an example for her. "Their marriage has not always been perfect," she said. "There have been better decades and worse decades, but they've always been close. When I see what they have, I know that what I want for myself is possible."

Children change marriages and marriages shape and affect children for generations to come.

CHAPTER NINE

~

Crisis!
"You've Got to Keep Living"

Conventional wisdom has it that when trouble comes, families pull together, helping one another through hard times no matter what the underlying differences that divide members. Religious teaching tells us that suffering leads to salvation and that pain purifies, freeing humans of such base emotions as lust, greed or envy. Romantic lore holds that tragedy deepens the love between a man and a woman, and that shared grief leads to a unity of souls.

All of the above are possible responses to a crisis in a marriage. None of the above acknowledges the feelings of anger, hatred, despair and hopelessness that may be other responses. Divorce statistics have not been refined enough to indicate just how many marriages break up because some unexpected crisis shatters the equilibrium a family has established, but I would wager that the numbers are not small. Although the marriages that last in spite of a tragedy or a sudden blow may emerge stronger as a result of the crisis, most carry with them scars of pain and suffering that never completely vanish.

What happens to a marriage when a crisis hits? To gather information, I sought out couples in lasting marriages who had experienced some devastating event that set their marriage reeling off course and questioned them about their reactions, about the factors that may have pulled them apart and those that drew them closer.

One couple had struggled for four years with infertility problems. Eventually they adopted twin girls, and when we met, they were happily involved in rearing their children. But they had not forgotten the unhappiness of those earlier years. Fewer remedies for infertility existed then (although that was only about twelve years ago), and little had been written in the popular press about it. For the wife, there had been almost unbearable shame and guilt when she first began to realize that she might have an infertility problem. Was she being punished because she had postponed having children early in her marriage?

After medical tests revealed that both wife and husband had low fertility potentials, each went through a stage of secretly blaming the other, goaded by their physicians. Her gynecologist, frustrated that the fertility pills he fed her and the painful hormone injections he gave her had helped her to ovulate but not to conceive, said more than once, "It's clear that the problem lies with your husband." His urologist returned the favor, assuring him that with the medication he was receiving, his sperm count was more than adequate to father a child. "I hated myself for thinking it," this woman told me, "but I couldn't rid myself of the idea that if I had married someone else, I could have been a mother. After all, there is more than one person in the world any of us can marry."

Although the same thoughts crossed her husband's mind, just as often he tortured himself with blame. "I wanted a baby terribly," he said, "but I wasn't obsessed the way Patty was. It was all she could talk or think about, and the more we spoke, the more miserable I became. I felt so guilty and inadequate. For a while I thought the best thing would be for her to leave me. I used to pick fights all the time, thinking, I guess, that if I could provoke her into leaving me, she could marry someone who could give her a baby."

He had begun to think the marriage could no longer work. He felt less than a man, and mixed with his guilt, he was also angrily resentful of his wife who, it seemed to him, "rubbed my nose in my 'unmanliness.'" The stresses on both didn't help their sex life, nor did the schedule their doctors set for them. Intercourse, the specialists taught them, had to be precisely timed just before the wife ovulated to guarantee the best chance of pregnancy. To establish the right moment, the wife had to take her temperature daily.

In some ways, the husband said, what finally saved their marriage was the misery of that daily temperature ritual and the rigidity of their "sex schedule." One day, after another month had passed and Patty was not pregnant, they just looked at one another and decided to call off the entire ritual. "I threw away my thermometer and canceled all my appointments with the gynecologist," she said. "I finally decided that my marriage was more important." Soon afterward, they began adoption procedures. Both concede that if adoption had been as difficult then as it is today, their marriage would have suffered still other pressures. But they maintain, and I believe them, that they would have found a way to cope because they had come to a new understanding about themselves.

Another couple spoke of the devastation to their marriage when the wife, Amy, became severely depressed. Amy is a private nurse in great demand because of her combination of efficiency and charm. When her depression began, she could barely drag herself to work. "I thought I was going slowly out of my mind," she recalled. "Sometimes I'd sleep all day, get up for a little while and then go back to bed. When I was awake, all I did was cry." She entered therapy for a few months, discussed relationships with her parents that had troubled her, felt much better and decided she was cured. When her symptoms returned, she undertook an extensive therapeutic program, "doing the work I should have done in the first place." Among other things, Amy began to realize that she was "tired of being superwife, supermom and supernurse." She had to learn to give up some responsibilities and some of the control she exercised over the lives of her husband and four children.

While she was learning this, however, her husband Nick was having to be superhusband and superfather. "She would cry for hours," he remembered. "I tried to keep a stiff upper lip but I was scared. I had weeks of sleepless nights. I was so worried that she would try to kill herself." Sometimes Nick would lie in bed next to his wife, cradling her in his arms like a baby until she stopped crying. He felt helpless and somehow guilty, as if everything that was happening to her were his fault. "I called her therapist," he said. "I offered to help, and I told him about my fears that I was to blame. He assured me I wasn't, but you know you still have those nagging doubts, you still blame yourself in a thing like this, although logically you know you can say, 'It has nothing to do with me.'"

Amy was well and back at work for about a year when I spoke with the two of them, but I had the impression that Nick tiptoed around her, as if afraid that the slightest pressure would set her back. Privately, when he wasn't commiserating with the despair she had experienced, he was a bit impatient about what he felt was her judgmental attitude toward her mother that had emerged from her therapy. "She came out of all this hating her mother," he complained, "and that disturbs me because I love her mother. I understand that there are things Amy experienced with her that I haven't. Still, I wonder. At some point you have to stop blaming your parents for everything wrong with you."

None of this would he dare say to Amy. It was as though her illness had left a crack in the marriage, not deep enough to shatter their union, but there nevertheless, a weak point that had not existed before. Nick couldn't be completely honest with her anymore, and that put a certain distance between them. If Amy stays well, the crack will probably seal over, bringing them close again. For now, they remain shaky in themselves and with each other.

A third couple were still in the midst of a trauma that had totally disrupted their lives. The husband, once an executive in a large publishing house, had been out of a job for two years. In his late forties, he was not an easy candidate for a new job. Although he had received generous severance pay, the money was quickly going. His wife, headmistress of a small private girl's school, had taken on tutoring assignments outside of school to supplement her income, now the only steady source of money in the family.

Both spouses were angry and sympathetic with each other at the same time. He was grateful to her for the extra workload she had assumed, but he hated feeling financially dependent on her. Although he conceded that she was right in expecting him to run the household because he was home and she wasn't, he resented buying groceries, cleaning the house and keeping track of their two teenage sons. He wanted to see himself as the executive he had once been, and spent as much time as possible writing applications and proposals for free-lance books projects to various companies. Meanwhile, she sympathized with his plight and his loss of self-esteem because of it, but she had little patience for his complaints. "Women can stay home and do all these things and that's okay," she said angrily, "but when a man has to do domestic chores, it's suddenly a state affair."

She was also scared—both were. What if he were never to find work? She had not bargained on being the breadwinner in the family; she liked the sense of freedom she had always had at work, knowing she could quit if she wished. He wanted her to have that freedom yet he suspected that even when he did get a job, neither of them would enjoy the security they had once had. The one glimmer of optimism both expressed was new insight into the other's life. "I understand the kind of pressure men are under," the wife said, "knowing they have to stay on a job, and they have to work to support their families." He, in turn, acknowledged "the pressures of being a working wife," with responsibilities at home and outside, which he had never completely comprehended before. Yet those perspectives give off only small rays of light at the moment, as the months roll by and the future remains elusive. "There is no way this will split us," the wife insisted. "We have too many memories stored up in the bank, too much between us. But if things ever get better, it will take us some time to get over what we have been through."

Sadnesses cannot be measured nor misfortunes weighed so that an outside observer can say, "Yes, yours is bad, but his is worse." Every person who suffers a severe illness, a major disappointment or a cruel setback in life can testify to the weight of his or her own burden. Yet, it seemed to me that those couples who had experienced the death or disabling illness of a child had gone through a special hell that nothing in our world could eradicate.

Describing the discovery of her son Jody's severe handicap, Helen Featherstone writes, in *A Difference in the Family:*

"When I was twenty-five, a friend told me that her brother had been killed in a motorcycle accident two years earlier. She said, 'Nothing bad had ever happened to me before.' I turned this statement over in my mind for a long time. What could she mean? Bad things happen to everyone—even the luckiest people. Two years later I learned that my newborn son was blind; on that day I remembered her words. Now I understood them. I knew that nothing bad had ever happened to me before."

In marriage, when a child is desperately ill or dies, all the strains that may already exist, all the differences that have shown themselves over the years, all the weaknesses and sore points become magnified to almost blinding visibility. The clarity can destroy the marriage; or it can bring new insights.

A woman described leaving her husband after the death of their daughter from leukemia. The separation came not from the child's illness or death per se, but from the husband's way of handling the tragedy. Shortly after the little girl's illness was diagnosed as being incurable, he began drinking heavily, and the drinking continued through the agonizing months of illness. He was fired from his job because of it, and then spent his time in self-pitying bouts with the bottle or in furious battle with his wife, whom he somehow blamed for the misfortune. The scenes between husband and wife were so exhausting that neither had energy to spare to focus on the real horror, the slow death of their only daughter. In a way, the fighting served to shield them from the full reality of the pain they were undergoing, but it also prevented them from supporting one another or helping their daughter cope with the terror of what was happening to her. With her death, any glimmer of love or sympathy that may have existed between them was gone. The wife left, and is trying to salvage a bit of herself in order to make a new life. The husband made a suicide attempt, and is now hospitalized in a psychiatric ward.

Two couples discussed earlier, the Winters and the Gilberts, both lost sons, the Winters to leukemia, the Gilberts in an automobile accident. Those losses have overshadowed every other problem in these couples' lives— the alcoholism of Claudia Winters, the alcoholism and manic-depressive illness of George Gilbert. Yet both marriages have remained intact, and in both the partners have strengthened each other in ways they could not have done before.

A third couple has a different story. It centers around a daughter who was supposed to have died and didn't, and around living with the consequences of a child's serious illness. For me this couple epitomize the stress, anxiety, anger, humor, love and courage that mark those marriages that endure in spite of and beyond a crisis.

The first time I met Tony and Marie Augustine was in their pretty suburban home in Oak Park, outside Chicago. Like others I had interviewed, they were somewhat nervous when we began, and spoke hurriedly, as if to get the whole thing over with. They began by telling me about all the couples they knew who had split because of the death or illness of a child, each remembering another incident.

"There was Eddie and Jenny. Their daughter was anorexic."

"Yeah, and then there was Holly and Joey. Their son died of an overdose of heroin."

"And what about Andy and Lisa? What happened after their kid got meningitis?"

"All these marriages went along fine until this one thing happened to their children. They even went through the crisis together. Then they broke up."

"They all broke up."

"And you," I asked, "how come you haven't succumbed as your friends did?"

"I've never considered divorce a viable alternative," Marie answered immediately. "It's different with this new generation. They consider divorce an alternative. But for people like us it's never an alternative. And when it's never an alternative, you don't consider it."

"But," Tony objected, "they all married the same time we did." He turned to me and, clasping his hands like a champ, said, "twenty-eight years in March," then went on: "Divorce wasn't a viable alternative when they got married either. Just like us, they never thought of it; but then it happened."

"So?" I asked.

"I can't imagine life without him," Marie answered. "I absolutely cannot."

"Me neither," Tony agreed. "I know the best thing that ever happened to me was marrying Marie. I'd be lost without her. Sounds mushy, huh?"

"No," I replied honestly. "It sounds wonderful."

"But wait." He held up his hand. "Let's be honest." He was beginning to relax. I would find, over the course of many hours, that Tony Augustine had a passion for honesty—and not only for honesty, but for exploring all the nuances of his feelings. It was as though, now that he was going to open up to me, he would ignore nothing, leave no bruise unexamined.

"Let's be fair," he continued. "I would be lost without her. But there have been times during this crisis in our lives when I seriously considered leaving. I didn't consider divorce. I didn't get to the point of thinking, 'After you leave you have to make provisions for your wife and children, and then you have a legal separation and then you have a divorce.' I didn't get to that point. I just wanted to get out and leave—run away. I have to be honest. I have thought of running away from it all."

A split second of silence was followed by Marie's laughter. "I wish you had told me," she said, "I would have said, 'Wait for me; I'll pack my bags.' "

I could see that as painful as the material we were going to discuss was, it would be possible to talk to these people. They had a certain verve, both of them, a warmth that came through even the most stressful moments of our meetings. And there were many such moments. The Augustines' account of their life and the life of their daughter Julie was a story of illness, despair, medical ineptitude and years of anxiety and heartache, stretching back to the 1960s and continuing today.

Twenty-year-old Julie is the Augustines' middle child. They have an older son, Alex, and a younger daughter, Linda. Like the other children in the family Julie had been a happy, chubby, delightful baby. And the Augustines, living modestly in their Oak Park home, were like hundreds of other middle-class couples, concerned about finances, busy with their children, occupied with the everyday matters of life.

When Julie was seven, she was stricken with a rare, incurable children's disease, in which the child usually deteriorates rapidly and then dies. Physicians predicted that she had, at most, eighteen months to live. Although they would treat her with every available medication, they saw no hope for survival.

"She's a special child now," the oncologist told Marie. "Hold on to her. Give her every drop of love you can, then you will know you have done your best."

Heartsick, the Augustines followed their physician's advice. They said nothing about Julie's illness or impending death to their other children—in any event, little Linda would have been too young to understand, and they reasoned that they could explain to Alex later, when the end was closer. For themselves, they hovered over their beloved child. They catered to her every whim, denied her nothing. "Such a short time," they told one another. "We'll have her for only a precious moment and then she'll be gone." And they wept together.

Miraculously, the eighteen months stretched to two years, then to three years, as Julie responded to new, experimental medications. Still the doctors predicted only disaster. "We'll keep her alive as long as we can," one specialist after another promised the Augustines, "but don't get your hopes up. There's no chance of long-term survival. It's amazing she has gone on until now."

"But what should we tell her?" Marie pleaded with the internist who followed Julie's case on a regular basis. Because of the medications she was given regularly, her illness was generally kept under control, but at the slightest cold or sign of fever—things that other children shrugged off—she was taken to the doctor and subjected to an array of new treatments. At times medications didn't work, and she would run dangerously high fevers accompanied by excruciating muscle pains. Yet nobody explained those fevers or pains to her.

"Say nothing to her," the internist insisted. "You don't tell a young child she's going to die. Just keep assuring her that she'll be fine. And keep watching her carefully; the slightest cold could kill her."

Time moved on, and Julie was twelve years old, still surviving, still under intensive medical care, still ignorant of the nature of her illness. She knew only that sometimes she got sick, and at those times, she could get anything she wanted from her parents (although she usually got what she wanted at other times too). She knew that she could count on being treated differently and more leniently than her brother and sister; that she couldn't play closely with other children because they might hurt her; that her teachers acted as though she were special, never demanding anything of her or scolding her no matter how she misbehaved in class. And she knew about examinations, about injections and about medications, one kind after the next. She had injections that made her bones brittle and others that made her break out in rashes, medicines that made her desperately nauseous, and others that made her blow up like a tub. She became known as a "regular" in the outpatient department of the local hospital because many of the medications had to be given intravenously, a painful process in itself. Since none of the specialists could say exactly what it was that kept her alive, she was given everything turned up by new research, in the hope that one thing or another would finally prove the right cure for her illness.

One day, soon after Julie turned thirteen, Marie overheard her speaking to a friend who had apparently asked why she spent so much of her time going to doctors. "I think my parents have volunteered me for medical experiments by scientists," she said nonchalantly. "They get extra money that way."

"It was horrible, horrible," Marie recalled. "We were so busy trying to protect her by not telling her what was wrong, we never even thought about all the fantasies she must be having, all the reasons she was giving herself for the craziness of her life. We decided now to tell her the truth, no matter what would happen."

Always dedicated to doing what was "right" and "best" for their daughter, the Augustines consulted a social worker for advice on how to tell the child she had a deadly illness. The social worker counseled them to break the news to the entire family, act very normal and at all costs avoid frightening Julie.

"We followed her advice exactly," Marie related, "just as we had followed the doctors' advice all along. We went away with all the kids for a weekend and we told them about Julie's illness. We were calm and reassuring—so much so that none of them realized how dreadful this disease was. Julie seemed relieved to find out there was something truly wrong with her, and we weren't simply tormenting her with medicines. She went back to school and she said, 'Hey, kids, I'm really sick!' There was a terrible reaction from the other kids. They went home and told their parents and came back treating her as though she were dead."

Julie became depressed and angry, enraged at her parents, her schoolmates, the world. She blamed Tony and Marie for not telling her the truth earlier, during all those years when she was suffering from medications, and then she turned around and blamed them for telling her the truth even now, forcing her to face the fact of her probable death. They responded by apologizing and explaining, apologizing for everything they did, explaining everything that had to be done to her. More than ever, they catered to her slightest wish.

Through it all, the experimental treatments continued. At one point during that same year of revelation, Julie received medication that made her ravenously hungry. She couldn't control her appetite, became so heavy that no clothes were large enough for her, then deeply depressed because of her weight. A psychiatrist the Augustines consulted about her weight recommended having her see a hypnotist who might teach her to hypnotize herself into not eating. Timorously, Julie walked into the hypnotist's office, her parents a step behind her. "Crazy to begin with," the Augustines later realized, the hypnotist stared at the enormously overweight teenager in front of him, snickered for a moment, then called out, "How's your sex life?"

"Sex life?" shouted Julie, without missing a beat, "I'm thirteen and I'm hungry." She glared at her parents. "Let's get out of here," she cried, "I want to go to McDonald's." With that, the three of them turned around and walked out of the hypnotist's office, never to return.

At the age of seventeen, Julie was pronounced free of disease. Her recovery was so rare, it was presented at a national conference of medical specialists. All agreed that she no longer showed any trace of illness, and that while nobody knew exactly what medication had cured her, all medication should be discontinued. Julie had been under treatment for ten years and was now considered fit to resume normal life.

The only problem was that she had never had a normal life and didn't know what it entailed. Sheltered by the shadow of death that had tagged after her, exempt from all responsibilities at home and at school, she had not learned how to get along with children or adults. She knew nothing about sharing or closeness, nothing about cooperating with family or friends, working hard to meet challenges and prove one's worth. Her expertise lay in making demands and manipulating others.

"You suddenly get smart," Marie said, "and by then it's too late. When I saw what was happening to Julie, I went to her teachers and pleaded with them, 'Please, please, treat her like anybody else; demand the same work from her that you do from the others.' They agreed with me, and they meant well, but they couldn't cope any better than we could. All Julie had to do was complain about a headache and she was excused from any assignments." She was intelligent enough to get by in all her courses, even in high school, but, said Marie, "She doesn't know anything. She doesn't know basic arithmetic, she doesn't know how to think. She's simply uneducated."

As uneducated as she was, Julie managed to get herself accepted to a small, midwestern college. Positive that she would not be able to cope with the demands of any college, the Augustines pleaded with her to drop the idea of going. Her response: "You don't think I can do anything." Then she sulked for days, reminding them that

her plight was their fault. Within three months, she had
returned from college. At the first tests, the first term
papers, the first expectations, she turned around and came
home. She wasn't about to be told what to do.

"Then," Tony traced the recent past, "she went ba-
nanas. She got a job as a waitress at a sleazy nightclub on
State Street." When she came home at all, it was usually
drunk or stoned. Many nights she simply stayed away.
"We knew she was sleeping around with anyone and
everyone," Tony said. And if they'd had any doubts, the
two abortions they were asked to pay for dissipated them.
It didn't help the family much when she took her own
apartment not far from her work. She continued to call at
any time of the day or night for money or advice, or to be
bailed out of some trouble.

With shaking voice, Tony told of an incident that had
occurred about a year before we met. Encouraged because
Julie had left her nightclub job and was working as a file
clerk in a downtown office, the Augustines had taken a
brief vacation. They had expected to hear from Julie at
their vacation resort on Marie's birthday—remembering
birthdays is an important tradition in the Augustine family. When they heard nothing, Tony called Julie's office.
He was told that Julie had not come to work for the past
few days because of the serious accident in the family.
Didn't Mr. Augustine know about the accident?

"Accident? What accident?" Tony screamed franti-
cally into the phone.

Linda, the Augustines' younger daughter, the secretary
told him, had been smashed up in an auto accident.
"You understand," Tony said to me, "that's my Linda,
my baby. She is the love of my life. I died when the
secretary told me that. If anything happened to my Linda,
I could not go on living." Of course, nothing had happened. Julie had made up an excuse to skip work for a
few days, but the effect of that lie, the shock he had
received, almost destroyed Tony. "I couldn't speak to
Julie for months after that," he said. "I couldn't look at
her. It was not only the terrible lie; the whole thing is
typical of the way she handles people, especially us."

There was more to come. A few months before I met
the Augustines, Julie had been discharged from a psychi-

atric hospital, where she had been a patient for four months, after making a serious suicide attempt. There had been some suicidal gestures before, but this time Julie had slashed herself badly. Tony and Marie were still stunned by that attempt. For years they had devoted their existence to saving this child's life, and now she was throwing that life away and they didn't know what to do about that. What would happen next? Where would she, and they, go from here?

At the time we met, also, the Augustines were trying to assess the results of the first vacation they had taken apart in all their years of marriage. Like so much else in their lives, the cause for the separation had been Julie.

Tony had been offered an opportunity by the printing firm for which he works to visit a large printing plant in Italy. It was to be a business trip with other members of the firm, and while the company would not pay for spouses, they were invited to join the group. Italian-American by birth, Tony was thrilled at the prospect. Assuming Marie would share his enthusiasm, he ordered two tickets to Rome, and was shocked when she turned hers down. Julie, it seemed, would be discharged from the psychiatric hospital shortly before the trip, and, said Marie, "one of us should be here so she can pick up the phone and say, 'This is what's happening to me today.'" To me she said, "I don't call her all the time, but if she does call, I think someone should be here to receive the call."

When Tony argued that Julie's psychiatrist did not feel it necessary for Marie to stay home after Julie's discharge, Marie's only answer was, "I've learned that doctors can be wrong."

Tony went on the trip alone, and both suffered. "I missed her desperately in the evenings," he said. "I had a great time during the day, but when evening came and the others went off in couples, I had no one to talk to. I had so much to tell Marie." She wanted to talk also, although her favorite topic of conversation, the single-minded topic of her life, is Julie. "I have such a need to share what is going on with Julie," she confided to me. "Sometimes when I call her and Tony insists that I shouldn't, I say to myself, 'There's no way I'm going to tell him what she said.' But then I do, because I have a need to tell; I have a need to share everything with him.''

Their different attitudes toward the Italian trip, really an extension of their different ways of handling Julie, epitomize the major conflict in the Augustines' life.

Tony complained: "I'm willing to just let Julie be now. Let her pull whatever tricks she wants to pull, but I don't want to be involved anymore. We have to let her try to function on her own. We have to let go, no matter what happens, but Marie won't do that."

Marie answered: "He wants me not to let Julie's doings affect my mood. He wants me to put her out of my mind, and I simply can't do that."

Tony rejoined: "It's not that. It's hurt me so hard, this whole thing with Julie—her drugs, her promiscuity, then her suicide attempts. There were times when I thought, 'I need Marie now but she's not with me. Her mind is only on Julie.' Julie comes first for Marie and I come second. But with me, Marie comes first—she's always first. I'm not sure who comes next. Not Julie, maybe Linda or Alex . . .''

Marie cut in: "It's ridiculous for him to speak that way. There are separate feelings a person has for a mate and separate feelings for children. They're not in competition with each other, these feelings. As far as saying that Julie comes first, ahead of the other children, well, it's simply not so. I get so much joy from them . . .''

Tony's turn to cut in: "You know I'm not talking about joy."

Marie again: "Well, when a problem presents itself, can you help think about that problem? I mean, if you have a sore on your arm, you don't think about your leg. It's something that invades every thought. That's what is on your mind—how am I going to deal with this sore?''

Tony, for the last word: "And I say forget about the sore. Think about me." To me: "We go through this all the time, but I still love her."

It's an argument that goes around and around, and over and over, the basic argument between them. It will continue forever, unless Julie suddenly changes and takes charge of her life, which is unlikely. In some way the roots of the differences in the Augustines' approach to

Julie go back before Julie existed, to the earliest days of their relationship.

They met, almost thirty years ago, at a resort hotel, where both had summer jobs as waiters. It was a case of love at first sight, at least for Tony. Marie was only seventeen. Tony, an "older man" at nineteen, had worked at the hotel before. When he and a friend were told that two new girls had joined the staff, he decided to take a look. What he saw was a thin, olive-skinned girl with black onyx hair dressed in black shorts and a black sweater. He looked at her, then looked again.

"See that girl in the black shorts?" he asked his friend.

"I see her," came the answer.

"Well, I'm going to marry her. I'm going to marry that girl."

Anyway that's how Tony remembers it happening, like "bells going off," although, he admits, "I've told this story so many times, maybe I made it up." What he didn't make up was his real interest in Marie, whom he began pursuing with determination. She lived in the Near North Side of town, he in the South Side, not a short distance apart for someone without a car. He had to take two buses and the El train to reach her house for a Saturday night date, but he persisted. Even when Marie insisted that they date other people as well because they were too young for a serious involvement, Tony persisted. They dated for more than three years and then they married, with both their parents' blessings. She was twenty, he twenty-two, about average ages for marriage back in the 1950s.

The slight unevenness in their feelings for each other, from their very first meeting, accounts in some measure for their never-ending differences about Julie. Tony has an all-encompassing love for Marie. She loves him too, with a love that is full and warm, and unswervingly devoted. But he adores her. "She still turns me on," he'd say, "all the time—I hope it lasts as long as I live." Or "Nobody has come along in twenty-eight years to change my feelings about her. I love her; I like her; I respect her." Whatever mysterious force seized him when he first looked at Marie and informed him that he would marry that girl continues to possess and direct him. Tony wants all of

Marie, as much of her as he can get, and that's never enough. "Sometimes I feel neglected," he said, "but she never feels neglected because I don't let her." And it's true. Tony will put Marie ahead of everything, including the children. She is not willing to put him ahead of Julie. And because he is unwilling to accept the second spot, they have running arguments about the management of Julie.

Yet there are limits to the arguments that keep them from becoming destructive, the kind of built-in checks and balances, discussed earlier, that parents in strong marriages seem to create for themselves. That is, if Marie were not as devoted and preoccupied with Julie and her problems as she is, Tony probably would be. For in spite of his bravado and bold assertions that he would leave Julie alone to fend for herself, he is deeply concerned and caring of her. He can permit himself to complain of being neglected by Marie because he knows she is not neglecting Julie, and he feels safe with that. Marie, on the other hand, firmly secure in Tony's love for her, knows that she can neglect her husband somewhat for their special child, and nothing terrible will happen.

They have choreographed a dance between them. Marie goes too far in worrying over Julie. Tony pulls her back. She allows him to pull her back up to a point—the point at which she thinks Julie will be in danger if left alone. Then she holds her ground, and he yields to her. Sometimes Marie goes further than she should in protecting Julie, and sometimes Tony becomes more stubborn than he should in demanding that she let go, and they reach a stalemate, such as the trip to Italy in which they both felt abandoned. Most times, however, they dance their steps well, synchronizing their motions around Julie.

The back-and-forth pulling over Julie has been carried into their social life, but here Tony has been firm and Marie has acquiesced.

"I give Tony full credit, *full credit*," she said, "for the fact that we have tried to live a normal life. He insisted that we must. We have seen examples of families that have given up any semblance of a normal life, where everything is child-centered. We didn't live that way."

"I've got to accept that credit." Tony didn't try to be

modest. "She's terrific about going out now, but you've got to admit, sweetheart, that it took a long time to get there. I felt we had to pull away a little. If I had lived and just worried about Julie all the time, I couldn't go on. I'd rather not be living."

"Yes, yes," she agreed. "Things that normal people in family situations do, we did. We went out, we went to parties and concerts, we took vacations . . ."

"Except when Julie screwed them up. She managed to screw up so many of our vacations by creating a crisis just before we'd leave."

"Still, we went. We kept going." Marie had to lessen the interference from Julie.

"Yes, we kept going. Lots of times I had to force Marie into going. She wasn't in the mood. I wasn't in the mood either, but I forced myself to go. You'd think, 'Oh my God, how can I see a comedy in the theater tonight?' And then you go and get involved in the comedy, and feel a little better. Of course, the day we found out that Julie cut her wrists, who's going to go out? So you don't go out then."

"Even then"—Marie had to point out that Julie had not destroyed them—"not that day, but soon afterward, we went."

"Yeah, I know. Life had to go on."

"We got dressed and went."

"Crying inside, but we went."

They are closer together in their ways of dealing with the burdens of their life than they initially appeared to be. They are also far more complicated as people. Marie the worrier, the overprotective and distraught mother, can be a pillar of strength to her husband in other areas. Tony, the happy-go-lucky one, is also given to depressions.

Tony likes to attribute his depressive streak to his mother, who always seemed sad and withdrawn, even from Tony, her only child. After her death, he discovered one primary source of her sadness: a thwarted love affair before marriage, from which she never recovered. It seems that when she came to America from Italy she had a boyfriend whom she had promised to marry. He and his family had emigrated to South America. He wrote to his love in Chicago, but her father intercepted the letters,

convinced that if she married that young man, she would
go to South America and the family would never again
see her. Rather than allow that, he preferred to see her
break her heart thinking the man she loved had forgotten
her. She married an American man, Tony's father, but
harbored her secret love within her for the next thirty
years, until she died. One of the reasons Tony is so fixed
on keeping some distance from Julie is his memory of his
mother, who had been smothered by her father and had
lived out her days feeling, Tony is convinced, that "life
had cheated her."

There are, however, other reasons for Tony's moods.
Julie, of course, is a major one. So is his work, and that,
again, is tied into Julie. Back in the days when Tony was
courting Marie, he was desperate to find a job so they
could marry. He finally landed a very good one at a small
printing house. "I was delirious about the job then," Tony
recalled. "I was making seventy dollars a week, quite a bit
for a beginner. I said, 'Oh my God, if I ever make ten
thousand a year, we'll be on top of the world.' Then when
I reached that goal, I said 'Twenty: all I want to make is
twenty thousand a year." Now, thirty years later, Tony
makes more than that goal of twenty thousand a year as a
production manager at the same company with which he
began, but he is dissatisfied with his work and his position. A few years ago, the management of the company
changed, and the new management made it clear that
Tony had gone as far as he could with this firm. Although
he thought about leaving, he knew he needed the health
insurance plan he had built up over the years to pay for
Julie's various hospitalizations. He stayed, and the awareness that he will never advance beyond where he is today
sets him to thinking that life has cheated him too.

Marie cheers him. Like many other couples, they
reverse roles when needed. He provides her with the
strength to step back from Julie; she gives him the strength
to believe in himself, in spite of work setbacks. Again and
again he said, "Money means something in our society. If
you don't have money, you haven't made it." And just as
often she interrupted to say, "I don't care about money. I
don't care about jewelry and big cars. I can look at a dress
in a window and admire it and forget it the next minute.

He can brood for a day because I can't afford to go into the shop and buy the dress I didn't want in the first place. Those things are meaningless; they're just *things*."

More than the words, her reassurances are an affirmation of her belief in him as a person in his own right rather than a person defined by achievement. Marie senses that Julie is not the only reason Tony holds on to his job. He has a great need for security, a need to be loved and cared for. Because he is not a gambler, he is not about to take a chance on starting his own business or looking for a job at this point. He needs her reassurances that she is not dissatisfied with his position in life.

"I know she doesn't care," he told me, "and she reminds me every time I forget about how much we have, how far we've come. When I get down and things happen, or I see all my friends passing me by because they're all higher up in their positions than I am, she reminds me that we had nothing to start with and now we have a house in the suburbs. I think about that especially in the winter when I make a fire in my fireplace and I sit in front of it. I can sit for hours and listen to music, and I think, 'My God, a boy from the slums of the South Side is just sitting in front of a fire in his own house and doing nothing.' I never even knew such a thing was possible. That's when I get back to what matters, and Marie helps."

They help each other, and that help is what has carried the Augustines through some of the worst moments of their life together. Sadly, they have received little help from friends in struggles with Julie's illness. In the early days, when they thought Julie would die at any time, they told only Marie's sister about the decree of doom that had been handed down to them. They spared their parents as long as they could, not only for the parents' sake, but, said Tony, "because we thought their anxiety would be one more burden on us." Eventually they did tell, and to this day Marie's mother cannot look at Julie without crying. Her sister has been wonderfully sympathetic, even inviting Julie to spend a summer at her country home with her family in order to give the Augustines a much-needed respite.

But friends, even close friends, to whom the Augustines might have looked for aid and consolation, have not come through for them. In spite of the emphasis of recent years on the role that friends can play as substitutes for extended families of earlier generations, the Augustines are not the only people I spoke with who felt abandoned by friends when struck by a crisis. Perhaps we expect more from our friends than many have the time or energy to give. Or in a situation like the Augustines', perhaps there are sorrows in life that friends cannot fathom, never having been in that place themselves.

Although the Augustines' closest friends knew that Julie had been ill and recovered, they knew nothing about the chaos and disruption of family life that followed the recovery, nothing of the agony that was crushing Marie and Tony every day. After Julie's most recent suicide attempt, however, the Augustines decided to open up their hearts to a few chosen friends. "No more secrets," Tony explained. "Enough. We decided we need support. This is driving us crazy. I mean we didn't put a sign up on our house, but we made up our minds to stop hiding things the way we always had."

Marie continued the narrative: "This past year and a half with Julie has been so bad, so incredibly difficult. The inside of you is so raw and hurts so much, that when we started talking to each other sometimes we would start fighting. I knew why. It's because you just want to strike out at somebody because everything is so rotten, and the only one who would take it or listen to you would be each other. At least I had someone to talk to. Whenever I would get another terrible phone call from Julie, I would call my sister, and get it all out of my system. But Tony had no one, so I said, 'Pick someone out; you have to talk to someone.' "

Tony chose an old friend to whom he poured out his story. That night he warned Marie, "Be prepared, Ben will tell Dana, and she'll surely call you tonight." Dana didn't call and neither did Ben, not for another three weeks, and then they barely asked about Julie. The Augustines revealed their secret sorrows to another couple while away with them on vacation. It was an extensive trip, taken while Julie was in the hospital, and Marie felt compelled to call her daughter or the hospital at least every other day. Again, the Augustines expected these friends to phone immediately after the trip to inquire about Julie, and again they were disappointed.

As a result of these disappointments, Marie and Tony have begun to force themselves to adopt a new attitude. They are learning, they say, not to judge their friends but to accept them as they are, recognizing that people do what they can, and those who have not experienced a tragedy may not have the capacity to understand those who have. A sensible attitude, but one that leaves them lonely. "I can't remember a time when we didn't have trouble," Marie said, "and what I've learned is, only I really know how he's feeling and only he really knows how I'm feeling."

With that knowledge Marie and Tony are able to talk to each other honestly, about everything and anything. "We never don't communicate," is the way she put it. And even in the worst moments, they try to make physical contact with each other. "There have been times," Tony said with a trace of anger, "when everything going on with Julie would louse up our sex lives." Marie continued, because it was about her that he was talking: "Occasionally that would happen. If it was a particularly bad day and we'd had bad news about Julie, I would lie there until all hours of the night, and, well, you just don't feel like it then. But even when we have arguments and Tony is angry, I always make it my business to turn his way and put my arms around him. It's easier for me to do than for him, but once I do, he always responds. We have to feel this is a separate part of life that's outside everything else."

They also try, as much as possible, never to attack one another no matter how heated an argument over Julie. That is one of the unwritten rules of their marriage, and if they do not always succeed in adhering to it, at least they know when they are failing. "If one of us slips," Tony said, "the other one says, 'That's not fair.' "

Whom Marie attacks—relentlessly—is herself. She blames herself for what Julie has become, for having listened to the doctors and for not having told Julie the nature of her illness years earlier. Had they dealt honestly with Julie's disease and allowed her to face up to it, Marie maintains, she would not have turned into the disorganized, helpless and hopeless person she is today. Marie's self-blame is not a unique reaction. Psychiatrist Kenneth Terkelsen told me that many parents of children with problems blame themselves even when it's clear they bear little responsibility for the problems. There is an almost magical wish to have been the cause of the problems, he said, a feeling that "if I caused it, I can make it go away."

Some of that thinking is at work with Marie, and Tony tries to stop it. He doesn't believe they can blame themselves for Julie's problems now, and he doesn't believe they should torture themselves in trying to make those problems disappear. What happened to Julie, he maintains, came from circumstances far beyond their control. Tony likes to remind Marie that at the time Julie first became ill, there were few parent organizations clustered around children with specific illnesses, as there are today. The Augustines had only their own instincts and the doctors' advice to go on.

"We had no choice," he insisted in discussing this matter of blame. "We had to do what the doctors told us." To which Marie replied with vehemence, "We followed like sheep. We were scared and we were dying for someone to tell us what to do. Yet look at me. I'm an intelligent woman. How could I let myself be so stupid just because some doctor told me to act a certain way? So what if he told me? That doesn't make it right."

People have gotten smarter, Marie said to me, and they no longer follow experts' advice blindly. "Now," she said, "I've become a crusader. If I hear about somebody whose child is ill, I speak to them and say, 'Please, listen to me; learn from my mistake. Treat your child like any normal child should be treated, with honesty. Tell that child the truth.' "

At one of our last meetings, I sought truthful answers from the Augustines to a question I had hesitated to ask earlier:

"Considering all that you have suffered in the last few years, have you wished sometimes that Julie would have died, as the doctors predicted?"

Marie didn't answer. Tony spoke slowly and hesitantly: "I only felt that way once. She'd had a relapse and was in such pain and going through hell in the hospital. I said, 'My God, that poor kid is suffering so much, maybe it would be better if she died.' She was just a little girl then and the pain was intense, yet she was being so stoic. I didn't know how anyone could live through that." Tony was silent for a moment. Then he spoke again. "Never, I have never wished her to die. I wished her to go away, or me to go away. Isn't it strange? If Julie had died within eighteen months, as the doctors predicted, we would have had a terrible tragedy. We would never have been the same—how can anybody be the same once he loses a child? But this thing that happened . . ."

His voice trailed off, then picked up softly, as though thinking aloud: "We were unlucky. She lived. Isn't that funny? We were unlucky because nobody prepared us for her living, only for her dying. Sometimes I fantasize about what our lives would have been like if we hadn't had the trouble with Julie. We could have had the greatest time; we could have been the happiest ever. I would have saved myself over a hundred thousand dollars I spent on doctors and hospitals. We could have gone places; we could have done things; we could have flown to the moon. We could have been terrific. But then, who knows? Maybe not. Who knows what life brings? Wish her dead? No, never, except for that one time in the hospital."

I believe the Augustines could have "flown to the moon" together had they not been grounded by the weight of Julie's illness and its consequences. As it is, they have had to stay on earth, constantly beset by problems. They have had to live with the fact that Julie will never have a normal life. She will always run into difficulties, unable to get along with others, incapable of being independent, angry at her parents and at herself, always at the risk of depression and suicide. They have had to face the knowledge that their other two children will never be the persons they might have been had there been no Julie in the family. Alex, their oldest child, has moved to Utah to join a company that builds solar energy houses, as far away as he could get from the heat in his home. Linda, the youngest, once a fine student, slipped in her schoolwork and became listless and depressed after Julie made her last suicide attempt. "This was the worst year of my life," she told her parents, and they knew she spoke truthfully.

And they have had to accept the limitations of their own lives that are constantly interrupted by Julie, constantly on call to bail her out of some new trouble.

They have lived with and accepted all these things. Why have the Augustines been able to stay together, to be close and loving and helpful to one another when so many couples fall apart in similarly devastating situations? One reason is because they *have* accepted their lot in life. As difficult as it has been for them, they have learned to live with less than they hoped for from their children and from themselves. Often, people whose marriages split as a result of a crisis are people who cannot live with the realities of what they have or whom they have become. They try to escape their ill fate by drinking, having affairs or simply walking away from the whole mess. Tony has dreamed of walking away, but he never did and never will. He is too committed, as is Marie, to making the best of the life he has.

Their ability to live life in spite of dreadful setbacks is another factor that holds them together. "If you don't keep on reading books," Marie said at one point, "and knowing what's going on in the world, you're not really living. You've got to know what's going on." Then she continued, "If someone said to me, 'We're facing this terrible thing,' with a child or whatever, I would say 'Keep on living—no matter what, no matter how hard, you've got to keep living.' "

Claudia and Jeff Winters, who lost a son to leukemia, had the same philosophy. They spoke about an old truck Jeff, a farmer, had bought while Todd was alive and how the two spent time together working on repairing that truck until the boy became too ill to work anymore. After Todd died, Jeff looked at the truck and said, "I owe the doctors so much, I'm going to sell that truck and get what money I can out of it. To heck with making it work now." Claudia calmly replied, "Fine. But you have to wait a year before doing that." Someone had told her, she remembered, that after a tragedy you should not make any major decisions for at least a year. Just about a year after Todd's death, Jeff began working on the truck again, forgetting about selling it. "It takes time," he said, "and then you start to pick up the pieces. Pick up, start again, and keep living."

Picking up and living, no matter what, is possible for the Augustines and the Winters because neither spouse in either marriage blames the other for the tragedy in their lives. Marie Augustine blames herself, and the two of them, for having followed doctors' orders as precisely as they did and not using their own judgment in handling Julie's illness. Jeff Winters grieves within himself, because he and Todd had never gotten along well before the boy's illness. And his guilt at his own impatience with his son's "adolescent foolishness" still clings to him more than two years after the boy's death like a cobweb whose threads stick to the face and hands no matter how firmly they are brushed away. Lynn and George Gilbert each bear a feeling of personal blame for their son's death by an automobile, because at the time of the accident both were preoccupied with their own heavy drinking problems. But in none of these marriages did one spouse turn around and point an accusatory finger at the other after their tragedy had occurred.

I know of a marriage where that is precisely what did happen, and the marriage broke up shortly afterward. In that situation, the husband had been driving the family car when it went out of control, injuring himself and his wife and instantly killing their seven-year-old son, their only child. Although the accident had not been his fault, his wife could not forgive him, and their life together became a nightmare of accusations and counteraccusations. In the midst of their profound sorrow, they could not find their way back to each other.

The Augustines know their way with each other because each is clear and open about hurts and angers, needs and resentments. They speak to each other about everything, and even when they disagree, which they do often about Julie, they have no hidden agendas; neither is out to "get" the other, and each knows just how far to go. Difficulties that arise after a crisis in a family most often center around this issue of dealing openly with the event. Sometimes neither partner wants to go near the subject, and then both may walk around isolated in their sorrow, unable to help each other or themselves. Sometimes one partner wants to talk and the other doesn't, hugging the unhappiness within. The marriage can become rough around the edges if the one who wants to talk turns into a nagger—"Let's plan for your new job" (when a job has been lost), or "Let's talk about why this happened."

The Winters had this last problem. Claudia needed terribly to talk and talk some more about Todd's illness and then his death. Jeff could not talk at all. "I take out my frustrations and anger and hurt and everything in my work," he explained. "I just worked harder after Todd got sick." Their closeness came, after a while, in being able to respect the different ways each of them handled the tragedy. "In some respects it was harder on me," Claudia said, "because I needed to be able to talk about it, and in some respects it was harder on him because he didn't want to talk about it." Because they understood one another's difficulties, each was able to lean over and draw nearer to the other's style.

"If either of us had gotten pickier," said Claudia, "it might have ruined everything. But the respect we had for each other's way of handling it carried us through. We'd be talking after dinner and Jeff would make a real effort to speak to me and listen to what I was saying and then he would say, 'Well, I just can't talk about it anymore.' And I would stop." Along with respect, there was such sensitivity one to the other that to this day Jeff can be dreamily stirring his coffee and Claudia will look at him and say, "You're thinking about Todd," and she will be right.

Claudia has also learned that when she couldn't speak to Jeff, she could turn to other people. Unlike the Augustines, she has two close friends with whom she teaches school and who are consistently sympathetic and available for listening. Having those friends has helped her, and it has helped free Jeff from a burden of communication he is not always able to carry.

Finally, Marie Augustine described herself as a crusader, helping people handle their children's illnesses in a more sensible way than she did. That crusading spirit seizes many couples who have suffered a tragedy. Often they discover that in forcing themselves to move toward others like them, they take some of the pressure off one another, making it easier to draw close again.

Claudia and Jeff Winters spoke with warmth about the many young people with physical and emotional problems who began coming to their home during Todd's illness and continued to come afterward. Emotionally drained themselves, they still felt, Claudia explained, "a responsibility to help these young people in the matter of mortality, of life and death." With that sense of responsibility they also found that their involvement in the lives of other young people helped pull them through their own misfortune. More than five hundred people came to the small Congregational church the Winters attend for a memorial service for Todd, many of them the young people they had aided. At one point, however, soon after Todd's death, it all got to be too much. One recently divorced young woman whose father had terminal cancer leaned on them so heavily that they finally had to say, "We just can't handle any more now." Nevertheless, they continue to speak on occasion to groups of parents of sick children, and to stay in touch with many of Todd's friends, and these contacts have helped them bear their loss.

An area of strength and support that had no meaning for the Augustines but has helped other couples is religion. Both lapsed Catholics, they found little personal comfort in religious teachings. When Julie first became ill, they did speak with a priest from a local parish, but his religious message didn't touch them. Claudia Winters, on the other hand, has uncovered a deep religious faith within her. In beating her alcoholism, she had learned, she said, to give herself up to a force beyond her, to say simply, "I can't do it myself; help me, help me." As a result, she has become a devout Congregationalist, and her church has become a "very special place" for her. When she looks back on the last ten years of her life, she senses a divine purpose in them, as though her alcoholism and recovery were preparation for the much worse ordeal of losing a son. God knew how to test her, she believes, and from that to teach her to handle the blackest events of her life. Jeff does not have this kind of faith, and when he speaks about what has occurred in his life, he speaks fatalistically—things happen and there is nothing much to be done about them. Yet he has been encouraging to Claudia in her religious search, and he says, simply, "Even in the worst of days, I never damned God and I never will."

Much has been written over the past few years about the stages of grief and mourning people go through when hit by a crisis or death in their own lives or in their families. Elisabeth Kübler-Ross was one of the first to plot out stages dying patients might move through as they adjust to the inevitability of their illness. They begin, she believed, by denying the illness and its seriousness, move on to being enraged by their lot in life, then to bargaining (as if to say, "I'll accept being blind, but just let me live"), depression, and finally acceptance. Other specialists have mapped similar stages for families subjected to a crisis, with stable families moving from disbelief to acceptance and coping.

These outlines for adjustment are useful because they highlight the fact that few people are able to accept and deal immediately with sudden interruptions in the everyday flow of their lives. Like all such theories, however, they tend to simplify the reality and mislead the troubled into thinking that the stages are like steps on a ladder, a vertical climb to accepting difficulties that leads to final peace of mind. Actually, many of the stages in dealing with a crisis go on simultaneously, rather than step by step. Even while a couple may be shocked and unwilling to recognize the severity of a problem, an illness, a job loss, a disabled child, they begin to find ways of coping with what is happening to them. And even when they have reached the stage of acceptance, most still wrestle with fears and self-reproaches, with dreams and fantasies of what might have been.

For the Augustines, there is always pain, in spite of their ability to cope and to live with what Julie's life was and is. Although they have handled the crisis in their lives probably as well as any couple, they have not moved from stage to stage in a straight line of triumphant resolution. Within the richness and fullness of their marriage, there exists a part that is weak and incomplete, a part of each and of the whole that is permanently damaged by the tragedy of Julie.

Has the ongoing crisis in their lives strengthened the

Augustine marriage—that is, has it brought them closer together than they would have been without it? In some ways, yes. By having shared the horrors of Julie's death sentence and then the results of its reprieve, they have shared an understanding of one another that they might not have had otherwise. Yet crisis has not made this marriage work. It is a marriage that works in spite of crisis. And it works because the Augustines, like other couples whose marriages have been disrupted by difficulties, have found that they can live with imperfections and with unresolved problems in their lives as long as they are living those lives together.

CHAPTER TEN

~

Therapy and Counseling
"A Bias Toward Marriage"

In a large conference room in the psychiatric wing of a metropolitan hospital, I joined a group of psychiatrists-in-training to watch a videotape of a couple during a session of marital therapy. I had been invited to the viewing by a psychiatrist on the hospital staff who had planned the teaching session, building it around videotapes of couples he had treated over the past few years. The room was packed, not only with young would-be psychiatrists, but with many senior staff members as well.

Not long ago many of these men and women would have looked down their noses at an invitation to a conference on marital therapy. The field, known for years as marital counseling, was dominated by ministers and social workers. Psychiatrists and psychologists were trained to deal only with individuals in therapy, and a marital problem was usually handled as a problem that resulted from a psychic disorder within one or both partners, best treated by analysis or therapy with each partner individually. Before 1950 there were perhaps twenty-five articles on marital therapy in the psychiatric literature, an indication of the low status of this area of treatment. After World War II, however, when marriages had risen in number and more couples began to seek help, the number of professionals in the field increased. Many began focusing on the problems of couples and families, along with those of individuals, and marital therapy became recognized both as a special field of therapy in itself and as a discipline within the broader area of family therapy, which treats all members of a family. By the mid-1980s, so many research articles had been written on various aspects of marital and family therapy that a reader had to sift carefully to separate the valid research from that presented mainly to promote a researcher's viewpoint.

Although I interviewed many professionals—psychiatrists, psychologists, social workers and sociologists—in the course of researching this book, I had hesitated about delving deeply into the techniques of family and marital therapy because I had always intended this to be a book about functioning marriages rather than a "how-to" backed by cases of problem marriages. Few of the couples I spoke with had been in marital therapy; some had had individual therapy either before or during the course of their marriage, and a number of those married during the late 1960s had attended EST meetings at the height of the encounter movement of the 1970s. The others had worked through the problems and crises of their marriages by themselves, and it was their ability to do so that I found inspiring and worth recording. Yet as my interviews continued, I met couples who, I believed, might have benefited from some expert help. I also met enough divorced people who said, "I wish I had tried harder," to make me feel a discussion of ways of trying harder with the aid of professionals is warranted.

On the videoscreen in the conference room of the large metropolitan hospital, I watched a couple fight with each other. The psychiatrist conducting the conference explained that the partners were in their late thirties, had been married twelve years and had a ten-year-old son. The husband, Jay, made a comfortable living turning out free-lance technical articles for a variety of industrial trade magazines while he struggled in his leftover time to write fiction. The wife, Hope, a gifted sculptor, had given up her work after their son's birth, but now, while he was away at school during the day, had taken up pottery making. She was successful enough to have her works exhibited and sold at craft fairs around the country. With their son demanding less of Hope's attention, however, she had found herself fighting with Jay almost constantly. At Jay's insistence they had sought therapy after a particularly bad blowup, and the videotape we were watching was made soon after they had begun.

The fight we were witnessing on the screen, the therapist explained, epitomized many of the issues that divided this couple. The story behind the fight was this: Two weeks earlier Hope had discovered a lump on her breast. With great trepidation she had a mammogram done. Although the X ray revealed nothing suggestive of cancer, and her gynecologist assured her the lump was most probably a common benign tumor, he did want to have a biopsy done. He scheduled her for a needle biopsy, a simple procedure carried out in the physician's office in which part of the lump is extracted for further study under a microscope. Jay had offered to accompany Hope to the doctor's office and wait for her, but she had been confident that she could manage herself. She went alone to have the biopsy performed and returned home to find a note from Jay saying he had gone to lunch with a magazine editor who might give him a new assignment. A few hours later, as Jay walked through the door of his apartment, he was greeted by an enraged wife. Hope was furious at having returned from the frightening procedure at the doctor's to an empty home.

As we watched the tape, the therapist stood at the back of the room, sometimes commenting as we went along, sometimes stopping the film to discuss what we had seen.

In the first segment, Hope and Jay sat on a couch in the psychiatrist's office. The black-and-white video blurred the couple's features, but even through the electronic haze I could pick up Hope's intensity, make out the tightness of her jaw, the skin taut against high cheekbones, the thin lips, dark eyes and hair and long, fine-boned fingers flitting in perpetual motion. Jay was stockier, short-legged and square. An old-fashioned crewcut flattened the top of his head but also visually enlarged his skull, and with both arms clasped about one knee he had the appearance of a fetus, all rolled up into himself. Hope's back was turned to Jay, on her right, as she faced the therapist, who sat, off-camera, in a chair on her left. Although she spoke to Jay, she didn't look at him, nor he at her. We watched and listened:

SHE (*shouting*): What the fuck did you go to lunch with Patrick for?

HE (*shouting*): I told you. I thought you'd just want to rest when you got home. But we're not getting anywhere. I'm sorry I came back so late.

SHE: Bullshit!

HE: There's no way to convince you anymore that I love you.

SHE: I don't care if you love me.

HE: I'm trying to state facts and realities, and we're not getting anywhere.

SHE: The relationship is all wrong. Everything is wrong. It's just no good. We'll never work this thing out.

The machine was stopped and the therapist spoke from behind us in the darkened room: "I let them go on at first because, as you could see, I couldn't break in at any point. They were too involved in attacking each other, or rather, she was attacking him. He was acting cool and distant, the factual one showing up her emotionalism. There's more of the same kind of accusation and anger for some time, so let's skip ahead a bit. In the segment you'll see now, they begin to plead their cases to me, which gives me a chance to serve as a go-between. Whatever I ask one, I'll ask the other in kind. Watch."

SHE (*turning toward the therapist who is off-camera*): He didn't have to go to that lunch, but he went.

HE (*looking straight ahead*): I was out to lunch maybe forty-five minutes to an hour, at the most.

THERAPIST (*off-camera, to Hope*): What did his being away mean to you?

SHE: He could not even spend time with me this morning; that's what it comes down to. (*Turning toward Jay*) You cannot spend time with me. (*Back to the therapist*) He had *nothing* to do. He didn't have to go hopping around to that lunch.

"Notice," said the therapist from behind us, "how she minimizes his work—'nothing to do,' 'hopping around' —while he minimizes her feelings."

THERAPIST (*off-camera, to Jay*): What do you make of this experience?

HE (*looking straight ahead, at no one*): There's no way I can convince her I love her except to wait on her hand and foot. I was out of the house possibly forty-five minutes to an hour, that's all. (*Turning to her*) You do this and you do it repeatedly. You set up rejections when they don't exist, and then you complain about being rejected.

SHE (*facing him, both staring at each other*): You cannot spend time with me. You cannot sit with me for two hours. That's the truth.

HE (*his voice softer*): You expected me to pick you up at the doctor's office, and you were right to expect that. You think it's silly to make normal demands, but you have a right to those demands, and I would gladly have gone with you or picked you up if you had wanted that. I only object when the demands are excessive.

SHE (*her voice calmer*): I didn't want you to pick me up because I didn't want to wait until you woke up this morning. But I was shocked and angry because you weren't home when I got there.

The video was shut off again, and the therapist addressed us once more. "You can see," he said, "that we've made a transition. Hope is using 'I' words instead of 'You' words. That is, she's speaking about how she feels rather than accusing him. Watch also their nonverbal communication. See how they're sitting. They were far apart before, but have begun to move closer." He laughed. "Jay, I have discovered, has a problem with authority. In these early sessions, he rarely answered my questions directly or looked directly at me. And he had a funny little habit of pushing his nose with his finger whenever I spoke to him or he responded to me or to something I had said to Hope. Sort of like thumbing his nose at me. See if you can pick it up." The screen lit up again.

THERAPIST (*off-camera, to Hope*): You're finally beginning to say what you want.

SHE: I was embarrassed to say I wanted him at the doctor's office with me. I've always been very self-sufficient in this marriage.

THERAPIST (*off-camera, to Jay*): Did you know she felt that way or did you feel she was testing you by going alone?

HE (*pushing his nose with his finger, staring ahead*): It's hard for me to know if she needs me if she doesn't say so.

SHE: How can you ask *if* I need you? If you love someone, you're *there*.

THERAPIST: You've been blaming one another excessively today. What do you think you were both reacting to?

SHE: I was scared. Doctors scare me. Cancer terrifies me. I was insecure so I was getting all worked up. Physically I felt exhausted. The fear exhausted me and I didn't feel strong and in control the way I like to feel. I was looking forward to a long afternoon together. That's the best part of Jay's working at home; we can be together when we want to. I wanted a lot of love; I wanted to be taken care of. When I found he had gone out, I felt abandoned. I needed him and he wasn't there for me.

HE (*covering his face with his hands, then turning to look at her*): I guess I made a mistake. I didn't know how you felt. I shouldn't have gone out.

THERAPIST (*off-camera*): You see, Hope, it's easier for Jay to respond to your needs when you tell them to him than to try to figure them out himself, especially when you deny them. And Jay, it's easier for Hope to tell you what she needs if she feels you are listening to her and not trying to get away from her.
(*Jay leans over and kisses Hope. She takes his hand.*)

Half-jokingly, we all applauded as the video was turned off. "What you need to complete this, doctor," called out one psychiatrist-in-training, "is some schmaltzy music as they walk off together into the sunset, a little Verdi or Tchaikowsky."

The therapist smiled. "I get cynical about quickie cures also," he said, "but I'm sure you all recognize that while this session had a happy ending, it was not the end of therapy for this couple. Patterns that have been repeated for years don't dissipate in one session. We made a beginning here. Jay and Hope both began to recognize that they can't operate on assumptions with each other without checking those assumptions out. For Hope that means speaking out about what she wants rather than assuming Jay will know her thoughts even when she expresses contradictory feelings. For Jay it means learning to open himself up more, to become less remote and more responsive to her instead of assuming she's always being emotional and demanding."

He paused. "We've worked on other issues also. Jay's need for power and control—his nose-thumbing at any authority—became important enough matters for me to work with him alone in individual therapy in addition to their joint marital sessions. Things are getting better for them in many ways."

Why have marital therapy? The obvious answer is in order to solve marital problems. The disclaimer to that answer is that not all problems can be solved in therapy nor should every couple that have a problem enter therapy.

Because therapy has become so accessible and because there is no longer a stigma attached to it as there once was, it has become, for many couples and individuals, a first resort rather than a last resort. Yet there are some couples, as there are individuals, for whom therapy can be a hazard rather than a help. These are the couples who use therapy as a substitute for maturity. They turn to a therapist to make decisions for them, to say things to each of them that they haven't been able to say themselves, to be a big daddy or mommy to lean on. For them, the therapist as intermediary (an acceptable role in many circumstances) becomes one more block to intimacy, one more form of distancing. And instead of exerting their own authority, they become dependent, like children, on the therapist's advice, giving up the opportunity to test their own strengths and abilities.

Such couples—usually they are young and newly married—have a better chance at success when they try to work at differences themselves, and in the process, get to know one another better.

Who, then, can benefit from therapy? Couples who care deeply about one another, but can't seem to get along; couples who have become overwhelmed by problems between them that they can no longer solve themselves; couples engulfed by tragedies—a job loss, a death in the family, an illness—who need support in coping; couples so caught up in anger or depression that they have forgotten the roots of their relationship, the reason they married in the first place, and want to rediscover those roots; couples who fight recurrent battles, rehashing the same issues again and again without being able to move on, to accept the differences between them or simply live with those differences.

Some couples come into therapy because they are crushed by external pressures: in-law interference, the impossible demands of two careers, problems with children. Some couples come into therapy because one or the other feels crippled by internal pressures: a violent temper, sexual inhibitions or dysfunctions, incessant anxiety. And some couples come into therapy as a way of ending a marriage both feel is over but neither has the ability to terminate. For such couples, marital therapy provides the last rites for a union that has been emotionally dead for years.

What can therapy do for couples who want to stay married? When it works well, it can help each partner recognize and understand more about the other's needs, fears and wishes, and act on that recognition. Like Jay and Hope, on the videotape, couples in therapy can find a channel for speaking to each other without outbursts of anger and resentment, for saying what they really mean to say without blurring their intentions or operating on false assumptions. Therapy can help a couple come to grips with the realities of who they are, separate from the fantasies and illusions they brought with them into marriage. It can help married people find strengths in their marriage that have been forgotten or covered over with quarrels.

Psychiatrist Henry Spitz told me about a couple who had come to see him after thirty years of marriage. Filled with accumulated angers, they spoke about the miseries of their marriage, each elaborating in great detail on the other's fault. Finally Spitz asked, "What do you like about each other? What are your strengths?" They looked at each other. "Nothing," said the husband. "I can't think of anything we like about each other." "No," said the wife, "I don't think there are any strengths in this marriage." Casually, to move them away from their accusations and recriminations, Spitz asked them about their work, their family, other background information. He discovered that they had built a successful business and worked in it together for twenty-five years, and had managed at the same time to rear three terrific sons, of whom they were very proud. "You were able to accomplish all those things together," said Spitz. "Surely you had great strengths in your marriage. Maybe we can rediscover them."

Therapy can also aid partners in gaining insight into patterns they may have carried over from their family backgrounds or from previous marriages, and in changing those patterns that have been harmful.

Marital therapy, in short, can effect wonders and miracles in a marriage—but it's the partners, not the therapist, who can create those wonders and shape those miracles by working hard to build up the marriage rather than tear it down.

What marital or family therapy *cannot* do is make over one partner to suit the ideals of the other. For almost every couple, therapy begins with each partner telling the therapist what is wrong with the other. "She's so caught up in her work, she forgets what it means to be human" or "He yells all the time; any little thing sets him off." Blame him, change her—these are the themes mates hum aloud as they go to greet a therapist. What they find as they become more involved in their meetings is that while each can and does change in the course of therapy, the change is never one-sided; it always requires movement on both sides. In fact if one person is determined not to change, and to continue to hang blame on the other, there's little chance of success in therapy.

Marital therapy *cannot* become a substitute for honesty in marriage. "I won't be the keeper of somebody else's secrets," said one social worker. "For example, if one partner is having an affair and tells me about it as a way of avoiding telling the other partner, I will refuse to become the confidante. I won't insist that the partner tell the other, and I won't reveal the secret, but I won't promise to protect that secret either, if the issue arises in the course of treatment." She went on to say that she tells clients her position at the very beginning. Sometimes that means that one or the other will hold back a secret from her, but at least, she said, "I'm free to conduct therapy as I see fit and what comes out comes out."

Another therapist, a psychologist, agreed that he would not reveal a secret, such as an affair, if told about it by one spouse. Nor would he necessarily insist that the partner tell the other about it right away. ("Being honest," he said, "can be one of the cruelest things ever.") What he would do is question the spouse about why it is that he or she can't tell, even though the couple is in therapy. He would wonder what the sense of marital therapy is if the spouse has to persist in keeping such a secret. Eventually, if the subject remained undiscussed, he would have to say, "There's no point in continuing unless you're clear with your partner."

Nor can therapy in an expert's office substitute for

dealing with issues in a couple's own home and lives. Couples sometimes use therapy as an excuse to slash at each other and to land precisely placed blows. "We're in therapy," they'll say, "and we're working hard at our problems," when in fact, what they are working at is killing each other. Therapy was designed for healing, not hurting, and unless a couple use sessions to get a better understanding of one another that can be carried over to life outside of therapy, they're wasting their time and the therapist's. A good therapist will make that clear.

And then, therapy, sadly, *cannot* resurrect a marriage that is already dead. If one party wants to end a marriage and refuses to participate in therapy, there's little hope for the success of the therapy even if that person comes to sessions. A man who divorced his wife after ten years of marriage because of vague feelings that he was missing out on something more had agreed to accompany her to a marriage counselor shortly before their final break. "This guy said to me," the man remembered, " 'Do you want this to work?' and I said, 'No,' and that was the end of that. I've now come to think that I should have given it more of a chance. But it was clear to this fellow that I wanted out, and nothing he could have done would stop me."

For some couples, in fact, a therapist's office becomes a safe ground for ending a marriage that neither has been able to end alone. Psychiatrist Aaron Stein described a couple who had scheduled an appointment with him— actually it was the wife who scheduled the appointment, explaining that her husband was reluctant about it, but she was sure she could get him to agree. She arrived a few minutes early and continued reassuring the doctor that her husband would appear at any moment. The husband did show up. He walked into the office, looked at his wife, and said, "The reason I'm late is that I just filed for divorce. My lawyer will be in touch with you." Then he walked out, leaving his stunned wife in the care of her marital therapist.

A less extreme case was that of a very passive man married for years to a highly aggressive and demanding woman. What he wanted from treatment, he said, was for the therapist to tell his wife to stop making demands on him. The therapist pointed out that that was not her role, and that if the couple entered therapy, a confrontation between them was inevitable. Issues that had not been discussed openly were bound to come out now, and each would either have to be able to change to accommodate the other or face the consequences of airing their grievances. The man seemed relieved. He anticipated that the "airing" would make the marriage evaporate, a thing he wanted but had not been able to do on his own.

What goes on in marital therapy? Much depends on the issues presented, the attitudes of the mates and the approach of the therapist. Couples bring a variety of problems to therapy. For young couples, troubles may grow from immaturity, from parental pulls and pressures, from social anxieties and sexual fears. Older couples speak about depression and about failures, about lost dreams and frustrated ideals, about marital boredom and competition with children, and about sex problems too. Remarried people carry with them their fears, their lack of confidence and inability to trust again after the failure of earlier marriages.

Most therapists begin by seeing both partners together. Some will agree to meet with one partner at the beginning if the other refuses to appear, but very soon will insist on seeing both. Others will not see one partner alone, even for an initial interview.

At first the therapist will listen to the couple, listen to hear what each is complaining about and watch to see how they interact. Many therapists will take a family history that begins with a history of the marriage. They will want to know when the couple met, how long they were engaged, whether they lived together before marriage and whether they had been married before. They will ask when the couple's problems began and what factors may have contributed to those problems, probing especially into relationships with children. Next, many therapists will collect information about each partner's family background. The couple might be asked to draw a family tree, showing connections with parents and siblings and discussing special factors in their families that may have influenced them.

With background information gathered, the therapist might ask a couple to speak of their own aims. Why have they come to therapy? What goals do they have? How are they willing to negotiate? What are they prepared to give to each other? Finally, the therapist makes an evaluation of the situation. Can therapy help this couple, and if so, what can they hope to achieve through it?

If the couple decide to go ahead with therapy, they will probably meet with the therapist together for a few sessions, then each partner will have private sessions, and then back together again.

Often a couple will seek help for a child who is depressed or having school problems or abusing alcohol and other drugs, and in the course of initial interviews about the child's problems, the therapist will determine that the child's symptoms result from animosities between the parents. In such situations the therapeutic plan might call for sessions for the parents alone and then broader family therapy sessions for the entire family, or family therapy and marital therapy sessions taking place interchangeably, and perhaps some individual therapy sessions for the child.

Sometimes the results of initial interviews lead to a recommendation that rather than joint marital therapy, one or the other spouse should have individual therapy to deal with a specific problem, and then see whether marital therapy is still warranted. Or the couple themselves might choose to undertake individual therapy in which both work separately on internal problems. This kind of separate therapy can be effective when spouses are so burdened with carry-overs from the past that they can barely deal with each other in the present. Here's how a secretary described the usefulness of her psychoanalysis in the early years of her marriage:

"I saw myself as a bitch; I always saw myself as the bad one and my husband was the good one, just the way I saw my parents—my mother was bitchy and my father was so good. But even though I perceived myself that way, I resented it, and we began having terrible fights about that—I really didn't want to come crawling back all the time and saying, 'Please love me; I'll try not to be a bitch; I'll be a good girl.' What I explored in therapy was that my own aggressiveness and wanting more and being critical of my husband's passivity were not necessarily bad. And the fact was that I wanted to let go of my image of myself as the bitch, but he somehow needed to see me that way as an excuse for his not pushing himself or trying to do more than he was doing. At my insistence, he got into therapy also, and good things happened to both of us as a result."

But there is great danger to a marriage when both spouses have individual therapy, separate and apart from one another and the marriage, and the danger is this: In individual therapy, each spouse becomes involved in a personal self and a personal past, and each therapist becomes, essentially, the advocate of his or her patient. Nobody serves as an advocate or representative of the relationship as a whole; nobody minds the store, as it were. A woman whose marriage broke up after she and her husband entered individual therapy on the recommendation of a marital therapist wondered what would have happened had they stayed in therapy together or at least had marital therapy along with their individual treatment. "Between us we must have spent thirty thousand dollars in divorce fees and negotiations on ending this marriage," she said. "Why couldn't we have spent that thirty thousand dollars on keeping it together?"

In marital therapy, the relationship, rather than either partner, is the patient. In my opinion, when partners undertake individual therapy, there needs to be somebody looking out for the relationship also. There needs to be a recognition that no matter how focused a partner may be on internal and past issues, life goes on in the present too. To keep that life going, some form of marital therapy should be continued along with individual therapy. Or at the very least, the individual therapists should maintain contact, occasionally setting up meetings of the partners either with both therapists or with one or the other. An ongoing marriage deserves that much advocacy.

For most family and marital therapists, the earliest sessions, after a couple's histories have been taken, revolve around problems in communication. At least, most couples begin by saying, "We can't communicate," or "She doesn't understand me," or "He never listens to anything I say." What those complaints really mean varies from couple to couple; they are shorthand ways of saying that something is wrong, the couple is "stuck" (to use a favorite word of the psychotherapists) and can find no other form of interacting than by fighting. Although good therapy goes beyond techniques of communicating or fighting in order to delve into underlying difficulties and motives, many therapists find that dealing with communication issues is the least threatening way to begin reshaping a troubled marriage.

On the most fundamental level, a therapist would point out, as the therapist on the videotape did, that many communication problems and conflicts can be avoided if partners don't view one another as mind readers, but say what they really mean. Psychiatrist Aaron Stein, who had an anecdote or case to illustrate every point he felt strongly about, told this one about a wife who complained that her husband didn't understand her:

"He never knows what I like," she said, "and never does things that I enjoy."

"Like what?" asked Stein.

"Well, I love the theater but my husband will never go with me and I don't like going alone."

"Have you asked him to go with you recently?" Stein asked.

"I'll try," said the woman, "but I know it won't help."

The woman returned to the doctor a week later, almost triumphant.

"You see," she said, "I told you. I asked him to go with me to the theater and he refused."

"What did you say to him?" asked Stein.

"I said, 'You wouldn't want to go with me to theater, would you?' "

Of course, Stein told me, hearing the question stated that way, the husband would surely refuse, but "had she said it more positively so that he realized how important it was to her, I know her husband would have gone with her. He's a very caring and reasonable man." Whether Stein's story was actual or apocryphal, it made his point: Partners have to be straight and clear so that each can pick up the other's wishes and expectations.

As for conflicts themselves, therapists try to help partners understand what they're fighting about and how they're fighting. A therapist will ask a couple why a specific fight took place. What did they hope to achieve and how did they go about trying to achieve it? The "why" is not meant to unearth profound global responses that trace the causes of every fight back to the roots of the relationship—"We're fighting because he never takes care of the kids even when I'm sick and dying." Instead the questioning is designed to keep partners fixed on the issues at hand, the cause of this particular fight—"We're fighting because he scheduled a meeting at the very time he was supposed to pick up Lisa, and I had to rearrange my schedule at a moment's notice in order to get her."

The reason for that focus is to help couples recognize that yelling and screaming can't undo the past, but working on a problem in the present can influence how that problem will be dealt with again in the future. The more capable a couple is of defining specific issues in each battle rather than dredging up every sore point that exists between them, the less destructive each fight will be and the more likely to bring about some change.

Some of the effects of the techniques and lessons of therapy were described by a couple, married fifteen years, who had had marital therapy about seven years ago, and considered it a turning point in their marriage. Their ability to learn how to speak and relate better to one another is what this couple, the Reins, emphasized, although other aspects to their therapy involved insights into the backgrounds and upbringing of each.

Ellen Rein, at forty, was one of the most beautiful women I had ever seen. With her smooth skin (not a hint of a wrinkle), honey-colored hair (not a trace of gray), and almond-shaped, hazel eyes (not a suggestion of puffiness), she had the kind of scrubbed, timeless looks that have nothing to do with fashion and will probably never fade with age. Yet it was her good looks that triggered off many of the marital troubles that sent her and her husband Donn into therapy. Even as a young child her beauty had set her apart from other children, and she grew up adored and indulged, catered to by her parents and her two older brothers, who loved to show off their beautiful little sister. Handsome enough himself and an only child in his family, Donn Rein had grown up with his own share of indulgence and coddling.

At first the marriage seemed a continuation of the charmed life both had enjoyed at home. The couple joined the local beach club, not far from their suburban home. There Ellen became known for her powerful tennis backhand along with her beauty, and Donn made new connections that he hoped would help him up the management ladder of the department store for which he worked.

In their third year of marriage they had a child, and soon afterward another, then another, with little time between. Within just a few years, their lives had changed completely. Especially Ellen's. Suddenly she had no time for tennis or beach clubs, little money for pretty clothes and parties, and barely a drop of energy for anything by the end of a day of caring for her three babes. Although she had a cleaning service that did heavy-duty household chores every week, she felt now that she needed more help, at least twice a week. Donn refused, arguing that they couldn't afford that kind of luxury. She responded by sniping at his cheapness and lack of concern for her, and he retaliated by mocking her self-indulgence and "narcissism," the results, he pointed out again and again, of her being beautiful and spoiled. If she wanted more help in the house, he argued, she should get a part-time job to increase their income. How could she get a job, she answered, when he was too tight to spend any money on a part-time housekeeper to care for the children?

For two years they bickered and fought: she complaining that her life had been turned upside down since the birth of the children, that she was expected to do all the giving while he went along his merry way; he arguing that he couldn't work any harder than he was and she was making unreasonable demands on him. For some reason that neither remembers, both sets of in-laws became embroiled in their children's fights, making matters that much worse. By the time the Reins went to a marital therapist, they had given up sex with each other altogether, they could barely speak without fighting, and Donn had been diagnosed as suffering from high blood pressure.

Like most couples, each approached the therapist by pointing out that the other needed help. He, in turn, insisted that he would not see either of them separately to begin with; he needed to evaluate them together. And he made a rule: They were not to fight at home, but must save their fights for the office so that he could see what they were fighting about and how they were fighting.

"It was the strangest thing," Ellen recalled, looking back seven years. "Here, we could barely say a civil word to each other, but when the doctor said we weren't allowed to fight at home, we managed not to fight. We didn't forget the issues, we just put them off until we got to his office. We were like children obeying a parent. I guess that's one of the things therapy does. It gives you an authority outside yourself to add controls that you're not able to impose yourself."

Therapy did more for the Reins. At the sessions to which they carried their fights, the therapist would intervene in the midst of their arguments to make them listen hard to what each was saying. Donn remembers at one of their earliest sessions hearing the therapist say to Ellen, "He can't hear you when you're calling him a bastard. Say something he can hear!" Whatever it was Ellen was talking about, she stopped short and reworded her complaint in a way that helped Donn listen without jumping to fight back. Once they were able to listen to each other, the therapist asked them whether each could see some legitimacy in the other's viewpoint. They admitted that they could, and he pressed them to think about what each could do to help the other out. "He told us," Donn said, "that the only way therapy could work was for both of us to get some 'goodies' out of it. That was the word he used." What he meant was that both needed to feel the other understood, and was willing to make some concessions, to negotiate.

Over several sessions they did negotiate, and they came out with a plan they both felt they could live with: Donn agreed to take more real responsibility for the children, not just to help out when asked. Part of that responsibility involved dressing and feeding them on weekends when he was home, and driving them wherever they had to be. He also agreed to stay home alone with them one evening a week, while Ellen went out by herself to spend the time however she saw fit. In turn, she agreed to stop nagging him about money and recognize that their finances were limited in spite of his managerial position. And part of that recognition involved a decision to go back to school to earn a teaching certificate as soon as their youngest child began school so that in a few years she could teach and supplement their income.

As important as the agreements they reached, the Reins feel, was the more honest understanding each attained of the other's position, and one that has carried over into their life today. Donn acknowledged that Ellen wasn't simply acting like a beautiful spoiled brat when she complained of the burden of spending all her time caring for three young children with little outside help. That acknowledgment meant a great deal to her. Ellen acknowledged that Donn was working as hard as he could but that there was a limit to how much he could earn. For the first time, in fact, she sat down with him and took a serious interest in their finances, and that interest and understanding went a long way toward relieving him of the pressures he had felt. Today, they are busy with their growing children and their own lives (Ellen is now a nursery school teacher), and they look back with affection on the therapist who helped them speak so that they could be heard and fight without destroying each other.

Beyond the issues of communicating clearly and fighting fairly, marital therapy offers a way for a couple to probe into deeper causes for the problems between them and to work at relieving those problems. How therapists approach a couple's problems depends on the orientation of the therapist. As the fields of family and marital therapy have grown, dozens of new theories and approaches have arisen, and it's worth a couple's while to find out what a therapist's philosophy is before getting involved in the therapy. For example, a man who bridles at any kind of authority may have great difficulty if he and his wife meet up with what is called "strategic therapy." In this approach the therapist is very directive, developing a strategy for solving specific problems in a family and giving parents and children prescriptions for how to behave in order to achieve that strategy. The authority-hating man might find himself in head-to-head combat with such a therapist, undermining all efforts to solve his family problems. On the other hand, a man who is hesitant or confused and welcomes some direction might find this kind of therapy the best mode for working out marital troubles.

Although few therapists are such purists that they stick rigidly to one technique or approach, most do have an orientation that they favor and that forms the framework for their attitudes and methods. By asking about that orientation, a couple can judge whether they will be able to work with a therapist.

Some therapists, for example, would devote many sessions to digging into each partner's family history and discovering the roots of current problems in their earlier backgrounds. Such therapists, whose orientation is a "psychodynamic" one, might see a couple individually for a while and then together, or might send one or both off for individual therapy in addition to their marital therapy. The goal of this therapy would be to have the couple gain insights into their pasts, and then apply those insights to the way they act in the present.

A therapist whose orientation is what is called "experiential" would put less emphasis on the past and more on the effect each partner has on the other—the way they experience one another. Like Ellen and Donn Rein, who described their marital therapy sessions above, couples in this form of therapy would explore the emotions and reactions each evokes in the other by the things they say and do. In this form of therapy, also, a couple might be invited to participate in group therapy sessions with other couples. The assumption is that listening to the way other spouses speak to one another might give them perspective into their own ways of relating, and help them change those ways if need be.

"Behavior" therapists, from a third school of thought, take a different approach altogether. This therapy concentrates completely on the present and on bringing about immediate changes without any interpretation of the past. Family histories and relationships are not examined at all. Instead the therapist looks carefully at each spouse's behavior pattern and develops a system of rewards and punishments to reinforce behavior that helps the couple and eliminate behavior that harms them. For example, if a

wife constantly interrupts her husband and the husband
sulks in response, she would be rewarded every time she
caught herself before interrupting, and he every time he
spoke out rather than withdraw into silence. The reward
might be dipping into the family budget for a personal
treat, or choosing the family entertainment for a month,
or anything else the two considered rewarding.

Then there are therapists who place special importance on the role of extended families. Such a therapist
would somehow involve a couple's parents, siblings or
other relatives in their therapy. Family members might be
invited to attend some therapy sessions, or partners might
be instructed to spend some time in their family homes
with their parents. The purpose of this kind of involvement is for spouses to learn to recognize ways they get
along with their parents that may be harmful to their
marriage. For example, a man who is sarcastic to his wife
and embarrasses her in public might discover, when he is
paying attention to such things, that he is treating his wife
just as his father always treated him. Or a woman so
driven to achievement that she has little patience for her
family might realize, in spending time with her mother,
that the older woman has constantly goaded her toward
accomplishment, perhaps to make up for her own sense
of inadequacy. Those realizations help spur change in
both partners.

Finally, if children are affected by a couple's problems, or have problems of their own, the entire family
might undertake family therapy. Many family therapists
refer to themselves as "systems" therapists, meaning that
they see the family as a unit, as a system, in which
anything that happens to one part affects the rest. Family
problems may come about because the system is too
rigid—in the words of one therapist, "If one member of
the family sneezes, everybody grabs for a handkerchief."
Or problems may result because various family members
act toward one another in disturbed ways—a father constantly enraged at the children, for example, with a mother
so indulging them they don't know where they stand.
Strategic therapy is a form of family therapy that works
out plans and strategies for solving a family's problems.

Which kind of therapy is best? That is a question that,

ultimately, a couple have to decide for themselves, for no objective answers exist. In his book *Couples in Conflict*, psychologist Alan Gurman seeks to evaluate the effectiveness of many different kinds of therapies. His conclusion is that while there are areas in which some may be more effective than others, the skill of the therapist carries more weight in the outcome than the particular philosophy any one therapist espouses. Therefore, the most important thing partners can do is find a therapist who inspires confidence in them, and then ask questions to see whether they feel comfortable with his or her approach.

How do they go about finding such a therapist? They can begin by getting recommendations. A family physician, a minister or a rabbi usually can supply the names of therapists for a family seeking help. If not, a good idea is to call the psychiatric department of a university hospital, outline the problem for the physician who is chief of that service and ask for recommendations. A social service organization is another good source of referral. Inquiries can be made to the social service division of Catholic Charities or the Jewish Board of Family and Children's Services or other community organizations that deal with family problems.

A family or marital therapist may be a psychiatrist, who has a medical degree, or a psychologist or a social worker. Whatever other degrees a therapist holds, however, the professional a couple should see for marital problems should have training in working with couples and families. From that viewpoint, a psychiatrist who has worked only with individuals in therapy may be less helpful than a social worker who has worked extensively with families. And that is something that needs to be considered when choosing a therapist.

Other considerations are called for. When I said that a husband and a wife should feel comfortable with their therapist, what I meant is they should feel the therapist respects them, is sympathetic to them and is listening to what they are saying rather than trying to impose his or her thoughts on them. If they wish, they should interview more than one therapist to find one who feels right for them. And if in the course of therapy, they begin to have doubts about what is taking place, they should not hesitate to ask for a consultation with another professional (therapists have a way of telling you you're "resisting" therapy if you begin to complain—best to check out doubts with a second opinion). If any couple decides after a few visits (two to three visits is a fair amount of time) that they have fallen into the wrong hands, they are under no obligation to continue with the therapist they have chosen, although it may be useful to state their objections and, before choosing somebody else, listen to the therapist's reasons for moving in certain directions. If they have chosen a therapist who seems to be working well with them, they may find improvements in their marriage within a few months.

Sex therapy is a subject in itself. Many couples who enter family therapy find that their sex life improves when the rest of their family life improves. But sex therapy is more directly called for when sexual problems make up the primary problems in a marriage and then cast a pall on the rest of the relationship. It's not always possible for a couple to judge for themselves whether their sexual difficulties result from other matters between them or whether the sexual frustrations are the main problems disrupting other parts of the marriage. That's why it's a good idea for couples with sexual dysfunctions to see a professional trained in both sexual and marital therapy. Such a therapist can evaluate the causes for sexual difficulties—whether they grow out of deep-seated anger and hostility, whether partners have become disenchanted or so bored with one another that they have lost interest or whether the problems result from misunderstandings on their part.

Alexander Levay of Columbia University described the last category—misunderstandings—as a common cause of sexual problems, and one that is the most hopeful to work with. A psychiatrist who does both marital and sex therapy, Levay exudes a kind of comforting warmth I would think puts his patients at ease almost immediately. "A man may be afraid when he is making love," he explained, "that he won't be able to keep up an erection, and if he can't keep it up, his wife will be very disappointed and then she'll be angry at him, and maybe she'll leave him or have an affair. So he's in great fear. And in his mind the only way a man satisfies his wife sexually is through intercourse, so he avoids any sexual contact. Meanwhile his wife has a completely wrong idea of his behavior. She thinks he is no longer attracted to her—she's too old, has put on too much weight, etc. He never tells her his fears; after all, a man isn't supposed to show any weaknesses. And she never discusses her hurt feelings with him. Yet this is a couple with whom a therapist can do a lot."

The first thing the therapist can do is "explain the man to himself and to his wife." Then the therapist can show the man how erroneous his thinking is, pointing out that intercourse is not *the* way of having sex, it's *one* way, and that some people prefer other ways, and can feel close and loving toward one another without intercourse. Based on such a discussion, what most therapists would do is give the couple some assignments designed to have them enjoy one another sensually—touching and caressing one another's bodies without culminating in intercourse. The purpose of these exercises is to cut down both partners' anxieties about performance and have them rediscover the pleasures of sex.

In recent years sex therapy and the assignments and exercises originally devised by William Masters and Virginia Johnson have come under attack for being too mechanistic and having little to do with love and emotion. Masters and Johnson themselves have been accused of exaggerating the benefits of their sex therapy and of the techniques they originated. Yet many sex therapists maintain that, in spite of shortcomings, Masters and Johnson were pioneers whose research and teachings created opportunities for treating sexual disorders in ways that had never existed before. They point out that there are mechanical aspects to sexual intimacy that couples can learn, and that beyond those mechanics, the process of helping one another relieve anxieties and distortions makes possible a very special kind of intimacy.

Part of a couple's ability to relieve anxieties in one another comes from education. So during the course of sex therapy, they are given a better understanding of human physiology than most had before they began. One thing they learn, in Levay's words, is that "for a woman an orgasm is both a satisfaction and a stimulation; for a man it is only a satisfaction." That is, a woman can get aroused again very quickly after orgasm and can have multiple orgasms while it would take some time for a man to become aroused again or to continue without any loss of arousal (except, perhaps, very young men).

Like sexual exercises, education is also meant to relax partners so that they don't make excessive demands on themselves or one another. Partners learn that neither needs to feel forced into arousal, nor does either one need to be deprived of sexual enjoyment. One can tell the other, I don't actually feel like making love, but I'll stimulate you and I'll satisfy you. Said Levay, "I use the eating analogy. If one of you is hungry and one not hungry, the one who is not hungry should not be forced to eat nor should the other be prevented from eating. And maybe you might help each other in the process—if you get hungry watching him eat, then eat something too."

Through sex therapy, also, a couple learn not to be ashamed of their bodies and their desires. Even in our liberated times, for example, children grow up ashamed and fearful of masturbating, although most do it. Sex therapists consider masturbation a "hidden asset" because it shows that the person has sexual desires and abilities. So when partners admit that each has been masturbating privately, they are encouraged to do it together as a beginning to overcoming embarrassment and fears of sexual closeness.

Because many sex therapists also have experience in general marital therapy, they often try to look at sex problems from a broader point of view. A therapist might ask a couple to describe the dreams they had at night before or after carrying out a sexual assignment, and through those dreams arrive at some understanding of the underlying causes for sexual difficulties. Or if a couple can't seem to do the exercises and assignments given, the therapist will probe to understand why not, to discover the deeper motives behind their inabilities and problems.

And what kinds of problems do sex therapists see? They seem to change over time. A few years ago, I've been told, one of the key couple complaints at sex clinics and therapists' consultation rooms was the woman's inability to achieve orgasm. Some women were distraught over their own lack of orgasm; some men over their inability to give their wives an orgasm. Today, those complaints have greatly diminished. Levay believes the outpour of information on the subject, in books, popular magazines, even television shows, have educated women and men, so that the issue is no longer a pressing one in marriages. The other possibility, it would seem to me, is that as the "Big O" has ceased to be the subject of absorbing public interest and to receive the publicity it once did, fewer couples feel so inadequate or concerned about it that they seek professional help.

Today, male performance problems have displaced those of females on the sex therapists' couches. So have general problems of low sexual desire on the part of both men and women. Here again, that subject, known as inhibited sexual desire (ISD) received a great spurt of publicity in the 1980s, giving the impression that it was some new problem of epidemic proportions. Actually, there have always been people, including married people, who had few sexual desires or interests, but the labeling of this characteristic as an official diagnosis by the American Psychiatric Association brought new attention to it. Since nobody has come up with a formula for what normal desire is, it is hard for experts to diagnose inhibited desire in a couple. But there are couples who avoid sex completely, and if they go to a therapist, it may mean that they have some sexual feelings and fantasies that they would like to get in touch with and act on.

In many cases, marriages that avoid sex are marriages that are trying to avoid performance problems that may have come along with sex. Or they are marriages in which the partners have become sexually bored with one another, and instead of working to relieve the boredom, they have given up on sex. In such marriages, sexlessness is an adaptation, said Levay, and desire isn't inhibited— it's abandoned in the interest of peace. By avoiding sex, the spouses preserve their relationship without crisis or disappointments, without reminding one another of what they're missing. Such an arrangement is a throwback to the way each spouse once lived in his or her original family, squelching sexual feelings toward parents or siblings. If through therapy, such partners can allow themselves to have a few good sexual experiences, to take a chance in order to get pleasure again, they may be able to reverse their adaptation and bring sex back into their married life.

Finding the right sex therapist calls for as much care and caution as finding any other marital or family therapist, with one addition: Many sexual complaints actually stem from physical disorders—hormone imbalances, poor circulation, chronic illnesses—or from medications taken to treat physical ailments such as diabetes or thyroid deficiencies. Before going to a sex therapist, a person should have a thorough physical exam to check out physical causes. If they don't exist, the best sources of referral for a therapist is a physician, a family or marital therapist, a friend who has been treated by a sex therapist or, again, a good teaching hospital.

~

Many people who wouldn't think of seeking out a marital or sex therapist when they have marital problems would find a way to speak to a pastor, a priest, or a rabbi. And counseling couples is, in fact, an important part of the work of any religious leader.

"People connect marriage with religion," said Rabbi Judah Nadich, spiritual leader of the Park Avenue Synagogue, one of the largest in Manhattan. "Marriage is a sacred institution, so when something goes wrong, the first person they think to call is a religious leader. I have had phone calls from people who are not even members of my congregation or observant Jews in any way." A Catholic priest and an Episcopalian minister agreed that they were often the first resource for a troubled marriage. But all agreed, also, that if they saw a serious family problem they thought needed professional therapy, they would refer that couple to the proper resources. Most religious leaders keep lists of referral possibilities so they can help congregants in such matters.

Along with counseling, many churches and synagogues offer premarital programs they hope will tone down expectations and prevent problems before they ever get started. In fact, the only premarital counseling most couples receive is done by clergy, and couples who do not have religious ceremonies rarely receive any counseling—few therapists are called on to do such early intervention.

The Roman Catholic church, with its strong stand against divorce, has been especially active in such programs, with many dioceses making them mandatory for engaged couples who want to marry in the church. In Providence, Rhode Island, for example, engaged Catholic couples must wait six months before being married. During that time, they are required to take at least forty-five hours of prenuptial training given by their church. The training includes an evaluation by the couple of their compatibility, a seminar on sexuality and fertility and an agreement by the couple to do some service for the community. Administrators of the diocese have found that a number of couples who go through the program cancel or postpone their weddings because they recognize that they are not ready for marriage.

An Episcopalian priest in New York has seen similar results. Reverend Barbara Blair gives every couple she marries a detailed questionnaire that asks things such as "What are your expectations from this marriage?" "What do you like most about yourself, your partner?" "Are there any secrets that you cannot share with your partner?" The partners fill out the questionnaire separately and then the priest discusses their answers with them together. In some cases, when the answers show very different expectations and orientations toward marriage, a couple may decide not to marry. In New Jersey, Lutheran Pastor Michael Fonner plays a card game with a prospective bride and groom. He labels six cards with six aspects of married life—sex, money, family, friends, property, children—and gives the partners each three cards face down, which they turn over one at a time and discuss for four or five minutes in terms of marriage. Each has two minutes to respond to the other's comments. Then the pastor talks with the couple about his perception of their attitudes. Occasionally, if he believes the two are making a mistake in marrying, he will refuse to marry them in his church.

The problem with all prenuptial counseling and evaluations is that most couples are, in the words of the Reverend Blair, "on a pink cloud" before they marry, hardly prone to question the wisdom of their marital decision seriously or focus hard on differences between them. That is why a number of churches and synagogues have now instituted counseling sessions for newly married couples into their first or second years of marriage, for whom the illusions and unreal expectations are beginning to wear thin.

This philosophy of intervening after marriage is under way rather than before has become especially popular among lay organizations. One of these, the National Association of Couples for Marriage Enrichment (ACME) has developed programs in which couples married for some time share their experiences with younger, newly married ones in an effort to help the latter get through rough spots. Among the most active of these programs is one carried out in Kansas City, Missouri, where regular classes are conducted for couples married six months to two years. Called "Growth in Marriage for Newlyweds," the program includes six sessions, which run about three hours each, on such topics as communication skills, resolving conflicts, sexuality and intimacy and understanding family backgrounds. Like marriage encounter groups, enrichment programs with lay rather than professional leaders seek to have couples learn from one another and to recognize that their own problems may not be unique.

How effective are enrichment programs or encounter programs, religious counseling and advice? Any form of solid marital education can be helpful to couples seeking to get a better understanding of themselves and their marriages. The danger in all lay movements of this sort is that people with serious problems may try to use them as substitutes for the more experienced professional help they need, with disastrous results to themselves and their marriage. The other danger, or at least detriment, is that couples with conflicts may fool themselves into thinking that by attending enrichment programs, they are working out their differences, just as some couples in therapy like to pretend to themselves that simply being in therapy and gaining insights mean they are solving their problems.

Changing in marriage takes time, understanding and de-termination. It doesn't happen in a weekend or a few weeks. Still, if a beginning is made through these pro-grams, and if some marital difficulties can be prevented by them, that is certainly to the good.

Ministers, priests, rabbis and leaders of marriage en-richment movements have one thing in common: they all work to strengthen marriages and help them stay to-gether. Therapists are different. They have been trained to be objective, to keep their own values out of their treat-ment of patients so that the individuals and couples who come to them can discover through therapy what it is they want and what they believe is best for them. As one therapist said, "From my viewpoint, divorce can be a successful resolution to a couple's treatment. A priest experiences the same resolution as a failure on many levels—a personal failure and a religious one." That makes good sense. Yet a Catholic priest, liberal enough to believe that the church should be more flexible about divorces, argued that while the stricture against divorce can be harmful when people are ill-suited to one another, it can also be a "healthy thing." That is, it "can prevent couples from rather peremptorily getting a divorce, and force them to take the whole thing more seriously." And that makes sense too.

I don't believe therapists should or have a right to impose their own views on their patients. Yet I liked it when a therapist told me, "I have a bias toward marriage, and I tell that to my patients." Such a bias means that the therapist will begin by trying to give the marriage every chance to make it. It means that she or he will recognize that couples come into therapy during a crisis, when the scales are tipped toward the negative, and some efforts need to be made to help them discover the positives in their marriage. Having a bias toward marriage means help-ing a couple hold on to their past history, the reasons they married in the first place, rather than give in to the angers of their recent history. And it means allowing the couple time to rediscover the strengths they have, knowing that there is always time later for a divorce, if in the end that is what they want.

I believe that a therapist should be neutral and impartial toward the partners, the two patients in the marriage, but that there is no breach of ethics in being biased toward the third patient, the marriage.

CHAPTER ELEVEN

~:~

Forever II
Some Conclusions

Durability, a psychiatrist said to me, is its own proof of a good marriage. That is, the fact that a marriage has lasted for many years is the ultimate statement about its ability to satisfy the partners, no matter what the marriage might look like from the outside. I do not agree with that assessment. Marriages may last a lifetime yet be filled with hatred. Why do they continue? Often for financial reasons—a woman (less often a man) cannot afford to walk out, so dependent is she on her husband's economic support, especially when there are children in the picture. Or for security—as bad as it is inside a marriage, fear of the outside, the unknown, keeps a couple bound together, even in their unhappiness. Many women, in addition, still feel that they must get their status and position in society from their husbands. Giving up that position means giving up their identity as Mrs. Somebody, leaving them insecure and vulnerable.

Sometimes a marriage lasts because of deeply neurotic needs: the couple need one another as whipping posts, to inflict pain or alternate roles of tormentor and victim. (That's not to say that all neurotic matches are bad. As an old saying goes, if the rocks in her head fit the holes in his, that's all right too. But the kinds of neurotic unions that lead to constant hurt, humiliation and misery, the kinds in which spouses continually tear away at each other, cannot be listed under the category of good or even acceptable marriages just because they have endured.) Some unhappy marriages drag on long after they have ended emotionally because of religious strictures, some "for the sake of the children," some because of family or community pressures. And some marriages continue simply out of inertia—there is no pressing reason to end them even though the partners have long since stopped feeling anything for one another, not even anger (older couples, who married perhaps forty or fifty years ago when divorce was strongly frowned upon, are more likely to endure such marriages than are couples married in the past twenty years or so when divorce has become far more accepted. Yet there are younger couples who remain in such marriages too).

Two marital therapists in California who have studied marriage among the elderly, James A. Peterson and Marcia Lasswell, classify long marriages in which the couple gain little enjoyment from one another but are resigned to living together as "survivor marriages," as opposed to "creative marriages," in which there is continual satisfaction and excitement. Like all such labels, these are somewhat oversimplified. Most marriages that endure include "survivor" times and "creative" times. Even the most creative marriage has its lulls and dead spots, and many seemingly shallow marriages are built around more complex emotions and attachments than meet the eye. Yet some marriages do simply survive, with little joy and little heat, and these can be distinguished from more satisfying long marriages.

To help make those distinctions, I interviewed several couples whose marriages had lasted for twenty-five years or more and then broken up. I wondered (1) why these marriages had lasted as long as they had before ending, (2) whether, had I met each of these couples before their divorce—say in their fifteenth or sixteenth year of marriage—they or I would have regarded their marriages as good, sound, working ones and (3) what had finally caused these marriages to end. The main impression I came away with was that most of the marriages that ended after many years had really ended for both partners years earlier, sometimes shortly after the marriage had begun, and for a variety of reasons had continued in form only. Had I interviewed these couples while they were still married, I believe the deadness that divided them would have been apparent, if not immediately, then after some hours spent with them.

Exceptions to these conclusions were long marriages that broke up after some catastrophic event, such as the death of a child, so shook their foundations that they could not continue, and those in which one partner experienced what is commonly known as midlife crisis and left to seek something different from what the marriage had always been. Actually, such a crisis doesn't happen only during middle age—it can occur long before or much later, when one partner assesses the marriage and wonders, "Is this all there is?" Some of these marriages that break up suddenly may have been superficial and devoid of feeling all along. In others, the longings for more may be based on vague fantasies and dreamy hopes that a new marriage will substitute for personal failings or somehow halt the inevitable slippage of time.

Aside from these exceptions, the long marriages that didn't last were, for the most part, marriages that had been empty all along. Why did they finally end? In some cases because one party mustered enough energy to decide that whatever reasons had existed for staying together were no longer strong enough to balance the dead weight of the marriage. More often some precipitating event shattered their fragile structure.

Typical of other late-in-marriage divorces was that of a forty-eight-year-old Roman Catholic woman, Gerri Dean, whose loveless marriage stretched out over twenty-seven years.

"By the second year into our marriage," she said, "I knew this was not good. I never felt I was special or important to my husband; I never felt we were connected emotionally. Even when we went out to dinner, he couldn't stand to be alone; he always invited other people along."

The couple had five children, but the only time this woman sensed any warmth or ties to her husband was when one baby died a crib death. "We consoled each other then, and it brought us closer," she recalled, "but the closeness didn't last. My next delivery was a difficult one and he didn't even come to the hospital with me. I rationalized that it was hard for him and he felt under pressure. But it was hard for me too."

The marriage went on year after year because in her family and religion, divorce was "unthinkable," and she lived in the hope that things would get better "if you try to work at it." What she discovered was that her husband was not going to change or work at the marriage. She began to fill up every moment of her life with children and with work. She went back to school, took a degree in nutrition and became the dietitian for a local hospital. And there she met a man with whom she embarked on an eight-year love affair.

Her marriage ended when her husband found out about the affair. He gave her an ultimatum: End the affair or be prepared for a divorce. "I chose divorce," she said. The divorce left her ostracized by her church and many community members, but her children have stayed with her and remained close to her. Her lover, a married man whom she continues to see, cannot bring himself to leave his wife and family. Still, Gerri has no regrets.

"Some things you can do something about; some things you can't," she said. "I realized after many years of trying that I could do nothing about my husband's coldness and distance from me and the children. Had I had a richer marriage, I could have grown and thrived. As it was, I felt shut out and shriveled up."

~

Marriages that last because they are satisfying to both partners, marriages in which couples can give positive rather than negative reasons for staying together, are usually more complex than those entrenched ones that just go on. These are the marriages that stay together both "because of" and "in spite of"—because of the emotional riches the marriage provides and in spite of difficulties that arise. The qualities that define these marriages have been discussed and described throughout this book. Now for some conclusions.

What are the characteristics of long, satisfying, happy marriages? As I've said before, there is no formula, no single recipe that when used in the right proportions will produce the perfect marriage, or even a working one. Rather, there are certain abilities and outlooks that couples in strong marriages have, not all of them at all times, but a large proportion a good part of the time. They fall, it seems to me, into eight categories:

1. An ability to change and tolerate change. Change is inevitable in marriage as in life. Partners become involved in work and pull back from work; children are born, go to school, leave home; spouses age, get sick, drop old interests, take on new ones, make new friends, live through the sorrows of old ones; parents get old and die; couples move from apartments to houses and back to apartments, from one town to another. Changes bring anxieties and disequilibrium. Yet in the strongest marriages, each partner is able to make "midcourse corrections, almost like astronauts," as one psychiatrist put it. That is, they are able both to adapt to the change that is happening in the marriage or in the other partner and, when called for, to change themselves.

Couples whose marriages have lasted fifteen years or more have lived through some of the most rapid and overwhelming social change in modern history. These people married at a time when marriage had a set form, when husbands knew that their work was to provide for the family and wives knew that theirs was to care for the home and children. During the course of these marriages, the world turned upside down. Marriage was ridiculed as a dying if not dead institution, to which almost any "alternative" was better for the "growth" of the individual. Husbands who played out the traditional roles they had been taught as children were now seen as "insensitive," dictatorial "patriarchs," while wives were "oppressed" in "stifling" marriages. And along with the rhetoric of a changing society came real change, a new emphasis on a woman's right to seek her own work outside her home and on a man's responsibility—and right—to shift some of his energies and time away from the outside to the inside of his home and to his family. The changes brought chaos to many marriages that had started out one way and then found all the premises on which they had been built cut out from under them.

In the marriages that have remained strong and viable, partners have had the flexibility to pick up what was useful to them from the barrage of slogans and confusions of "facts," and change their marriages and themselves to incorporate new ideals that made sense to them. Even the marriages that have kept the most traditional forms, as many have, have had to make concessions to the mood of the times, if not within the marriage itself then in the couple's outlook and their attitudes toward their children. The Flahertys, one of the most conventional couples interviewed, maintained that Peggy Flaherty's place was in her home, and her work the work of running the family finances and caring for her husband. Yet they strongly encouraged their two daughters to develop occupations— one is a dental technician, the other a nurse—and to continue working after they had families of their own. (True, these are typically "women's" occupations, but the very idea of a married woman working had once been anathema to Tom Flaherty.) Although practicing Catholics themselves, they have succored and supported one daughter who is divorced, recognizing, they said, that she had a right to rid herself of a bad marriage and seek her own happiness.

Much greater changes have taken place in the couples who have shifted their life patterns as social values have shifted. The women who have gone to work or back to school years into their marriages have come to see themselves as different beings than they were in their earlier days. They have not discarded their old selves; they have developed a different part of them. But in doing so they have changed their marriages. Their husbands have accommodated to those changes—some more willingly than others—and in doing so, many have changed themselves. They have changed the way they behave by taking on household tasks they would not have dreamed of touching when they first married, and by rearranging their schedules to make room for their wives' schedules. More important, they have changed inwardly, many of them, truly acknowledging their wives' strivings, ambitions and accomplishments outside their homes. One tiny manifestation of these changes in long marriages are the numbers of no-longer-young men I see at dinner parties automatically getting up to clear the table or serve a course while their wives sit and chat with guests. They are not self-consciously carrying out some carefully formulated contract. They have incorporated this domestic behavior into their way of being. For them, such acts are not merely gestures; they represent an inner change.

But there is an attitude toward change in long marriages that goes far beyond the social issues. There is this: People who stay happily married see themselves not as victims of fate, but as free agents who make choices in life. Although, like everyone else, they are influenced by their own family backgrounds, for the most part they do not allow their lives together to be dominated by their earlier family lives apart. Because they choose to be married to one another, a choice they make again and again, they are open to changing themselves, pulling away from what *was* in order to make what *is* alive and vital. In other words, as much as they are able to, they try to control their lives, rather than drifting along as the patsies of destiny.

A man whose marriage had gone through a rough time for a while spoke about his decision not to leave even when the couple's troubles reached their worst. "Had I left," he said, "I would have missed out on something good. There's a sense of optimism in staying married and watching this incremental change going on. You think, 'Well, some things have changed a little; I'm going to stick around to see what will happen next.' "

Now, it must be said that every change a partner injects into a marriage is not necessarily acceptable, nor can every change be incorporated within it. Sometimes one partner changes so drastically that all the shared ideals and values on which the marriage was based become flooded and washed away by the change, so much so that the marriage cannot continue. The wife of a movie star described with great sadness the end of her marriage of twenty-six years. At the height of his movie success, her husband had become a heavy user of drugs, especially cocaine, the favored stimulant of Hollywood stars. The drugs, she said, had changed his personality, "scrambled his brain" so that she no longer recognized the person he was beneath the person he had become. He had taken up now with much younger women, most of them groupies who follow stars from place to place. "I feel like a widow," this wife said. "I'm in mourning, for my marriage and for the man I married. I went along with everything that came into our lives: our move from a small town to Hollywood, his sudden stardom and the fears and insecurities his success brought him. With it all, we were close and loving to one another. We had grown up together, we had memories and connections and we were able to continue growing together. But now, I don't know him anymore, and I'm mourning my loss."

In the best of marriages, change takes place in a context. It is contained within the boundaries of the marriage as both parties have known it. Within those boundaries each partner acts and reacts, bending to the changes in the other and in the world outside. And even while they change and sway, couples recognize that some things cannot change and should not change—and that leads to the second characteristic of long-term marriages, and its major paradox.

2. An ability to live with the unchangeable, which means to live with unresolved conflict when necessary. The simultaneous acceptance of change and of lack of change in long marriages is summed up by the words of a shopkeeper, married thirty-eight years: "You have to know when to holler and you have to know when to look away."

A statement made by many couples when asked about the "secrets" of their happy marriage was, "We don't expect perfection," or some variation thereof. They would go on to explain that their marriage had areas that were far from perfect, qualities in one another that they wish could have changed but they have come to recognize as qualities that will never change. Still, they live with those unchangeable, and sometimes disturbing, qualities, because, as one woman said, "The payoff is so great in other areas." We have been so bombarded with advice books and articles about "solving" problems and "overcoming" adversity, about "improving" our marriages and becoming "ideal" mates that we often forget that it is possible also just to let things be, without solution or improvement.

On a superficial level, I think of a woman who described her misery early in her second marriage because of her husband's unbelievably ear-shattering snores. Night after night she lay awake listening to his nasal roars and wondering how she was going to survive this marriage. For a while she tried slipping out of bed in the middle of the night to sleep in the living room. But she didn't sleep well there, and, anyhow, she wanted to be in bed with her husband. Then she prevailed upon him to seek medical help to control the snoring. The doctors had nothing to offer, and the night sounds continued unabated. Finally, she stopped complaining and bought some ear plugs. They do not block out the noise completely, but they help. The snoring problem, she has decided, will never be solved, the plugs make it possible for her to live with it as best she can, and that is as much as she can do.

On a more serious level, long-married couples accept the knowledge that there are some deep-seated conflicts— about personality differences, habits, styles of dealing with things—that will never be solved. In the best of situations, they stop fighting about those issues and go about their lives instead of wasting their energies on a constant, fruitless struggle to settle differences "once and for all." Not long ago, at a time when marriage was under perpetual attack, this very quality of marriage, its imperfectability, was at the crux of the arguments against it. People spoke of marriage as a form of "settling" for something less than ideal, as "compromising" with what one wanted from life. Yet this ability to live with the imperfect is, it seems to me, the essence of maturity. Mature people are able to accept the limitations life places on them and work around them. And in the "working around," in finding ways to live with difficulties, they may experience some of the most creative moments of living.

Couples who get pleasure from their marriages often say that they do so because they focus on the strengths of the marriage, not its weaknesses, on compatibilities rather than dissonances. With that outlook they are able to enhance what is good so that it becomes the core of the marriage while the negatives cling only to the periphery.

Among the many remarried people I met who wished they had "tried harder" in their first marriages, some are finding their remarriages successful because they *are* "trying harder." They are maneuvering their marriages around imperfections and unresolved conflicts they were not willing to tolerate the first time because this time they are determined to make things work. An anthropologist, Kent Lawrence, said it had been a shock to him to find himself wedded in his second marriage to a wife who was a "scrapper," ready for a good fight any time. His first wife was not a fighter, and rarely had either of them raised their voices. Now he faced regular combat, especially over matters relating to ways of raising the children she had brought with her from her previous marriage. Had this been a first marriage, he said, he might have given up on the whole business. But "I didn't want to break up a second marriage that early, having broken a first one. I would have gone through my life consumed with guilt about being someone who isn't capable of staying married to people." And how did they resolve their differences? "We never actually resolved them. I pulled back and waited things out. As the kids got older, I developed a better rapport with them, and that improved my relationship with my wife." In short, he made himself live with the imperfections of the second marriage. Was he "settling"? I don't think so. He had become mature enough to get the best out of what he had, and that turned out to be quite a lot.

Actually, realizing that some things are unchangeable and irresolvable is not only one of the "secrets" of long marriage, but also, it would seem, one of the "secrets" of long life. I said earlier that people whose marriages end because of a crisis, such as an illness or a financial disaster, often are people who cannot live with the realities of their existence. They are destroyed by haunting dreams of what had been, might have been or should be. Along these lines, research in psychosomatic medicine, stressing the effects of emotions on an individual's well-being, has led to the concept that people can literally "eat themselves up alive" with regrets and frustrations, emotions that can be linked to a variety of physical diseases ranging from colitis to cancer. The point is not that we must all sit back and let life wash over us without trying to shape and control what happens to us. The point is that we can best control our lives—and our marriages—by acknowledging that some things will never be perfect and some things cannot be turned around, and apply our strengths where they can make a difference.

3. An assumption of permanence. Most marriages, first, second or later, begin with the hope and expectation that they will last forever. In the marriages that do last, "forever" is not only a hope, but an ongoing philosophy. The mates do not seriously think about divorce as a viable option. Certainly there are "divorce periods," times of distancing and anger, but even if divorce itself crosses the minds of the couple, it is not held out as an escape from difficulties. One can argue, with some truth, that couples married more than ten or fifteen years ago don't think about divorce because it was not as prevalent a part of our culture in earlier days as it is now. But that's not the complete story. Many couples married during those earlier days have divorced, and for many younger couples permanence is a built-in component of marriage, as it had been for their parents.

This attitude that a marriage will last, *must* last (not because some religious authority or family member says so, but because the marriage is that important to the couple), tempers a husband's and a wife's approach to conflicts and imperfections. They see the marriage as an entity in itself that must be protected. Or as family therapist Salvador Minuchin said, "A marriage is more than the sum of its parts. In marriage, one plus one doesn't equal two; it forms something different, something that is much more than two." And for the sake of that "something" that is the marriage, these couples are willing to make compromises and sacrifices when necessary. In today's terminology, they are committed to the marriage as well as to one another.

The commitment, however, is *not necessarily equal* at all times. In marriage after marriage, I had the impression that one partner more than the other was the "keeper of the commitment." One usually seemed more willing to give in after a fight or more prone to compromise to avoid the fight altogether and hold the marriage on a steady keel. That partner may have been the more dependent one, but was just as likely to be the stronger and more mature one, the one more able to swallow pride, break stalemates and see the other's point of view. But I also had the impression that the caring and dedication to the marriage was strong enough on the part of both partners that when the "commitment keeper" pulled back, or refused to be the conciliator on some issue, the other moved in and took over that role.

Along related lines, it was clear that the commitment to the marriage was not always top priority in both partners' lives at the same time, but it was usually top priority for one or the other at different times. In traditional marriages, especially, women spoke of going into marriage with the idea (and admonitions from their mothers) that it was up to them to keep the marriage going and to make it run smoothly while their husbands became preoccupied with their work world. Although many women have continued to hold that position, in other marriages, as the women have become more involved with their own work or schooling, the husbands have moved in to become guardians of the relationship. These shifts haven't always been easy or smooth, but they have been able to take place because of the underlying assumption on the part of both spouses that the marriage will last, and in the lasting needs to be watched over.

It should be pointed out that the commitment to marriage by long-married couples is usually a commitment not only to a relationship, but also to marriage as an institution. Mae West's famous remark that "marriage is an institution, and who wants to live in an institution" makes sense when the institution is seen as a static, stifling edifice. But to couples who value marriage, it is regarded as an institution that adds stability and order to life, transmits ideals from one generation to the next and provides a structure within which a woman and a man can entrust their souls to one another, knowing that they will be sheltered and protected by its permanence.

An important legal question is raised by the assumption of permanence in a marriage, and a Wisconsin lawyer named Allan Koritzinsky called me to raise it after seeing a reference to this book in the byline of an article I wrote. The question was, should couples entering marriage do so on the assumption that the marriage will last, and therefore make no legal contracts between them (other than their marriage vows)? Or should they begin marriage with the recognition that their union may well end in divorce, and therefore sign a prenuptial agreement spelling out their property and financial rights in case the marriage dissolves? (Some agreements also spell out details of housekeeping, such as who washes the dishes and who walks the dog, but these are generally not enforceable by the courts.)

The benefits of prenuptial agreements are clear-cut: they leave nothing to chance or to the vagaries built into some of the equitable distribution laws that have been passed in most states. They also cut down litigation expenses for both parties when a divorce does take place. And yet, when I took a quick survey about this issue among lawyers I know, I found them generally opposed to prenuptial agreements, especially for first marriages. "The prenuptials are great for business," one lawyer said, "but I don't think they're too terrific for marriage." And she went on to describe the fights she has witnessed when engaged couples tried to hammer out their agreements.

I tend to agree with this lawyer's assessment, and would argue for taking a chance on love without the legalities. For one thing, the process of deciding how to split assets and property before a marriage can start the marriage off on a note of dissension that undermines it from the beginning. For another, setting forth conditions for the breakup of a marriage before it begins certainly builds in the idea of impermanence, the very antithesis of the assumption of continuity upon which long marriages are based. People who argue in favor of prenuptial agreements compare them to life insurance. Yet life insurance is preparation for the inevitability of death; the death of a marriage should not be seen as inevitable at a time when it is just being born. Finally, prenuptial agreements tamper with the foundation of trust upon which strong marriages are built. The detailed spelling out of "yours and mine" diminishes the concept of sharing, which is, after all, what marriage is about.

All that has been said, however, I would qualify in the case of remarriages in which there are children of former marriages whose inheritance and other financial rights need to be protected by prenuptial agreements. Remarriages that partners enter into with a burden of hurt and mistrust carried over from a distressing divorce might also fit under this "qualifying clause." Better to begin with peace of mind by spelling out conditions than to let old suspicions poison a new union.

So, to answer the lawyer from Wisconsin: I believe marriages should begin on an assumption of permanence untarnished by agreements that anticipate dissolution, a belief tempered by some concessions to the practicalities of remarriages.

4. Trust. This is a word used again and again by couples, and it means many things. It means love, although people tend to use the word "trust" more often than they use "love." In part this is because "love" is an overused word, and one whose romantic meanings have overshadowed the deeper, more profound meaning of the love that binds married people. In larger part it is because feelings of love may wax and wane in the course of a marriage—in times of anger, for example, few people can keep in touch with those feelings—but trust is a constant; without it there is no true marriage. Trust also implies intimacy, or, rather, it forms the base for the closeness that couples in good marriages have established. But couples use the word "trust" more readily than "intimacy" or "love." And I believe they do because "trust" sums up much of the dynamic of a marriage, the back-and-forth interaction from which everything else grows. Trust in marriage allows for the sense of security and comfort that mark long and satisfying unions. Trust also makes possible the freedom marriage provides, the freedom and "right," in the words of psychiatrist Aaron Stein, "people have to be themselves and have their own feelings." Each partner trusts the other with his or her core self, trusts that that self will not be ridiculed or violated, trusts that it will be nurtured and protected—safe. And in that safety lies a special kind of freedom.

Intimacy, as I have said, is built around the trust partners allow themselves to have in one another. Once that trust exists, there is no set form intimacy must assume. I cannot say that every couple in a strong marriage communicate with one another as openly as the much-publicized communication ideals of our society would have them. Some do. Some are open and loose with one another, ventilating feelings and sensations freely. In other families, one partner, or both, may be more closed off, less able or willing to pour out heartsounds. But these marriages have their own ways of being intimate, which grow from the trust between partners. It may be that one partner is the expansive one while the second is more silent, relying on the other for emotional expressiveness. Or it may be that both act somewhat restrained in revealing sensitivities, yet they understand one another and feel comfortable with the more limited interchanges they have. I found many styles of relating among long-married couples, and no one seemed better than another as long as each couple was satisfied with their own style.

The trust that lies at the heart of happy marriages is also the foundation for sexual enjoyment among partners. When mates spoke about sexual loving, they almost always spoke about trusting feelings that had expanded over the years. "Sex is richer and deeper for us," said one woman. "We trust each other and we're not ashamed to get pleasure." Trust is also the reason invariably given for a commitment to monogamy, as in "I may be tempted, but I wouldn't want to violate our trust." When a partner has had a fling or brief affair, trust is the reason most often offered for having ended it or for avoiding further extramarital involvements. In short, trust is regarded by many couples as the linchpin of their marriage.

5. A balance of dependencies, which is another way of saying a balance of power. I prefer "dependency," even though "power" is a sexier word, with its implied comparison between marriage and politics. I prefer "dependency" because it better conveys the way couples see and regard one another. They speak of needing each

other and depending on each other, and in doing so, they are not speaking about the weaknesses of marriage, but about its strengths. In the best of marriages, partners are mutually dependent; interdependent is another way of saying that. They are aware of their dependencies and not ashamed to cater to them, acknowledging openly their debt to one another.

A person who best expressed the positive benefits of dependency in a marriage was a widow, a political person, who had gained prominence in her community for holding office at a time when few other women had. Her husband of thirty years, an attorney, had died about a year earlier. "First," she said, "there are the small dependencies. You know, how do I look in this dress or should I wear this belt or that one? Then there are the bigger things. My husband was an enabler—he helped me to be what I could be and what I was by encouraging me. And he opened my eyes to new things. For example, a new Supreme Court decision would come out and it would become an instant part of our lives because he would have all sorts of opinions about it that we would discuss and eventually I would incorporate. Now I'm not always sure what I think about some of the decisions being handed down. It's not that I lost part of myself by depending on him for this kind of thinking; it's that I would never have developed this interest to begin with. You have just so much time, energy and intellect, and it's so good to be able to depend on your spouse to fill in the gaps. Our dependencies enriched both our lives."

There has been a great emphasis on egalitarian marriages in recent years, marriages in which both spouses share economic earnings and power and both share household duties. Let us hope these marriages increase in number. However, an impression that grows out of this emphasis on economic egalitarianism is that emotional egalitarianism automatically follows and that, by contrast, in traditional marriages the dependencies are all one-sided: the woman depends totally on the man. This is not what I found among couples in solid, long marriages. Mates in nontraditional marriages as well as those in more traditional ones shared emotional dependencies. Rarely were husband and wife equally dependent on one another at any particular point. Rather, the dependencies tipped back and forth during the course of a marriage, each spouse nurturing the other as needed, so that over time, a balance was established, and that balance kept the marriage strong and stable.

Dependency, it needs to be added quickly, does not mean an obliteration of self. One thing I consistently became aware of was that no matter how close or how interdependent a couple, each spouse retained an individuality, a sense of self. If one or the other had lost that individuality and become completely submerged or exploited by the other, one or both partners usually expressed deep unhappiness in the marriage. Again, even in the most traditional marriages, where a woman's social identity may be tied to her husband's occupation or profession, the women who spoke most convincingly about the satisfactions of their marriages were women who viewed themselves as individuals, and who did not rely on their husbands to make them feel worthy.

An elderly woman I know was married for almost fifty years to a powerful, dynamic, charismatic business tycoon. "He thinks he's God," people often said about him, and so he behaved with both friends and family. His wife, beloved by the same friends and family, acted gracious and gentle, never upstaging her husband, always quietly in the background. After the husband died, this woman, who had not participated in her husband's business ventures, moved in and took over his many financial enterprises. She ran them with an iron hand, and seemed to flourish with each new challenge. "How could she have stayed in the background all those years?" I once asked her son. "She had to squelch her true self and act like a dependent little woman." His answer was: "You're wrong. She loved being married to 'God.' She always knew who she was and so did he. It was just more exciting to her to be in the background with him than in the foreground by herself. But she never lost her own identity."

In biology the term symbiosis refers to the living together of two organisms in an intimate relationship in which each may be of great benefit to the other. I always considered symbiotic relationships in nature to be particularly happy and cooperative ones. One that typifies others is the camping out of microscopic protozoans in the digestive tracts of termites, where the protozoans break down the wood eaten by the termites. This picnic for the protozoans helps the termites digest their wood while it provides nutrition for the protozoans, keeping everybody fat and satisfied. Unfortunately, I've discovered that psychologists do not think of symbiosis in quite such a felicitous way. They describe symbiotic relationships among humans as ones in which people (usually families) become so closely involved ("enmeshed" is their word) and dependent on one another that they become almost indistinguishable one from the other. I like the biological picture better: the protozoans seem to know who they are and so do the termites. Their relationship is one of mutuality (that is a biological term) in which each depends on and benefits from the other.

It would be nice to reinstate the word symbiosis in its more positive meaning into marital relationships because it so aptly describes the mutual dependencies and support of wives and husbands. There is one problem, however. The termites and protozoans and other symbiotic pairs usually cannot live by themselves, without one another. As attached as partners in long marriages are to one another, I had the impression that they could live alone and manage if necessary because each remains an individual, whole and intact, in the midst of their partnership. So, perhaps we can say that there exists a symbiotic relationship, in the best meaning of the word, between partners in a marriage, except that, if they had to, each could survive without the other. They simply do not choose to.

6. An enjoyment of each other. Wives and husbands in satisfying long marriages like one another, enjoy being together and enjoy talking to each other. Although they may spend evenings quietly together in a room, the silence that surrounds them is the comfortable silence of two people who know they do not *have* to talk to feel close. But mostly they do talk. For many couples conversations go on continually, whether the gossip of everyday living or discussions of broader events. And they listen to one another. I watched the faces of people I interviewed and watched each listening while the other spoke. They might argue, become irritated or jump in to correct each other, but they are engaged, and rarely bored.

They enjoy each other physically also, and sexual pleasures infuse many marriages for years and years. I could sense a sexual electricity between some partners. A different kind of warmth emanated from others, a feeling of closeness and affection. They held hands, they touched, they smiled and they spoke of sex as "warm and loving," as one woman said, "maybe not the wildness of our early marriage, but very pleasing."

They laugh at each other's jokes. Humor is the universal salve and salvation, easing tensions and marriage fatigue. "If you can laugh about it," everyone said, "you know it will be all right." And for them it is.

They find each other interesting, but they do not necessarily have the same interests. And that was a surprise. Far fewer couples than I expected spoke about sharing interests or hobbies. Typical of many others were the Augustines, who confessed, almost guiltily, their different interests:

"I'm afraid if you're looking for answers to long marriages, this is not the place," said Marie Augustine.

"Why not?" I asked.

"Because we don't share everything the way you're supposed to."

"I'm not sure you're supposed to. What don't you share?"

"Interests. For example, he likes to sit when we're on vacations and I like to run."

"And I like music and she likes the theater," Tony Augustine joined in.

"He can spend hours studying old coins. And I can spend hours catching up on weeks of newspaper reading," Marie continued.

"What do you do about these differences?"

"We work out arrangements that suit both of us," Marie answered. "With vacations, for example, one summer we run, meaning we travel and run around a lot and that makes me happy, and the next summer we sit. We go to a resort or rent a house in the country where we can look at the view, and that makes him happy."

"We also give each other space, as the kids say," Tony added. "Sometimes I'll go up to the room in our attic and devote all evening to listening to music alone."

"It's odd," Marie said. "I can walk into that room and he'll just be sitting there, and I'll say, 'What are you doing?' and he'll say, 'I'm listening to music.' Well, that's not me, just sitting and doing nothing, listening to music. But I'll go to concerts with him. We go to many concerts because of him."

"And I go to the theater because of her. But we don't say it that way as if we're sacrificing for each other. We go together because we like being together and actually, we each get our own kind of enjoyment out of the other's interests."

"Yes," agreed Marie. "We would never say, in terms of vacations, for example, 'Okay, I'll go run while you go sit.' That wouldn't be any fun for us."

Some other couples make fewer concessions to one another's interests. They might take separate vacations or go to movies or lectures with friends rather than with one another, and they find that for them that separation works better than forcing themselves to put in time at activities that one or the other hates. And for some married people, having separate interests makes each more interesting to the other. The only danger in this kind of separateness, especially for new marriages, is in its extreme. Spending a great deal of time apart is bound to cut into the closeness a husband and a wife build up. It also shuts off opportunities for them to get to know one another and, if not enjoy, at least appreciate and learn from the other's interests and obsessions. As in so many areas, couples in strong marriages try to find a balance between participating in one another's activities and going their own ways.

But if sharing interests is not a prerequisite for a rewarding marriage, sharing *values* is. Values refer to the things people believe in, the things they hold dear and worthy. The philosopher Bertrand Russell explained their importance in marriage well when he wrote, "It is fatal . . . if one values only money and the other values only good works." Such a couple will have trouble getting along, let alone enjoying one another's interests or ideas.

Mates who feel well-matched share a common base of

values even when they disagree about other things. One couple described having their biggest arguments about money. He loves to spend whatever they have on clothes, records and the theater; she watches every cent, wearing the same dress again and again. Yet they had an instant meeting of minds when it came time to buy a cello for their musically gifted daughter. They bought the best they could afford, even using a good part of their savings, because they both valued their child's music education above anything else money could buy. Another couple, who love antique Oriental ceramics, think nothing of living in a dingy, run-down apartment while they spend their modest earnings on beautiful ceramic vases that they track down and buy together.

For some couples, religion is the value that informs everything else in life. Those couples were in a minority among the families I interviewed, as they are a minority in our secular society. But those who did value religion considered it the strongest bond in their lives, and many attributed the happiness and stability of their marriages to that bond. I found it interesting that marriages in which both partners valued religion, even if the partners were of different faiths, had fewer conflicts over religious issues than same-faith marriages in which only one felt a religious commitment, especially if the other partner was disdainful of religion.

For all marriages, sharing values enhances the intimacy and mutual respect spouses feel, adding to their enjoyment of one another.

7. A shared history that is cherished. Every couple has a story, and couples in long marriages respect their own stories. They are connected to each other through those stories, and even the sadnesses they shared are a valued part of their history. "Our life is like a patchwork," one woman said. "We pull in red threads from here and blue threads from there and make them into one piece. Sometimes the threads barely hold, but you pull hard at them and they come together, and the patchwork remains whole."

The attachment couples have to their histories is not necessarily a sentimental or nostalgic attachment, but an affectionate one that sees significance in the past and in all the times spent together. George Gilbert said it nicely. His marriage, with one of the most troubled histories of all, had been filled with the traumas of manic-depressive illness and alcoholism until some years ago when he made himself stop drinking and his illness was brought under control by medication. "You know," he said, "you talk about this and you talk about that, and it sounds so chaotic, the alcohol and the rest. But still, in the midst of it all there were good times. In 1970, at the height of my drinking, we went to Cape Cod with our three sons and we got an acre of land. We put out a camper and we rented a canoe and we had a glorious time. Sure, when you reflect you think of the bad things—the flashing lights and the arms wrapped around the porcelain in the bathroom when you're hung over and sick. But there was so much else, even then. There was still a lot of fun, still a lot of humor, still a lot of good loving for both of us."

For the past two decades and more, educators have complained that young people are ahistorical. They have little sense of history and less interest in trying to learn about the past. They live in the present and they live without memory, a collective memory, of Watergate or Vietnam, of McCarthyism or the Great Depression. That absence of history, that amnesia, as it were, for all that came earlier, adds to the rootlessness that many of the young feel. To exist without a past, without a framework of history, makes life in the present that much more difficult. And while many factors are involved in the high divorce rate among young couples today, I believe their indifference to history is one more contributor. It's easier to end a marriage because of immediate problems when you don't see it as part of a larger fabric that stretches backward and forward, an entity that has a reality and history of its own.

People in long marriages value their joint history. When their ties in the present get raggedy, they are able to look to the past to find the good that they shared, rather than give in to the disillusionments of the moment. Their sense of history also gives them a respect for time. They know, by looking backward, that changes take time and that angers vanish with time, and they know that there is time ahead for new understandings and new adventures.

8. Luck. It has to be said, because everyone said it. With it all, the history and the trust, the willingness to change and to live without change, people need a little bit of luck to keep a marriage going.

You need luck, first of all, in choosing a partner who has the capacity to change and trust and love. In their book *Marriage and Personal Development*, psychiatrists Rubin Blanck and Gertrude Blanck make the case that marriages work best when both partners have reached a level of maturity before marriage that makes them ready for marriage. They are quite right. The only difficulty with their case is that few people are terribly mature when they marry, certainly not people in first marriages who marry young, and not even many people in second marriages. Yet many marriages work because partners mature together, over the years of matrimony. So, you need a little luck in choosing someone who will mature and grow while you, too, mature.

And you need a little luck in the family you come from and the friends that you have. A horrendous family background in which parents abuse their children or offer no love can set up almost insurmountable obstacles to the ability to sustain a marital relationship. Yet there are couples in long, happy marriages who did have devastating backgrounds. Often they were able to break the patterns they had known because of the encouragement of an aunt or an uncle, a grandparent, a teacher, a friend. They were lucky in finding the support they needed.

Then, you need a little luck with life. A marriage might move along happily and smoothly enough until a series of unexpected events rain down on it. A combination of illnesses or job losses, family feuds or personal failures might push the marriage off-course, when without these blows, it could have succeeded. Every marriage needs some luck in holding back forces that could crush it.

These aspects of luck may be out of our power to control. But the good thing about luck is that it is not all out of our control. Many people who considered themselves happy in marriage also spoke about themselves as being lucky. Since they seemed to have the same share of problems and difficulties as anyone else, sometimes even more than their share, I came to think that luck in marriage, as in life, is as much a matter of attitude as of chance. Couples who regard themselves as lucky are the ones who seize luck where they are able to. Instead of looking outside their marriage and assuming the luck is all there, in other people's homes, they look inside their marriage and find the blessings there. They are not blind to the soft spots of their marriages—nobody denied difficulties; they just consider the positives more important. So they knock wood and say they are lucky. And I guess they are. They have grabbed luck by the tail and have twisted it to their own purposes.

Throughout the writing of this book I have been haunted by one interview. It was an interview with a woman, divorced four years earlier, after thirteen years of marriage, by a husband who realized, he said, that "It could be better." The woman, Daisy Copley, spent a year in numbed shock. Then she turned the tables on her husband. She left the big house in the suburbs in which she had remained to care for the couple's three children, left the house and the children and informed her husband that he must return to watch over them. From now on she was going to live a new life, free of all responsibilities.

"I was supposed to be there standing by the sink in my apron and being Mommy, while he went off and did whatever he wanted to," she said, in telling her story. "Only I stopped being Mommy. I became the weekend father, Mr. Goody-Two-Shoes. It was wonderful. Now he was doing the laundry and making dinner, and I was coming on Sunday and taking them out, and they would shout 'Mommy's here! Mommy's here!' For the first time in fourteen years I felt like a person."

To go with her new self, she developed a new philosophy, and it is the philosophy by which she now lives:

"I don't rely on anyone but myself. I have my own needs and my own goals and I don't want to sublimate them for anybody else. I won't make compromises in my life anymore. I have had three men ask me to live with them in the last four years, and I have said no. I want to live with myself. I will share some of my time and space with people I care about, but I won't have anyone else calling my shots. I stopped wearing a watch two years ago. I never know what time it is because I don't need to know what time it is, and I don't care what time it is."

And Daisy contrasted her life to her mother's life:

"My mother remarried after my father died. Now she can't go anywhere without her new husband. She can't stand to be without him for five hours. She told me I should remarry while I'm still young. I said, 'Hey, Ma, I am really happy; I don't want to remarry.' My mother and her husband have decided they want to be buried together. They're going to dig up the graves of his wife and my father and rebury them so that they can all rest together, forever. Me, I want to rest alone. That's right. *I want to rest alone.* Forever."

My first reaction to Daisy Copley was one of great sympathy. I could sympathize with her walking out on her big house and kids after being so badly hurt by her husband. She's angry and bitter, I thought, and she has a right to be. My second reaction was irritation. She may have a right to be bitter, but does she have to be so self-centered? My third reaction was to go past her anger and self-involvement and think about what she said. When I did, it disturbed me. It disturbed me because I knew she was right about many things. She should not marry again if freedom and independence are what she wants, because marriage curtails both. No matter how egalitarian a marriage, no matter how much individuality each spouse maintains, neither is ever completely free. Always, in a marriage, each partner needs to maintain an awareness of the existence of the other, always conscious of the other's needs, the other's expectations. Married, you do need to wear a watch, at least figuratively, because your time is not always your own.

What then does marriage offer to make up for the loss of independence, for the assumption of responsibility for someone other than yourself? That is the question, most clearly articulated by Daisy Copley, that has haunted me, the question in back of my mind as I listened and relistened to the tapes of long-married couples speaking about their lives, as I thought about their marriages and mine.

My answer, finally, is this: Marriage may place limitations on our independence, but it expands the essence of who we are as human beings.

On its most immediate level, marriage expands us because it nurtures and protects in a way that nothing else does. Because of the security a good marriage provides, it allows each partner the courage to take risks, to venture into the unknown, to stretch as far as one can in the outside world, knowing that there is a place to come home to, a safe place with room enough to be oneself.

Marriage adds depth to one's being, the depth and understanding that come from looking into oneself in order to understand another. A woman, a professor of philosophy, newly married, described marriage as "even harder than philosophy." It was hard, she said, because it forced you to confront yourself, to sort out what you believe and care about, what you consider important and what trivial. "You could run away," she said. "You can get a divorce and run away when things get really hard. But you still have to confront yourself. If you run away, you run into yourself."

Marriage is filled with challenges, not least of which is the challenge of simultaneously being a whole person and being part of the larger entity that is the marriage. Meeting the challenge means living for oneself but also living outside of oneself. It means being selfish sometimes and selfless at others, and becoming a more complex human being in the process of trying to find a balance between the two.

To be married is to be connected to a past and a future, to be a family with private jokes and special stories, to have secret codewords and rituals. "There's a kind of tenderness that comes from living a long time with somebody," said a woman, "realizing that they are not going to live forever and neither are you but you are in this life together. With all the millions of people around, you're still going to try to make things good for that one person. There's a kind of gentleness that comes after a while, not having everything just happen but finding out what pleases somebody, and making that happen."

Marriage has its faults, God knows. It has its pains and tediums, its rages and despair. But when it works, it has its moments: of adventure and passion, of calm contentment, of companionship and of profound love. Married people think nothing can compare to those moments.

Not everybody needs to be or should be married. Plenty of people have rich and splendid lives without marriage. Daisy Copley will probably be one of those people.

But me, I don't want to rest alone. I want to rest—and run and laugh—with my husband at my side. Forever.

EPILOGUE

∾

Happy New Year

> *Their marriage is a good one. In our eyes*
> *What makes a marriage good? Well, that the tether*
> *Fray but not break, and that they stay together.*
> *One should be watching while the other dies.*

HOWARD NEMEROV, "COMMON WISDOM"

Rosh Hashanah Eve. We are at my parents' home for the Jewish New Year festival. We have spent this holiday with them since the earliest days of our marriage, and even when we lived hundreds of miles away, we often flew here to be with them. Every year we say to each other, "This is the last time we're doing this. Next year we're staying home." We prefer our community and synagogue to theirs. We would rather be with our friends than their friends during our holidays, rather entertain than be guests, rather go about the business of our adult lives than become children home for the holidays again. Then Rosh Hashanah approaches and with it the stocktaking of a new year: They're old. How many more years will we be able to do this? Suppose this is the last time. How can we disappoint them?

So we pack up, my husband, my daughter and I, and arrive at their home on Rosh Hashanah Eve, staying until the holiday ends two days later. After sundown of the second day we drive home, feeling good and congratulating ourselves aloud on having begun the New Year with the exemplary deed of honoring the elderly. And inside, unsaid, I am aware that respect and good deeds are only a small part of my own reasons for our annual Rosh Hashanah trek to the home of my parents. The larger part has to do with my wanting to hold back time, to savor still the incredible sweetness of being a daughter, someone's child even now, especially now, when I am so far away from childhood.

This year all sensations seem heightened. I am aware of the broken cord of a Venetian blind that probably broke years ago. I notice faded spots on the sofa fabric, and stains on the rug. Damn it! How did everything get to be so old? And my parents. They've turned into fragile wooden dolls, stiff and lined with age, liable to be toppled by the slightest whiff of air. She walks slowly, with pain, her knees knobbed by arthritis; he shuffles along on his cane, dragging his right foot while his right arm hangs useless at his side, both limbs numbed by a stroke suffered some fifteen years ago.

I ask my father a question.

"Huh?" he answers.

I repeat the question.

"Huh?" he repeats.

"Speak louder," my mother says. "He can't hear you very well."

"Cut it out," I say loudly. "What's the matter with you two? Somebody would think you were old or something." I hope it comes out sounding like a joke, but I can hear the edge in my own voice. Why did they have to get so old?

"Yeah," my mother says, picking up on my unspoken thoughts. "You think old age is so terrific. They talk about the sunset years. Look at us. In one eye I can't see because of my cataract and I can hardly walk. Daddy barely walks anymore, it's so hard for him, and he can hear only when you speak loudly. Some sunset. It's no fun growing old, let me tell you."

"But," my father says, "think of the alternative."

They both laugh. It's their standard joke. If he doesn't say it, she does. When you think of the alternative, it is better to be alive, even if you are old.

My mood changes. They don't resent getting old. They are not trying to hold back time. They think of themselves as lucky; in some remote corner of their consciousness they think they may have beaten the system (although even to acknowledge such a presumptuous thought is to tempt fate). Well they have, so far. A few months ago they celebrated their sixtieth wedding anniversary. "The only thing I ask for," my mother had said, "is that we can celebrate next year again, our sixty-first together. We have to take things a year at a time now." Then they asked for a little more. He wished them both good health for another year. She wished for peace of mind. "First of all you have to have a mind," he said, making light of the one fear that overshadows all others for them, the fear of senility, of losing their wits and control of their minds and bodies.

They have lost none of that control despite their years. If they forget some names or recent occurrences, their lapses are more than compensated for by their memory of the past and by the clarity of their reasoning. Recent research into aging has shown that, contrary to popular opinion, the mind does not deteriorate with age but actually continues to develop. While memory of the immediate might diminish, wisdom and the ability to think conceptually continue to expand well into old age.

My parents have become wiser over the course of their marriage, and happier.

Things were tough when they married back in the 1920s. He, a Jewish immigrant from Russia, had arrived in this country at the age of fifteen to work along with his father at odd jobs that would provide the necessary money to bring his mother and four younger brothers to the "Golden Land." At the age of fifteen, she, the daughter of immigrants, had left school to work in a factory so that there would be enough money for her brothers to go to college and enter professions. (It never occurred to her to expect the same for herself, a girl. "I was so proud of

hem," she once said. "How many boys from the Lower
East Side made it to college in those days? And my brothers did.")

They married when she was in her early twenties, he
six years older. Her parents had no more cash than did
his. The wedding was a small gathering of family and
friends in a rabbi's house, where the wedding meal con-
sisted of, my mother recalls, "a piece of herring." She
remembers it as "sad; a terrible wedding; we were so
poor"; he, as just the kind of wedding he wanted because
"I was too shy for a big affair, even if we could have
afforded it." Their memory differences fit their personality
differences. She sees the realities, including the negatives;
he tends to idealize, to emphasize the plusses.

But both present the same picture of the crushing
event of their married lives, the death of their first child, a
son. He was born in the third year of their marriage and
died a year and a half later. A beautiful and bright baby,
he walked and talked before he was a year old, a source of
pride for his parents. Then he died of pneumonia, snatched
away, my parents say, by a death that should have been
avoided. They blame themselves; they blame the doctor.
They recognize that medicine was not as advanced then
as it is now, that penicillin didn't exist, and yet my father
says, "He shouldn't have died." They never came to terms
with that death. Or maybe they did, but they never put it
out of their lives. "At first," my father said when I asked
him about it, "I thought about it all the time, twenty-four
hours a day. When it rained I thought of my baby buried
in the ground and I hurt because of the rain coming down
on him. I knew it was irrational, but I thought that way.
Then, of course, with time, the pain tapers off and it isn't
as sharp. But there is a cloud that pursues you all your
life. You never forget it. Even today, more than fifty years
later, I would say that not a day goes by that I don't think
about that child, about what he would have been like and
what he would be doing now."

I have never seen pictures of that baby. They probably hid the photos away. And they moved to a new
apartment soon after his death, to try to put the tragedy
behind them. Did they speak of their aching sadness to
each other? I have the impression that they didn't, or not

very much. With today's emphasis on communication and sharing we would probably say that they should have. But that was not their style, and they had no pressing need to speak about what each knew the other was feeling. They carried their suffering around silently within them, and in their silence they drew closer.

I had asked my parents about that baby (I'm not sure I know his name) a few months before their sixtieth anniversary. I was interviewing them, as I had interviewed dozens of married couples, tape recorder and all. I spoke with them separately, and after an initial awkwardness at being interviewed by their daughter, each relaxed and answered my questions honestly, I believe, about both the problems and pleasures of their life together. In the problem department what they spoke of was poverty, and ambition.

Every Thursday afternoon, in the early years of her marriage, my mother would visit her mother, and would carry home with her a "little spring chicken" for dinner that night. Every Friday evening she and my father would have Sabbath dinner with his parents and brothers. For the rest of the week, she would manage her meals on the ten dollars of household money her husband gave her out of his salary of twenty-five dollars a week. "I should have gone out to work," my mother said. "I was so worried that people would talk about us if I worked. There were some married women who worked, but not many, and none of our friends." It didn't occur to my father to have his wife work to supplement their income. "That just wasn't done," he said. "In our society, a woman who held on to a job after she married was looked down upon." So, I suspect, was the man whose wife had to work to make ends meet.

Instead, he worked long hours and she sat home alone, waiting for him. Even after she had children, she felt "so alone" (my brother was born about two years after the baby died and I a few years later). My father was building a small business manufacturing and selling men's clothing. He left the house at six o'clock in the morning and returned at ten o'clock at night, Sundays included. Over the years, their living standard rose, but his work hours remained long and hard. Each time business improved, he expanded, putting himself under new pressures. During World War II he prospered, along with other small businessmen. Then he extended his interests out of town, building a string of clothing stores in the South, outlets for the merchandise he manufactured in his New York factory. The expansion led to a different kind of time away from home. Once a month he would go "on the road" to check on his stores, and she would "sit and wait" for him to return.

"I spent so much of my time waiting for him," she recalled when we spoke. "That's another time when I should have gone out to work, when the children were older and he was traveling so much. That was the mistake I made. It wasn't a matter of money anymore, but I didn't have to be so lonely."

"Did you ever ask him not to travel?" I asked her.

"I was too proud to ask him not to leave me. But he knew how I felt."

"I knew she got angry when I went away," he said when we were alone, "but I didn't think she had a right to that anger. I wasn't off playing; I was working, trying to make the business grow so that one day I could retire with a lot of money."

He didn't retire with a lot of money. He retired with enough for them to live on, but modestly. Huge clothing-manufacturing chains had spread into cities throughout the United States and gobbled up the smaller entrepreneurs like my father. "I had wanted to be rich," he said, "not for the money alone, but because being rich represented power and prestige. There was so much I could accomplish with money—I could give large sums to charity, build synagogues, help the poor. I wanted to be able to do those things and also to build a reputation and be important.

"But it wasn't worth it," he went on. "Even if I had made it big, the sacrifices weren't worth it. I sacrificed my home life and my own life for the sake of making a reputation. I became a slave to my business. It was like the story of the mountain that had gold in it. Every year the climber thinks, 'I'll reach that gold. If I don't make it this year, I'll reach it next year, and then I'll be finished.'

So he goes on reaching, reaching, reaching for the top, but he never gets there."

It was a bitter image. "Are you bitter about not getting to the top in your business?" I asked.

"No, not bitter. I was disappointed for a long while. But now it's more a matter of being sorry that I didn't have the pleasure of spending more time with my wife and children. I loved them so much; I loved being with them. Mama didn't understand then that I hated going away as much as she hated my going. But I thought I was building our future and I was wrong. I gave up too much. If I had it to live all over, I would do it differently."

Not a unique story. I still hear versions of it: from a young wife about to leave her husband because of his obsession with his career; from a middle-aged man, frustrated because now that he is ready to devote more of his time to wife and family she is busy hustling her way to the top of a newfound career. Would my father, or anybody, really do it differently if they had it to do over? I don't know. The good thing about a long marriage, however, is that there is time within it for other ways of doing things, for other marriages.

When I look at my father now, I can hardly remember the businessman he once was. What I see is a gentle scholar whose greatest pleasure comes from studying and teaching the Bible, the Talmud, and other texts of the Jewish tradition. The link between the two, the businessman and the scholar, is a certain stubbornness of character, a tenacity that leads him to single-minded concentration on pursuing his goals. His goal changed more than twenty years ago from wanting to accumulate wealth to wanting to accumulate knowledge, and the second goal has been by far more satisfying to both of them.

The change began with his retirement, and that came when the business turned downward and he knew it was time to get out. Soon after he stopped working, he picked up on intellectual interests that had lain fallow for almost forty years. As a child in Russia he had studied in a *heder*, one of the all-day Hebrew schools most Russian Jewish children attended. While most found the rigor and rigid discipline of those schools stifling, my father had been lucky in having as his teachers two brilliant young men who later became scholars and leaders in America and Israel. He loved learning, and took pride in his ability to quote vast portions of the Bible and Talmud by heart. He had continued his studies for a while after he came to the United States, then had to give them up as he and his family struggled to survive. With his retirement he went back to those studies and found that he remembered more than he thought he had and that he loved knowledge more passionately than he realized.

The change in him took my mother by surprise. She had become a voracious reader over the years—magazines, novels, biographies, everything—in part to fill in for her aloneness. But "for years he barely even read the paper," she said. "He never had time. I had no idea that he remembered so much from his background. I never knew how intellectual he was."

Soon after my father stopped working, my parents began to travel, go to the theater, attend lectures, and do many other things for which there had never been time, the kinds of things my mother, especially, loved to do. "I would say that we've had a happy marriage," she told me, making sure to set the record straight, "even though there were unhappy times in it. But the years since he retired have been the happiest of them all. We've done so much together. We've been very happy."

"In spite of his stroke?"

"In spite of the stroke, although that has been hard for us."

The stroke caught him on a hot August day about six years after his retirement. It came as a shock, as illness always does, knocking him down at the very moment when he felt in his prime, free of business worries and filled with energy. It slurred his speech and left him with a paralyzed right arm and partially paralyzed leg. It also killed all further hopes of traveling.

"He was angry for a long time," my mother said. "He resented it terribly. 'Why me?' and that kind of thing. Instead of movies and lectures or tours abroad we spent our days with him in therapy exercising his arm and learning how to walk again."

"And you," I asked, "did you resent giving up everything you finally had? Did you feel cheated?"

"Cheated? Oh no. You don't feel cheated. You don't feel that at all. You feel sad, so sad seeing him that way."

"But you gave up so much also after he got sick."

"What did I give up? What did I lose? Nothing. None of those things were important. Only he is important."

They began to spend their winters in Florida after his illness because the cold months in the North were too difficult for him. He looked around him during their first winter and dubbed the area in which they stayed an "intellectual wasteland." Determined to correct matters, he delved more deeply into his Jewish studies. He taught himself to write and type with his left hand, worked harder at speaking clearly and began a series of adult education courses in his community. He continued the courses back home during the spring and summer. My mother frets about his courses.

"He works so hard at his preparations, and I get terribly upset if he doesn't get a good turnout of people. I get nervous for him too."

"But he enjoys the teaching?"

"He loves it."

"Are you interested in what he teaches?"

"Oh yes. I always find him interesting."

"Don't you ever get bored when you hear him tell the same joke or teach the same lesson over again?" I asked her. "I watch you sometimes when he's speaking, and you look so interested. How do you do it?"

"I am interested. And then, I'll tell you," she said, laughing, "I have a terrible memory. I forget what I've heard, so it always seems new to me."

It's a good explanation, although not necessarily true. She finds him interesting and funny, and when she has heard what he has to say before, she acts as though she finds it interesting or funny because that makes him happy. Is she more dependent on him than he on her? Probably she used to be, and much of her unhappiness at being alone in the early years probably came from that dependency. It would have been better for her to go out to work and make her own happiness. But for years now he has been dependent on her: to help him dress (although he is adamant about doing as much as is humanly possible with one hand himself), to cut his meat when two hands are required, to care for him. She watches over him, strong-minded and determined, concerned about his eating, worried that he might fall, always preparing herself for another stroke, or worse.

Yet they are more essentially intertwined and more equal than their roles of "traditional husband and the wife who cares for him" would imply. They entertain each other, he with his studies and teachings, she with everyday events culled from her reading of several newspapers and a pack of magazines every week. "We have so much to talk about—" he said, "the children, the grandchildren, the friends we have made, the outside world. We never run out of conversation." And they respect each other. "We had our arguments and fights," she said. "You know me with my temper. But we always had respect for each other, and the respect was part of our love."

Sometimes they become cranky with each other. He complains about her continuing frugality, a trait that goes back to the early days when she had to stretch a very lean budget. "I had to argue with her to give the painter a decent tip," he called to tell me one day. "Why does she worry about money when we have enough to live on?" But he knows they have enough to live on because she has always watched every penny. She complains that he doesn't eat enough or take good care of himself. Once, visiting us, he lost his balance and fell. She cried, "Oh no! You see how he is? He just won't be careful." It's more comforting to her to hold him responsible for his physical condition than to face the fact that much of it is out of his control.

Mostly they try to please one other. "You realize over the years," he said, "that you really want to do things for each other. At first you're *obliged* to do things, later you *want* to. We got accustomed to living together, and we shaped our lives together, shaped them up to one single point, to one entity, and that is our marriage."

Is it a "creative" marriage or a "survivor" marriage (to use the sociologists' latest categories for marriage among the elderly)? Neither. Both. I don't know. They have had a long life together and many marriages within, and they treasure all of it.

*　　*　　*

I watch them on Rosh Hashanah Eve as they prepare for the holiday. My father has spent most of the afternoon dressing, a slow process for him. He is ready to leave for synagogue now to pray for the New Year. My mother will go with him tomorrow, but tonight she is putting last-minute touches on the holiday meal. He walks over to her for final inspection. She fixes his tie.

"Remember," she says, "if you get tired walking, stop and rest. You don't have to be the first in the synagogue."

"But I don't have to be the last either," he answers, teasing about her constant worries.

She brushes a piece of dust from his shoulder. He leans down and kisses her on her lips.

"Happy New Year," he says softly.

"Happy New Year," she answers. She looks at him for a second, then kisses him back. "And next year again."

BIBLIOGRAPHY

This list includes a selection of current research and thought on marriage and family living. It also includes all sources—books, articles, and monographs—referred to in the text.

ALVEREZ, A. *Life after Marriage*. New York: Simon and Schuster, 1981.

ATKIN, EDITH. *In Praise of Marriage*. New York: Vanguard Press, 1982.

"At Long Last Motherhood." *Newsweek*, March 16, 1981.

BANK, STEPHEN P., and MICHAEL D. KAHN. *The Sibling Bond*. New York: Basic Books, 1982.

BELTZ, STEPHEN. "Five Year Effects of Altered Marital Contracts." In *Extramarital Relations*, edited by G. Neubeck. Englewood Cliffs, N.J.: Prentice-Hall, 1969.

BERGER, BRIGITTE and PETER L. *The War over the Family: Capturing the Middle Ground*. Garden City, N.Y.: Doubleday, 1983.

BERGMAN, INGMAR. *Scenes from a Marriage*. New York: Pantheon Books, 1978.

BERMAN, ELLEN M., and HAROLD I. LIEF. "Marital Therapy from a Psychiatric Perspective: An Overview." *American Journal of Psychiatry* 132 (June 1975): 583–592.

BERNARD, JESSE. *The Future of Marriage*. New York: Bantam Books, 1972.

BETCHER, R. WILLIAM. "Intimate Play and Marital Adaption." *Psychiatry* 44 (February 1981): 13–31.

BIENVENU, M. J. "Measurement of Marital Communication." *The Family Coordinator* 19 (1970): 26–31.

BIRD, CAROLINE. *The Two-Paycheck Marriage*. New York: Rawson Wade, 1979.

BLANCK, RUBIN and GERTRUDE. *Marriage and Personal Development*. New York: Columbia University Press, 1968.

BLOCH, DONALD, and ROBERT SIMON, eds. *The Strength of Family Therapy: Selected Papers of Nathan W. Ackerman*. New York: Brunner/Mazel, 1982.

BLUM, LEON. *Marriage*. Trans. Warre Bradley Wells. London and Philadelphia: Lippincott, 1937.

BLUMSTEIN, PHILIP, and PEPPER SCHWARTZ. *American Couples: Money, Work, Sex*. New York: William Morrow, 1983.

BOWEN, MURRAY. *Family Therapy in Clinical Practice*. New York: Jason Aronson, 1978.

BRECHER, EDWARD, and the editors of Consumer Reports Books. *Love, Sex, and Aging: A Consumers Union Report*. Boston: Little, Brown, 1984.

BRYAN, C. D. B. "Sex and the Married Man." *Esquire*, June 1984.

CARTER, ELIZABETH A., and MONICA MCGOLDRICK, eds. *The Family Life Cycle*. New York: Gardner Press, 1980.

CHERLIN, ANDREW. *Marriage, Divorce, Remarriage*. Cambridge, Ma.: Harvard University Press, 1981.

COLLINS, GLENN. "Why Long-Term Marriage Can Succeed." *New York Times*, November 9, 1981.

CUBER, JOHN F., and PEGGY B. HARROFF. *The Significant Americans*. New York: Appleton-Century, 1965.

DICKS, H. V. *Marital Tensions: Clinical Studies towards a Psychological Theory of Interaction*. New York: Basic Books, 1967.

DINNERSTEIN, DOROTHY. *The Mermaid and the Minotaur: Sexual Arrangements and Human Malaise*. New York: Harper and Row, 1976.

DOWLING, COLETTE. *The Cinderella Complex*. New York: Summit Books, 1981.

EHRENREICH, BARBARA. *The Hearts of Men: American Dreams and the Flight from Commitment*. Garden City, N.Y.: Doubleday, 1983.

EPHRON, NORA. *Heartburn*. New York: Alfred A. Knopf, 1983.

EPSTEIN, JOSEPH. *Divorced in America*. New York: Penguin Books, 1975.

ERIKSON, ERIK. *Childhood and Society*. New York: W. W. Norton, 1963.

FEATHERSTONE, HELEN. *A Difference in the Family*. New York: Basic Books, 1980.

FIELDS, NINA S. "Satisfaction in Long-Term Marriages." *Social Work* (January-February 1983): 37–41.

FRAMO, JAMES L. *Explorations in Marital and Family Therapy*. New York: Springer, 1982.

FRANK, ELLEN; CAROL ANDERSON; and DEBRA RUBENSTEIN. "Frequency of Sexual Dysfunction in 'Normal Couples.' " *New England Journal of Medicine* 299 (1978): 111–115.

——— and SONDRA FORSYTH ENOS. "The Lovelife of the American Wife." *Ladies' Home Journal*, February 1983.

FRANKE, LINDA BIRD. *Growing Up Divorced*. New York: Linden Press/ Simon and Schuster, 1983.

FRIEDAN, BETTY. *The Feminine Mystique*. W. W. Norton, 1963.

GAY, PETER. *The Bourgeois Experience: Victoria to Freud*. Vol. 1. New York: Oxford University Press, 1984.

GLENN, NORVAL D., and CHARLES N. WEAVER. "The Contribution of Marital Happiness to Global Happiness." *Journal of Marriage and the Family* (February 1981): 161–168.

GOITEIN, S. D. *A Mediterranean Society*. Vol. 3. Berkeley: University of California Press, 1978.

GURMAN, ALAN S., and DAVID G. RICH. *Couples in Conflict: New Directions in Marital Therapy*. New York: Jason Aronson, 1975.

HYMOWITZ, CAROL. "Wives of Jobless Men Support Some Families— But at Heavy Cost." *Wall Street Journal*, December 8, 1982.

JACOBY, SUSAN. "Maternal Madness: How Women Live with Childlessness . . ." *Vogue*, March 1984.

KOMAROVSKY, MIRRA. *Blue-Collar Marriage*. New York: Vintage Books, 1967.

KRAMER, RITA. *In Defense of the Family*. New York: Basic Books, 1982.

LEDERER, WILLIAM J., and DON D. JACKSON. *The Mirages of Marriage*. New York: W. W. Norton, 1968.

LEVINSON, DANIEL. *The Seasons of a Man's Life*. New York: Alfred A. Knopf, 1978.

LIFTON, ROBERT JAY. *The Broken Connection*. New York: Simon and Schuster, 1979.

MACE, DAVID R., ed. *Prevention in Family Services*. Beverly Hills, Calif.: Sage Publications, 1983.

MINUCHIN, SALVADOR. *Families and Family Therapy*. Cambridge, Ma.: Harvard University Press, 1974.

NEILL, JOHN R., and DAVID P. KNISKERN, eds. *From Psyche to System: The Evolving Therapy of Carl Whitaker*. New York: Guilford Press, 1982.

O'BRIEN, PATRICIA. *Staying Together: Marriages That Work*. New York: Random House, 1977.

OFFER, DANIEL, and MELVIN SABSHIN. *Normality and the Life Cycle*. New York: Basic Books, 1984.

OFFIT, AVODAH K. *Night Thoughts: Reflections of a Sex Therapist*. New York: Congdon and Lattes, 1981.

PAOLINO, THOMAS J., JR., and BARBARA S. MCCRADY, eds. *Marriage and Marital Therapy: Psychoanalytic, Behavioral and Systems Theory Perspectives*. New York: Brunner/Mazel, 1978.

PARENS, HENRI, and LEON J. SAAL. *Dependence in Man—A Psychoanalytic Study*. New York: International Universities Press, 1971.

PINES, MAYA. "Children of Divorce." *New York Times*, April 13, 1982.

POGREBIN, LETTY COTTIN. *Family Politics: Love and Power on an Intimate Frontier.* New York: McGraw-Hill, 1983.

"Princeton Reunion Puts '73 Women in Limelight." *New York Times,* June 6, 1983.

QUINN, SALLY. "Marriage: The New Switch." *Vogue,* January 1981.

RICE, DAVID G. *Dual-Career Marriage.* New York: Free Press, 1979.

ROSE, PHYLLIS. *Parallel Lives: Five Victorian Marriages.* New York: Alfred A. Knopf, 1983.

ROTHMAN, SHEILA M. *Woman's Proper Place.* New York: Basic Books, 1978.

RUBIN, LILLIAN B. *Intimate Strangers: Men and Women Together.* New York: Harper & Row, 1983.

———. *Worlds of Pain: Life in the Working-Class Family.* New York: Basic Books, 1976.

RUSSELL, BERTRAND. *Marriage and Morals.* New York: Horace Liveright, 1929.

SAGER, CLIFFORD, et al. *Treating the Remarried Family.* New York: Brunner/Mazel, 1983.

SCHULTZ, TERRI. "Does Marriage Give Today's Women What They Really Want?" *Ladies' Home Journal,* June 1980.

SHEEHY, GAIL. *Passages: Predictable Crises of Adult Life.* New York: E. P. Dutton, 1976.

SHORTER, EDWARD. *The Making of the Modern Family.* New York: Basic Books, 1975.

SHREVE, ANITA. "Careers and the Lure of Motherhood." *New York Times Magazine,* November 21, 1982.

SINGULAR, STEPHEN. "Master Diarist Max Frisch." *New York Times Magazine,* October 11, 1981.

SKOLNICK, ARLENE and JEROME, eds. *Family in Transition.* Boston: Little, Brown, 1980.

SPANIER, GRAHAM, and ROBERT LEWIS. "Marital Quality: A Review of the Seventies." *Journal of Marriage and the Family.* (November 1980): 825–839.

STONE, LAWRENCE. *The Family, Sex and Marriage in England 1500-1800.* New York: Harper & Row, 1977.

STREAN, HERBERT S. *The Extramarital Affair.* New York: Free Press, 1980.

TAVRIS, CAROL. *Anger: The Misunderstood Emotion.* New York: Simon and Schuster, 1982.

TODD, JUDITH. "Predicting Marital Success or Failure." *Human Sexuality* 16 (July 1982): 69.

TOFFLER, ALVIN. *Future Shock.* New York: Random House, 1970.

TOMAN, WALTER. *Family Constellation.* New York: Springer, 1976.

U.S. Department of Health and Human Services. *Duration of Marriage before Divorce.* Washington, D.C.: National Center for Health Statistics, 1981.

VEROFF, JOSEPH, et al. *The Inner American: A Self-Portrait from 1957–1976.* New York: Basic Books, 1981.

VISHER, JOHN S. and EMILY B. "Stepfamilies and Stepparenting." In *Normal Family Processes,* edited by Froma Walsh. New York: Guilford Press, 1982.

WOLFE, LINDA. *Playing Around: Women and Extramarital Sex.* New York: William Morrow, 1975.

YANKELOVICH, DANIEL. *New Rules: Searching for Self-Fulfillment in a World Turned Upside Down.* New York: Random House, 1981.

INDEX

ABOUT THE AUTHOR

FRANCINE KLAGSBRUN has written more than a dozen books, including *Too Young To Die* and *Voices of Wisdom*, and was the editor of the best-selling *Free To Be . . . You and Me*. Her articles have appeared in many national magazines, and she has lectured widely on family and social issues. She lives in New York with her husband and daughter.

MEN WHO HATE WOMEN—
AND THE WOMEN WHO LOVE THEM

By Dr. Susan Forward and Joan Torres

a Bantam hardcover

It is the stuff of dreams. The relationship usually starts with a rush of passion and commitment—on both sides. Here at last, the woman thinks, is a man who is truly interested in her, who is romantic and sexy and wants, even, to marry her. But the dream quite soon becomes a nightmare. While still persuaded that she loves and is loved, the woman finds her self-esteem under attack. She is criticized, belittled, restricted in her friendships and work life, watched over and controlled, and blamed for everything that is going wrong. And she takes the blame. After all, she is with a wonderful man.

MEN WHO HATE WOMEN explores the complexities of these relationships and answers such crucial questions as: What is the initial attraction? Why do the women stay? What in the man's past causes him to treat her this way? What in the woman's past makes her susceptible to him? And, most importantly, how can a woman break her near-addiction to the misogynist, regain her self-respect, and either rebuild her relationship or find a better one in the future.

Dr. Susan Forward, one of the nation's most sought-after experts in the field of broadcast psychology, is the host of her own program on ABC's TalkRadio Network and the author of BETRAYAL OF INNOCENCE, a book on sexual abuse and the victims of incest.

Look for it in bookstores or use the coupon below for ordering: